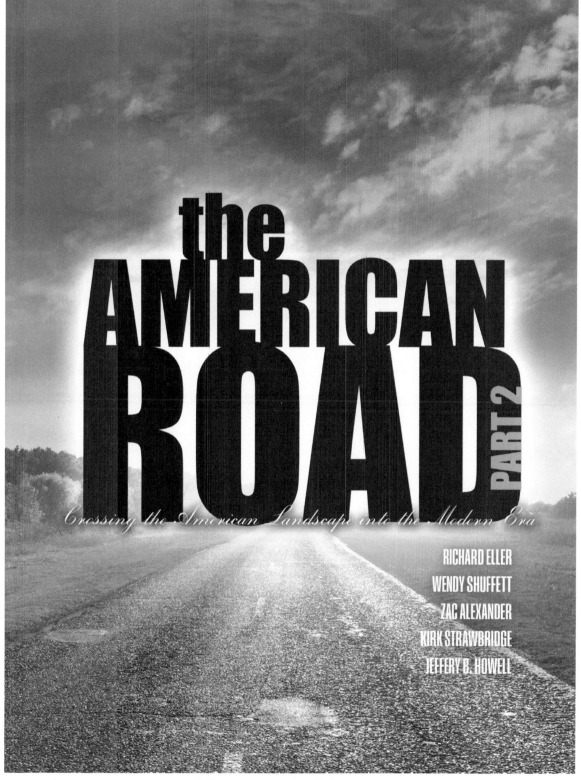

the AMERICAN ROAD

PART 2

Crossing the American Landscape into the Modern Era

RICHARD ELLER

WENDY SHUFFETT

ZAC ALEXANDER

KIRK STRAWBRIDGE

JEFFERY B. HOWELL

Kendall Hunt
publishing company

CONTENTS

TEXTBOOK INTRODUCTION

Roads connect us. Not only do they carry us to work and play, but they also bind us with each other. They reveal our wishes, strengthen our ties, and offer us our next adventure. It's been that way since humans first stepped onto this hemisphere. While technology has yet to make time travel possible, *The American Road* nonetheless takes you on an exciting journey through our nation's past. The story of America is a fascinating one, and to understand where we might be going we must have a sense of where we have been. The great southern writer William Faulkner once stated, "History isn't dead, it's not even past." When events occur they never literally repeat, but the spirit and atmosphere in which they happen continue to resonate now and in the future.

On July 4, 1776, the country's leading statesmen signed the Declaration of Independence. This document proved revolutionary because of its justification for independence and what it articulated about humanity. In the preamble, Thomas Jefferson states, "We hold these truths to be self-evident, that all men are created equal, that they are endowed by their Creator with certain unalienable Rights, that among these are Life, Liberty and the pursuit of Happiness." We are hard pressed to find more powerful words written in the English language. However, as revolutionary and eloquent as they are, Jefferson's vision was only partially realized after a civil war, and later a civil rights movement. America has traveled from a nation with slavery as part of its heritage to a land that witnessed the election of its first African-American president in 2008. The pathway of a nation that is, "indivisible, with liberty and justice for all" is a work in progress, but Jefferson's vision was never dead, nor is it past.

The issue of racial justice and equality is only one of many pathways that *The American Road* examines. Others concern the broad subject of war and peace. In his famous "Farwell Address" in 1796, George Washington stated that the "great rule of conduct for us regarding foreign nations is in extending our commercial relations, to have with them as little political connection as possible. So far as we have already formed engagements, let them be fulfilled with perfect good faith. Here let us stop." While the exact meaning of Washington's words remains controversial, it is clear that he was concerned about America's proper role in the world. At the turn of the eighteenth century, the United States was hesitant to involve itself internationally. However, it shed its conservatism beginning with Matthew Perry's 1853 naval expedition to Japan. In the following decades, America engaged in diplomatic and military matters all over the globe. These policy choices often connected to each other and led to more complex future events. By the end of the first half of the twentieth century, the United States had fought victoriously in two world wars, and in the process, became a global superpower. However, that new position would come with a high price.

In 1965, the United States entered a war in Vietnam which eventually cost tens of thousands of American lives. While the number of military personnel lost was less than experienced in World War I, World War II, or the Civil War, Vietnam was and continues to be one of our most controversial conflicts. Questions have abounded during the post-Vietnam War years: Why did our government feel the need to involve its citizens in an area of the world that is over 8,500 miles away from its shores? Was communism a real threat to America, and if so how so? Was it in our national interest to allocate numerous human and material resources to this conflict? The questions of when, where, how, and why America involves itself in overseas matters are ones we have faced before and will continue to confront in the future. The road to safety, security, and living up to our ideals is a challenging one, but it will likely face even greater obstacles if our past is not part of our conversation now and in the future.

As a superpower, America faced many global challenges with energy and a sense of purpose. On July 20, 1969, Apollo 11 made humanity's first landing on the moon. Not only did it swell the nation with pride, but it led to numerous scientific and technological advancements such as Landsat, the longest-running program for the acquisition of satellite imagery. The millions of images collected by this program have provided valuable data used in agriculture, government, agriculture, business, with numerous other applications.

There are many beliefs, events, ideas, people, and places that make up our nation's history. *The American Road* addresses what we think are the most vital aspects of these issues. By reading and learning about our past, we find connections to who we are today. The trip is not always smooth. Along the way, there are many bumps, turns, potholes, and yes, dead ends. But, the journey is worth the effort. Indeed, it is only by traversing our past that we can learn how to build a better road to the future for all who call America home.

WEBSITE INTRODUCTION

History begins with an **experience,** quickly moving to the written word to be chronicled and interpreted. But the highway between the two **travels** in both directions. We all need to see, feel and listen to the past to appreciate its **value**. Hearing and watching Jimi Hendrix is much different than reading about him as a unique guitarist. The same goes for anything of relevance that occurred before our time. We need the written word to begin our journey into the past of this nation, but to really **comprehend** it, to turn it back into something **real**, we need a sensory connection to it as well.

The website that accompanies this book offers an important element to understanding history, the ability to make an influential/emotional/meaningful **connection** to the past, as well as an intellectual one. In many ways the website can give you an experience in historical study that is absolutely **vital** to grasping why all this happened the way it did and why it matters.

Get ready to watch the authors of "The American Road" **unravel** the events that turned the United States into the nation we know today. **View** the images that have come down to us from those years, depictions that illustrate the passions of many from an earlier time. As you click these items, you will **enliven** your understanding by bringing the process full circle, back to an experience to which you can **relate** and from which you can **grow**.

CHAPTER ELEVEN

The New South

Chapter 11: Key Concepts

- What is the greatest cultural impact of the New South period and what is your reasoning behind this choice?

- How would you evaluate the impact of the populist movement during this period?

- How did the concept of race relations evolve during this period? What was the most important development that impacted this area of society in this era?

The New South has been defined by many different things, depending on when and where one looks. After the end of Reconstruction, it is probably correct to say that most of the country viewed the South as a problem—a place that refused to become fully American-ized. It has been disproportionately violent while remaining poor by the standards of the nation. Many have criticized white southerners as especially racist and backward-thinking people. Often, it has seemed that the Civil War and Reconstruction did little to change the region. Yet, historians, if we are to believe their terminology, specify there was something new about the South. Indeed, the South would change in many ways and continues to do so in the present.

There has been, along with the criticism, an enduring fascination with all things southern. As humans tend to do, things that seem strange or exotic are subjects of inter-est. The South, especially before the creation of Old West myths, had been romanticized in stories and various legends. It is possible to both admire and revile a place like the South. It seemed like there was something to appreciate about a place so steadfastly stuck in the past. This is especially true as Americans increasingly left rural and/or agrarian lifestyles and embraced modern American life. Southerners usually have been quick to point out that they comprise a different, unique part of the country not like the rest. At times, it seemed like the South did not want to be part of America. This has had both positive and negative results.

The New South was a place of contradictions and perhaps still is, currently. Nowhere was racial violence so casually accepted nor quite as extreme. Nowhere were racial cus-toms, legalized or not, so rigidly enforced. Southerners fiercely protected their traditions but also seemed hospitable and friendly most of the time. They welcomed outsiders, unless someone violated local custom. Southerners have been among the most patriotic Ameri-cans and eager to serve during wartime. Yet, the South after Reconstruction often seemed anything but American. At various times, the South appeared like anything but a western-ized democracy—as millions of its citizens were disenfranchised and kept as a permanent subclass. Many have even remarked that the South has been more like Old World Europe than any other part of the United States. Family ancestry and tradition remained a core part of southern culture well into the twentieth century.

The New South was a place where tension was a part of everyday living and was one of the defining features of the region. Tradition and custom remained so strong in the South, one had to work hard to make sure to follow public expectations. Eventually, the term "Bible Belt" would be a frequently used term to describe the South. Indeed, evangelical religion was a dominant part of the culture. Most southerners went to church or at least professed strong religious belief. At the same time, southerners were a sporting people who enjoyed competitive contests, gambling, drinking, and brawling on a Saturday night. Racial stric-tures, even before legalized segregation, marked practically all parts of the South. Black men could not assert themselves in public without the expectation of reprisal. In certain situations, blacks and whites were not to associate as friends or equals. Interracial sex was taboo. Yet, black and white southerners continued to do all of these things even during the worst era of racial relations. The South was a paradox of a place intensely religious but often violent and hyper-masculine. It was racially divided with a history of blacks and whites intermixing, and yes, sometimes working together. This mix is probably not that rare in the history of the world, but these did make the South a singular place within America.

The Bourbons

Owing to attempts at modernization, the South undertook a pathway that would make it less distinct and more like the North and West. The South was never quite as antiprogressive as those perceived outside of it. During Reconstruction, the Redeemers had begun to realize that the world had changed, and in many ways, had left the Old South behind. The obsession with defending cotton-based slavery meant that the South had not developed things like internal infrastructure and education. They began to persuade others that it was possible and desirable to become more like the North in terms of prosperity. This would mean the development of industry, among other things.

Southerners also were concerned with a more direct task of rebuilding after the Civil War. The war destroyed, more than just property, but also the foundations of white superiority. The central tenet of southern slavery was that blacks were unfit for freedom and were inferior. Race relations could still be negotiated, but almost always with blacks as the property of others. Afterward, no one was sure how the new order would function. Certainly, there were various responses ranging from acceptance of emancipation to the diehard rejection of it. Most Redeemers took a conservative approach. Thus, they did not want black equality but neither did seek to stir animosity between whites and blacks. In the 1880s, race relations were much better than the period before, or certainly, afterward. Still, peace usually depended on black southerners remaining "in their place" as subservient to whites.

During and after Reconstruction, Redeemers were often called Bourbons. This was not a term of endearment and was most used to disparage Redeemers. Bourbons can be summarized as conservative Democrats who tended to support limited government interference in the affairs of Americans. They were usually pro-business—favoring free competition instead of government control of things like the railroad. Bourbons tended to be from the middle or upper classes. The term itself refers to the French Bourbon Dynasty who kept reemerging in France after the French Revolution. They, like conservative southern Democrats, never seemed to accept the will of the people and manipulated them for self-interest, opponents argued. They were said to have "learned nothing and forgotten nothing." The Bourbons appeared to have not learned any lessons of the Civil War. The idea of states' rights had been defeated in the Civil War, many believed. Bourbon critics often thought they were another reincarnation of the stubborn planters who started the Civil War.

New Industries

Democratic leaders sincerely wanted to improve the South, but they faced an uphill battle. There was not much capitol in the South for investment. It is also true that southerners had little experience doing most of the work required to work in or manage a factory. However,

North Carolina led the way in the tobacco industry. Washington Duke served in the Confederate Army but was not a fan of secession. He found success in the tobacco industry, starting at the bottom and eventually creating a full-fledged factory and moving it to Durham in 1874. Duke became one of the most successful southerners of the New South. His fortune allowed him to donate $100,000 to Trinity College. Later, it was renamed Duke after its namesake. Duke put many of his competitors out of business mainly due to his cigarette making.

Duke University Chapel is located on the campus of Duke University in Durham, North Carolina and seats 1800 people

Steven Frame/Shutterstock.com

Other industries emerged during Reconstruction. The furniture industry began to thrive around the same time tobacco was flourishing. Manufacturers came to the South and were usually warmly received. This was true in several states, but ultimately North Carolina passed all others in the production of furniture. In several states of the former Confederacy, new factories also produced materials for houses, such as bricks and door and window frames. Mass production of this kind soon began to supplant artisans who had long made these kinds of materials. At first, products mostly went to southern homes, but southern businesses soon were shipping their wares to other regions. Thus, in this way southern culture began to mimic the ways of the North.

Southern mining even began to compete with established operations in places like Pennsylvania. In northern Alabama, and especially Birmingham, the iron and steel industries became very profitable and successful. The city was founded in 1871 and named after the steel-producing mecca of Birmingham, England. Also called "the Pittsburg of the South," it was one of the major railroad hubs of the Deep South. Birmingham had an abundance of coal, iron ore, and limestone which are the core components of making steel. Mineral deposits, mining, factories of iron and steel, and railroads all went hand-in-hand and supported one another. The latter was important in order to ship goods to other places.

What the South was destined to become looked dramatically different from the way it did before the Civil War. Cities like Birmingham would increasingly become the norm. Instead of open spaces, plantations, and small farms cities such as Birmingham and Atlanta dotted the landscape with mills and skyscrapers. Yet, this process took time, and many farmers resisted the transition from farm to factory. However, many southerners were struggling after the Civil War, so some had little choice. Owing to the loss of property, the destruction of fields, and the loss of forced black labor, thousands of southerners found it difficult to survive. Factory work offered opportunity and a consistent, but low, wage. In the early southern factories, whole families often worked together.

For southern textile workers, their jobs became tied to where they lived due to the growth of mill towns. By 1900, roughly 90% of southern textile workers lived in what were often called "company" towns. Here, an owner provided homes, a local store, and sometimes recreation among other things. There were usually places for family gardens and communal lands for grazing. Houses were small, and in general, the towns retained an air of the country life. Mill towns have become infamous for cases of abuse and mistreatment from owners toward the workers. Southerners who lived in them, however, had mixed opinions about mill towns, and not all were bad. For employers, it was beneficial for entire families to work in the factories. In the opinion of most owners, providing a safe and healthy environment for employees benefitted everyone. The problems of this situation may be obvious. Workers could be more easily controlled and persuaded not to leave their jobs once they were linked with almost everything else that one did.

Farmers found the structure of mill towns and family labor that was comparable to life on the farm. To survive, the entire family worked. There was neither a great deal of travel or mobility in the rural South, so families were accustomed to doing things together. Owners used this traditional way of life to transition families to a life in the mills. All members worked in the factories. As well, some people remained in farming part time while also working in an industry.

Living in mill towns always offered a mixed bag of experiences that both helped and hurt southerners. In many ways, the South was a traditional, communal society. Kinship groups of extended family retained close ties and often lived with or near one another. The South was more of a public than a private society. That is to say, public behavior, keeping personal and family honor intact, and upholding community values was still very important. In mill towns, families often cooperated with one another such as helping when one member was ill. At the same time, towns were restrictive of individuality and disapproving of any behavior that violated what the majority thought was right. One did not have unlimited choices in mill towns to be individuals—at least not as much as in a large northern city. One could feel constantly spied on, and gossip was the norm. These had long been staples of southern culture that continued with the mill towns.

Despite some similarities with the life they had known, owners found it a challenge to completely indoctrinate southerners into the mill lifestyle. Farming was seasonal and something of an inexact science. Farmers certainly worked hard, but not in the same way all the time. There were years when the harvest exceeded expectations and those which were lean. Farmers had some control of when they worked and at what pace. Mill owners, to some degree, had to change the agricultural mindset into an industrial one. Instead of the clean rural air, workers often breathed in the steamy, sometimes poisonous, conditions in the factory. The degree to which mill owners used traditional paternalism in the factories is debatable. Supervisors conducted the day-to-day task of ensuring whether work was completed. Sometimes viewed as overly harsh, workers approached the owners to complain. Perhaps this could be seen as a relationship like southern planters enjoyed over most people in the Old South; perhaps not. It was not always the case that laborers had direct access to the person who owned the mill. Historians debate whether the industrial South was a continuation of something old or a sharp break from tradition.

Whether this industrial life was more old or new, owners and investors in the cotton mills looked at their work as something of a "Cotton Mill Crusade." It was considered something of a crusade because it was believed that it could rescue the South from its antiquated, aristocratic past. More importantly, mills could create, it was thought, a middle class of prosperous managers—much like in New England. For the poor, it could save them from the grinding life of tilling the soil. It could give the poor consistent and guaranteed employment. Like the mill towns, it was advertised that poor southerners would have cleaner and healthier places to live in the cities. Northern capitol often was the driving force behind the rapid factory growth. Partly, this was because they could pay southerners less to work, which still remains a factor in the present.

New South boosters certainly hoped northerners would invest in building a southern industrial base, and Henry Grady was chief among them. Booster is a term for the energetic, optimistic, southerner of the late nineteenth century who tried to heal old Civil War wounds and put the South on a more modern course. Grady was the most visible and effective. The Georgia newspaper editor is often credited with the term "New South," in fact. He promoted the idea that a new day had dawned and the South was ready for progress. He chiefly aimed his comments at northerners with the funds to help a region that was still far behind other sections of the country. Grady's most well-known moment probably came during an 1886 speech to the New England society of New York. He assured the crowd that "The Old South rested everything on slavery and agriculture, unconscious that these could neither give nor maintain healthy growth. The New South presents a perfect democracy . . . " Hopefully, boosters like Grady wanted, not just more factories, but the development of the southern railroads. For the most part he got it, as by the end of the century thousands of miles of new track had been created. Grady's forecast for the future and grasp of the present was not as accurate as he made it seem, however. Grady was a very good propagandist who tended to overlook or obscure southern shortcomings.

Henry Woodfin Grady (1850–1889) American southern journalist and publisher of the ATLANTA CONSTITUTION. Used his influence to advocate economic development following the devastation of the Civil War

Everett Historical/Shutterstock.com

Grady's boosterism did not change the reality that factory work was very hard and not all were treated equally. Black men were often given the most laborious work in the worst conditions. Children started young and were given the least important tasks. White men received the highest wages, usually followed by white women, black men, and then children. Workers tended to labor on average 12 hours a day for 6 days each week. Southerners typically received lower wages than their northern counterparts in the factories. Workers had almost no protections and could be replaced. Disease was also a problem for both poor farmers and factory workers. Generally, poor southerners, no matter their occupation, survived on a poor diet. For some, this meant almost entirely subsisting on corn-based foods. As a result, there were outbreaks of pellagra that was a highly dangerous disease contracted from lack of Vitamin B.

Despite the rapid move toward mill towns and textile work, the South remained largely rural with many areas of large-scale plantation agriculture. During Reconstruction, blacks resisted a carbon-copy return to working in gangs on plantations as they did during slavery. Even for freedmen that stayed on the plantation, they demanded some changes. This caused the widespread "shortage of labor," that planters decried, but in reality, it was just that labor now had some power. Eventually, most poor farmers returned to the powerful grip of the planter class. It was not just sharecroppers who suffered. Tenant farmers were another class of southern agricultural workers. They rented land for cash. Yet, the same punishing laws of the credit and crop lien systems (a mortgage on one's crop) often reduced tenants to peonage. The cash poor South had trouble rising out of generations of hopelessly indebted black and white farmers.

Race and the Law

Southern governments began to introduce laws directly aimed at limiting the options of black laborers. The Black Codes had long been overturned, but laws that kept the spirit of them returned once southern states had been redeemed. Vagrancy laws forced blacks to sign labor contracts that were enforceable by the courts. For a black person, vagrancy usually meant one was trying to make a living in some way other than working for a white landowner. The South also cracked down on labor agents. These were often northerners who came south to recruit for northern industries. These were executed by charging outside agents extremely high fees to be licensed. If people did not conform to these race-based prescriptions, the chain gang was often the result.

Unfortunately, convict leasing became a frequent outcome for black southerners who did not comply with racial norms. The practice became commonplace during the 1880s and continued until the first decades of the twentieth century. The lease law in southern states enabled some convicts to be rented out to work to nongovernment individuals. There were no limits on how or for how long prisoners could be forced to work. They had no protections. Those who worked usually did so in horrible conditions or at jobs that were intensely laborious and dangerous. An untold number of black men, and children, were simply worked to death. Southern law clearly targeted black men, and courts were not on their side. Men convicted of petty theft could then be worked much like a slave, for years. In fact, convict leasing looked and operated much like slavery. The local power structures in the South were in agreement about the need for convict leasing and worked for its enforcement.

The state most infamous for this practice was probably Mississippi. In 1901, it created a penitentiary better known as Parchman Farm. It was literally created to work and feel like a plantation. It was thought to be a more humane method to control leasing as well as the black population. Parchman had its own fields where prisoners were to grow their own food. Yet, in Mississippi, one could be sent to Parchman for little to no reason but color. If the state needed more convicts to loan, authorities simply rounded up more people. Convict leasing was a legally sanctioned way to reimplement the Black Codes, or one might say, slavery.

New Possibilities

Given the racial stratification one might assume that the Bourbons established complete dominance, but there were challenges to the traditional order. Early Unions tried to make inroads in the South to improve the conditions for both industrial and agricultural workers. They had limited and varied successes. Organizations like the Knights of Labor and the United Mine Workers attempted to organize in some southern states. In Alabama, both groups were present in the 1880s. Each group found some receptive prospects in the mines around Birmingham. Here, black and white miners worked together with more of a sense of equality and camaraderie than in most occupations. For the most part, unions in the South were segregated and not biracial. However, among the miners there appeared some opportunity for racial cooperation.

The moments where white and black could come together, and truly institute reform, were beaten

Terence Vincent Powderly (1849–1924)portrait is surrounded by 32 smaller portraits of the Leaders of the Knights of Labor and scenes of labor

back by racial fears. It made sense that poor southerners would unionize, probably more so than people elsewhere. On average, they were the poorest people in the country. White and blacks had mostly the same concerns. Race—baiting was often used to divide, however. Union organizers were accused of being communists and fundamentally ignorant and uncaring of the South's traditions. Both of these were incorrect. For the Bourbon Democrats, labor organizing simply could not be tolerated. This was a direct threat to their dominion.

Other type of political movements challenged the Bourbons who redeemed the South. In Virginia during the 1870s, people were increasingly unhappy with the government. The Republicans were not well organized or influential. The Redeemer government had not steered the state toward responsibility. The government was in debt, the economy was poor, and people were upset. Former Confederate General Thomas Mahone led a new movement in Virginia who were known as Readjusters. His coalition included poor white farmers, middle class, ambitious men, and black Virginians. This was a significant development. This was the kind of turn in southern politics that could be used to defeat the conservative elite. While the Redeemer class was preaching limited government, poor farmers were crying out for reform. The middling sort likewise saw the Democratic elite as past their prime.

Beginning in 1879, the Readjusters had a few years of success. They controlled every aspect of state government until the mid 1880s. For a time, Mahone hoped to join ranks with the Republicans. This was probably the mistake that led to their downfall. The Bourbon Democrats warned that any cooperation with Republicans would lead once again to the dark days of Reconstruction. They preached that the Readjusters would create some form of black domination. Thus, Virginia was redeemed once again, but state politics in Virginia was not as solidly Democratic as others in the South. Mahone and supporters showed what was possible in the former Confederate states.

It should also be remembered that black southerners were still voting during and after Reconstruction. Democrats could not simply ignore this voting bloc. A majority of black males were still voting as late as the 1890s in most states. There still existed, as well, a group of southern elites who were former Whigs or sympathized with the Republican program. These saw reforms as needed such as better education and more federal money for internal improvements. Democrats were anxious and always strident to prevent an alliance against them. Race was the easiest and most powerful weapon in the hands of the Party.

The National Farmers' Alliance and Industrial Union was certainly the most important of its kind in the South. The organization began in Texas and could claim over a million southern members. The Alliance included both small farmers and some planters. The Alliance fostered a cooperative spirit and advocated for many reforms. Farmers had been struggling for years, in part, because a surplus of crops was driving down prices. The Alliance advocated for government aid to farmers. They favored cooperative programs whereby farmers could pool their resources in case of a drought or some other calamity. They tended to disapprove of the railroad interests, complaining about high prices for shipping. The Alliance pushed for government regulation or ownership of something as important to farmers as the railroad. Generally, the Alliance preached that all the power in the country was shifting eastward toward financial centers and captains of industry. Southern farmers responded to a group that told them the elites were aligned against them.

These issues were not really addressed by the Bourbon Democrats, and the possibility of a third party seemed alive in the early 1890s. Black southerners created the Colored Farmers' Alliance. They were not formally affiliated with the National Alliance but did often meet at the same time, though at different places. There were moments when it seemed that both branches of the union might work together. However, the Colored Alliance was in a precarious position between Republicans and Democrats, and neither fully accepted them. In short, joining a union was a bold move for black southerners that alienated everyone. At the same time, the white Alliance basically did the same. Throughout the 1890s, their numbers dwindled. A farmers' union was something that most southerners viewed with some degree of suspicion.

Populism

The Populist Party was more of a threat to the established order in the South. The Populists represented a real opportunity for southern and Midwestern farmers to mold something that could be successful, long-lived, and dangerous to the Democrats and Republicans. The Populists represented a protest against falling agricultural prices and a national shift toward corporations, banks, and cities. Among their ranks were members of the National Farmer's Alliance, the Grange (a farmer's union), and disgruntled former Democrats. Populists gladly proclaimed the idea of themselves as the "People's Party." They tended to believe that rich city dwellers did not have their interests at heart and maybe were even conspiring against farmers. They attacked almost any wealthy institution not associated with farming. Populists preached that silver and not gold should back American currency. Their enemies tended to smear them as cranky, jealous of others, and most likely not mentally stable. In the South, the Populists had a significant appeal in the 1890s.

Populists had the opportunity to welcome black southerners into their ranks. The primary opponent of southern Populists was the Democrats—and they had made their stance on black rights well known. However, Populists could start anew without race-baiting while welcoming black farmers into the fold. For the most part, they did not. They feared scaring the average white southerner by openly embracing blacks and the issues that mattered to them. In other words, Populists feared that race could lose them elections. However, behind the scenes, there was some degree of friendless if not unity between white and black Populists. The concern was to openly embrace race issues, so they tended to avoid them. Basically, Populists were trying to walk a fine line between offending either race.

Tom Watson was less concerned with upsetting the feelings of southerners compared to the average Populist. Watson was probably the most important southern Populist. He was a writer, newspaper editor, and attorney from Georgia. Watson was one of the few who occasionally expressed what everyone already knew: poor southern farmers, no matter the race, had the same interests. He served in the House of Representatives as a Democrat until 1893 and soon switched to the new Party. Watson had the advantage of publishing his own newspaper, *The People's Party,* which served as his mouthpiece for scathing attacks on all he viewed as enemies. He considered himself a Jeffersonian proponent of agrarian interests over industries and their wealthy investors and owners. He was an impassioned speaker on the stump. Watson was outspoken and highly critical of what Populists often called "moneyed interests."

THE SURVIVAL OF THE FITTEST.

The survival of the fittest. Cartoon celebrating the victory of the gold standard against the populist inflation promoting silver standard

William Jennings Bryan, Democratic party presidential candidate. Cabinet card, October 3, 1896

Populists would play a role in the presidential election of 1892. The Democrats nominated Grover Cleveland while the Republicans ran Harrison. The Republicans were unpopular and somewhat disorganized. They had been behind the McKinley Tariff of 1890 that was hated by average Americans. Republicans lost support from black southerners due to measures that had largely deprived them of their voting rights. Populists nominated the experienced politician James Weaver from Iowa. Populists earned 8% of the total vote, but most of those were from the Midwest instead of the South. Cleveland beat Harrison and became President.

The election of 1896 presented a great opportunity for the Populists. The Panic of 1893 was the worst economic disaster to that point in American History. The common man suffered, so Populists were hopeful for a stronger national following. The Republicans chose William McKinley to represent their party. McKinley seemed almost uninterested in the race and let party regulars do his campaigning. Young William Jennings Bryan, at 36, was the star on the rise. Although a Democrat, he sounded more like a Populist. Bryan pitted the poor versus the rich and agricultural western and southern regions against the East and its financial centers. In one of the most famous orations in American History, Bryan delivered the "Cross of Gold Speech" at the Democratic convention. In short, Bryan said the gold standard would crucify average Americans by making them poor. He campaigned vigorously and was probably the greatest public speaker of his day. Populists figured Bryan represented them better than anyone else and chose to join the Democrats in supporting him. It was a fatal mistake. After the defeat of Bryan, the Populists were never the same. They divided on whether to remain independent of Democrats or work with them against Republicans.

The decline of Populism was just one part of a process that was slowly ensuring black southerners would become a permanent subclass. Conservative Democrats survived the rebellion from below and ruled most of the South for decades to come. With their victory, solidly Democratic state government began to roll back black rights until they were almost nonexistent. Through amendments, new constitutions, or other legislation states passed laws intended to get around the Constitutional protections for former slaves enacted during Reconstruction. The disenfranchisement of blacks was the primary goal, and it was accomplished. Removing them for voting went a long way toward creating the "Solid South" of Democratic domination.

The most infamous state to achieve disenfranchisement was Mississippi—with its Constitution of 1890. The ways in which this was accomplished became the template for others to follow, and it was known as the "Second Mississippi Plan." Eliminating black voting was the primary topic of conversation at the constitutional convention. Poll taxes were fees one paid in order to vote. The problem, many complained, was that they also eliminated some poor whites from voting. The grandfather clause was added that allowed one to vote whose grandfather could do so before the Civil War. Obviously, this would not include blacks. Moreover, in order to vote, Mississippi implemented a law stating that one had to pass literacy tests. They did not invent this idea, as South Carolina already had their own version of them. These tests hurt blacks more than whites, as they had a much higher illiteracy rate in the South. However, Mississippi and other states added the "understanding clause" that allowed someone to vote who could interpret an important document like the Constitution. This was a blatant ploy to allow pollsters to decide who could vote or not based on color. Mississippi was the pioneer in subverting the Constitution without saying directly that the majority of black citizens could no longer vote. The Second Mississippi Plan was adopted by every southern state in the 1890s and moving forward to the next century.

Whatever was left of southern Populism after 1896 moved increasingly toward antiblack attitudes and the kind of methods of the Second Mississippi Plan. Populism did not necessarily die with the Party, itself. Some southern politicians adopted Populist rhetoric and outlook though affiliated with the Democratic Party. Ben "Pitchfork" Tillman was a Democrat, but because of his views, often was assumed to be a member of the Populists. He used the kind of direct, folksy appeals to the common man that the Bourbons despised. Tillman served as governor and long-time senator of South Carolina. Tillman made his hatred of black southerners very clear in his speeches. He, like many populist-types, began to see disenfranchisement as a means for whites to talk about the real issues without having to worry about the concerns of blacks. Tom Watson felt the same. Once a public spokesman on blacks' behalf, after 1896 Watson announced his opposition to black civil rights. He also had an intense hatred for Jewish Americans. In many ways, the failure of Populists in 1896 left Watson a bitter man.

The Emergence of Jim Crow

In 1896, a landmark Supreme Court ruling would further stack the deck against black southerners. Plessy v. Ferguson began as a test case to try to inviolate a New Orleans law that whites and blacks had to sit in different train cars. Concerned citizens of New Orleans

Everett Historical/Shutterstock.com

Melville W. Fuller (1833–1910), eighth Chief Justice of the United States Supreme Court from 1888 through 1910. The Court decided in favor of racial segregation in the Plessy v. Ferguson case of 1896

persuaded Homer Plessy, who was classified as black, to board the white car and get arrested. Plessy had some black ancestry but was very light-skinned. The idea was that lots of people were of mixed race and creating separate, rigid categories did not make sense and could not be used as the basis for legal segregation. Plessy's lawyer also argued that his client had been denied equal protection under the law as guaranteed by the 14th Amendment. The Supreme Court ruled against Plessy in a seven to one decision. The Court said Louisiana law had not violated his civil rights by offering separate accommodations. Here was established the precedent that separate but equal was the law of the land. This decision was one of, if not, the most important decision(s) in American History. It meant segregation could legally take place in limitless ways, and it did throughout the South. Racial segregation would be the norm in the South until at least the 1960s.

In essence, the Court sanctioned white southerners to create a society where blacks could be discriminated against every day and in all aspects of life. There are two basic classifications of segregation. One is written into law and the other operates via custom. The latter existed before Plessy v. Ferguson in some form, but historians disagree to what degree and when it started. Segregation of this type could be, for example, the refusal to allow blacks to live in white neighborhoods. It is clear, though, that segregation was not nearly as ingrained in the South before 1896 as after it. Widespread segregation did not immediately occur after Reconstruction. In addition, during slavery blacks and whites intermingled even if those relationships were unequal. After the Court's decision, legal segregation would often be referred to under the term Jim Crow. This was a catchall phrase that symbolized the oppressive, racist system, including segregation, which pervaded everyday life in the southern states.

Two years after the Court's decision, the Wilmington, North Carolina riot affirmed that racial relations in the South were getting worse. The town had been known as one where blacks and whites mostly had a peaceful coexistence. In 1896, a coalition of Republicans and Populists won many state and local offices. Democrats were determined to erase these results in the next elections in 1898. They used race-baiting to suggest that black men would sexually assault white women unless people did not restore the state to pure Democratic rule. The racial rhetoric was ratcheted up to such a degree that whites in Wilmington made war on their black neighbors. A mob attacked and burned a newspaper press owned by a local, outspoken black man named Alex Manly. Next, they began to randomly target and kill black residents. Officially, the death total of Wilmington's black citizens was 25, but it was possible that many more died. An editorial from the pro-Democratic local paper, quoting Georgian Rebecca Felton, revealed the fear and hostility that could have promoted this kind of massacre. It was printed, "If it requires lynching to protect woman's dearest possession from ravening, drunken human beasts, then I say lynch a thousand negroes a week . . . if it is necessary."

The Atlanta Race Riot of 1906 was comparably as tragic as Wilmington. Atlanta was a bustling community that New South boosters envisioned for the future. It was also one of the centers of a new class of a successful black middle class and cadre of intellectuals. Its black universities and churches were places of sharing ideas and seeking refuge from the Jim Crow world. Race relations worsened during the election for governor between Hoke Smith and Clark Howell. The candidates each had a rival newspaper in Atlanta that Smith and Clark used to smear the other. Both committed to white supremacy, the candidates stirred up antiblack sentiment in order to win the election. Stories about the rapes of white women by black men, likely false, were reported. For three days, mobs of angry whites roamed Atlanta killing and injuring dozens of black residents in response. Indirectly, the riot was caused by a general upsurge in the mobility and outward assertiveness of Atlanta's black population. Church leaders especially were important figures to the black community. Black business-owning was on the rise. As often was the case in this atmosphere, indiscriminate, racially motivated violence was the result.

Race riots and lynchings were characteristic of the time period most consider the worst for race relations in the history of the nation. Historians call the era from roughly 1890–1914 the nadir of black/white violence and racism. In the South, this was the worst time of race-based lynchings. Usually, people think of hangings, but lynching is any extralegal execution of someone, without a trial, for some perceived wrong. Most lynchings in the South were directed toward black men. Many things could incite this to happen. Relationships between black males and white females were strictly prohibited in the New South. The stereotype of black men having an uncontrollable lust, and being likely to commit rape, was persistent and common. Other things prompted lynchings such as black businessmen competing with whites, an insult toward any white person, an actual crime, or many others. His-

IDA B. WELLS.

Ida B. Wells, woodcut, 1891

torians estimate that many lynchings occurred around the same time as an economic downturn in a community. Thus, a lynching could have been due to collective white frustration and anger. They very often were public entertainment and even advertised beforehand. Hundreds or even more people sometimes attended the grisly spectacles, including children. Black men were sometimes burned before or after their executions. Mutilations frequently occurred. Body parts were taken as souvenirs and even sold in local shops.

Ida Wells was a black activist who vigorously worked to bring attention to the lynchings going on in the South. She was born in Holly Springs, Mississippi in 1862. Naturally tough and unmovable, she was once literally dragged off a train for refusing to give up her seat to a white man. In Memphis, Wells became an editor of the newspaper *Free Speech and Headlight,* and in 1892 three of her friends were lynched because they were competing with another white business. From this point forward, Wells dedicated her life to the cause of civil rights and especially that of trying to end the murders of innocent black southerners. In response to the Memphis killings, Wells suggested that blacks move out of southern cities that would not protect their constitutional rights. Later in Chicago, Wells wrote *Southern Horrors: Lynch Law in All Its Phases* to expose the southern practice of which most northerners were not aware. Wells also worked in the cause of female suffrage and against segregation. Wells was one of the founders of the National Association for the Advancement of Colored People (NAACP). In 1930, she even ran for the state legislature in Illinois. Her tireless efforts did little to stop southern lynching in her lifetime. The practice seemed to be condoned or at least tolerated by most white southerners.

Perhaps no white southerner during the early twentieth century was more outspokenly in favor of lynching and against black civil rights than James K. Vardaman of Mississippi. He became governor of his state in 1903. Vardaman had long black hair, was known as a great speaker, and earned the nickname, "The Great White Chief." A self-styled Populist, Vardaman was the enemy of the Bourbon elite and railed against them. He also may have been the most public, explicitly racist southern politician who has ever lived. Among many of his statements condemning blacks, he infamously remarked "if it is necessary every Negro in the state will be lynched; it will be done to maintain white supremacy." He considered black southerners unfit for equality, because they were "lazy, lying, lustful animal[s], which no amount of training can transform into a tolerable citizen." Mississippi planters like the powerful Leroy Percy worked to stop Vardaman's political career.

There were very tangible reasons why someone like Percy hated those like Vardaman. In this period, southern politicians who were of the Populist mold used, not only race-baiting, but appeals to class to win elections. Southern politics was a battlefield as much about the rhetoric as the issues. Within white society, there was a huge economic gap between planters with important family lineage and the dirt-poor farmer who struggled to feed his family. Both the Populists and the Bourbons were equally as committed to maintaining white supremacy, but they disagreed on how to achieve it. For poor whites, free blacks were competition, but for planters, they were the vital workforce that allowed their plantations to function. Southern, white elites preferred to minimize disruptions to the work routine, so this meant steering away from provocative language or anything that might prompt black anger in return. In other words, business runs best without instability of any kind. Planters preferred the paternalistic approach left over from slavery. Vardaman was not a paternalist, as this was bald hatred.

Someone like Percy feared that his black labor force might simply leave, and these fears came true. The 1927 flood of the Mississippi was a cataclysmic disaster, not just for Percy's state, but for those further north as well. In the Mississippi Delta near Greenville, thousands of black tenants and sharecroppers were displaced from their land. Desperate and fearful, planters used black labor to build levees in order to protect their plantations from the overflowing Mississippi. Once the levees were breached, Percy refused to evacuate the workers who were now caught on top of them. His concern was that once gone, they would never come back. Afterward, black Deltans held animosity toward Percy. The flood deeply strained the way in which black laborers viewed Percy and other Mississippi planters, so they began to leave by the thousands. Percy was devastated. He had spent a lifetime trying to cultivate a good relationship with those who tilled his soil. He had even stood up to the Klan and successfully prevented them from recruiting in Greenville. The incident was just one that contributed to the Great Migration of black southerners from the South to the North.

Washington and DuBois

Mass exodus of blacks from the South was something, years earlier, Booker T. Washington counseled against. Washington was among the last generation to be born into slavery. No black man in America had more influence or more respect from all quarters. His *Up From Slavery* told the story of his life, was widely read, and remains a classic. However, Washington was a prolific writer and speaker, as well as an educator. In 1881, Washington was named the first leader of the new Tuskegee Institute in Alabama. From here, Washington created a national network of white and black allies. He was personal friends with Republican politicians and visited Theodore Roosevelt in the White House. Until his death in 1915, Washington worked to educate and help black southerners. However, Washington did so through shrewd politicking and maneuvering. He believed black southerners could prosper in the South and should seek to remain there.

Booker T. Washington (1856–1915), African American educator and leader. Ca. 1900

Washington took the mantle of leadership from Frederick Douglass, who died the same year the great leader of Tuskegee made his most famous speech. At the Atlanta Cotton Exposition in 1895, Washington outlined his ideas about how his race could prosper while reassuring whites that blacks should not be militant about civil rights. Ever since, the speech has been known as "the Atlanta Compromise." Washington continually asked both whites and blacks to "cast down your bucket where you are." To blacks, this meant to seek to stay and work in the South and not seek prosperity elsewhere. For whites, Washington was advising to hire and help black southerners while not looking for sources of outside labor. In addition, the speech is known for his argument that blacks should postpone full equality in favor of gaining economic ground. In other words, he pledged that black southerners would accept segregation and disenfranchisement in exchange for education and good jobs. Certainly, many whites found this message acceptable. In other words, Washington was not offering subjugation but rather compromise.

W.E.B. DuBois was the chief critic of Washington's program. DuBois, the first black graduate of Harvard, did not believe in compromise of this nature. Part of it was the contrasting backgrounds of the two. DuBois was from Massachusetts and an intellectual. Washington was born in Virginia and spent most of his time in the South. Where Washington hoped for small gains in what he understood was a hostile land, DuBois tended to see widespread discrimination and looked for more comprehensive solutions to racism. Both had intellects of the highest order. DuBois argued that without basic equality, whites would be able to strip away all rights. Like Washington, DuBois had a wide circle of friends, so both headed two different networks of individuals which supported their leader's views through the press and otherwise. DuBois lived long after Washington's death. DuBois was a scholar as well as a civil rights activist.

DuBois' 1903 *The Souls of Black Folk* is one of the most important and insightful meditations on race ever written. In it, he introduces new terms and concepts that helped to define how people consider race. His "double consciousness" explained how black people had two separate identities due to their skin color. They were defined how other people saw them, and according to DuBois, that was usually negative. *Souls* outlined many of his views about how black Americans, and not just southerners, should approach the struggle for civil rights. Some have viewed him as an elitist, because of his idea that the "talented tenth," that is the brightest and best among black Americans, should lead the rest to rise to their level. Education was the key. He disagreed with Washington who advanced the idea that blacks should focus on vocational training. Instead, DuBois believed that blacks should strive to receive well-rounded education at the highest levels of universities. He famously predicted that the problem of the coming century would be that of "the color line." By this, he meant not just in America but referred to racism all over the world. In his classic work, DuBois also prefigured the coming Harlem Renaissance. He celebrated black achievements, most notably, in music.

Artistic Achievement

Despite the hardships of the Jim Crow era, the musical legacy that derived from black southerners remains one of the greatest in the world. Maybe it was partly due to suffering, in fact, that people produced the sounds that have traveled around the world. It is hard to imagine forms that have been more admired than jazz, blues, ragtime, gospel, and others—and these principally originated from poor black people across the South. One cannot trace the lineage of American music in full without eventually leading back to Africa. Most famously, syncopated rhythms of the African drum survived in some form and can be heard even in styles today. Certainly white southerners have contributed much, as well. Early pioneers of country included Alabaman Hank Williams and Mississippian Jimmie Rodgers. In the South, white and black styles were often mixed to produce something even better, as usually happens when cultures merge together.

No musical style is more synonymous with the South than blues and jazz. They are of course related. Without question, the jazz center of the country has always been New Orleans. Jazz is often free-form and improvised, and it has many subcategories. In a multicultural city like New Orleans, southern, African, Caribbean, and European influences were stewed together to create an art that is easier heard than described. Blues is likely even more identifiable as southern. By the name alone, most assume that it is strictly music about hard times and wallowing in misery. This is true to some degree, but that was not really the point of why it was created or played. People have said that jazz was more uptown and the blues was rural. The latter actually was the music of weekend parties in small clubs called juke joints. These occasions allowed people, perhaps frustrated or tired from their regular existence, to enjoy life without interference. Blues could be slow or up-tempo and take on almost any topic. Lyrics were often racy filled with metaphor and double-meanings. Most of what it was, is now lost to history, unfortunately. It is difficult to pinpoint when it started, but the genesis of what became the blues was formed during the first few decades before World War II.

Without question, the most respected bluesmen came almost entirely from the South. For many black southerners, this music offered a different kind of life other than sharecropping. Bluesmen traveled around the southern circuit of small clubs and sometimes played on street corners. They were often dangerous men who lived tumultuous and short lives. Charlie Patton is sometimes considered the first bluesman, only because more is known about him than some who likely lived and died anonymously. The Mississippi Delta produced an unusually large number of legendary blues artists, like Patton. Muddy Waters (McKinley Morganfield), Howlin' Wolf (Chester Burnett), and Robert Johnson were all from the region. Many consider Johnson as the greatest blues artist of all time. He died at 27 before ever receiving fame in his lifetime. Johnson's work has been admired and played by the most well-known rock musicians who have ever lived. His music was a marvel and his life, mysterious. As the story goes, Johnson sold his soul to the devil in order to play in a style that most agree was simply better than his contemporaries. Other places in the South produced great bluesmen, like Blind Lemon Jefferson from Texas and Blind Willie McTell of Georgia.

CLARKSDALE, MISSISSIPPI, May 8, 2015: Guitars show the junction of US 61 and US 49 often designated as the famous crossroads where, according to legend, Robert Johnson sold his soul to the Devil

Pierre-Jean Durieu/Shutterstock.com

In addition to music, literature flourished in the South during the first half of the twentieth century. Among the best authors were Eudora Welty, Robert Penn Warren, Richard Wright, and Zora Neale Hurston, but the reigning king of southern literature will probably always be William Faulkner. One of the greatest and most successful authors in American

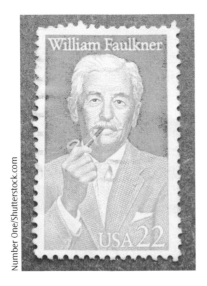

Number One/Shutterstock.com

History, Faulkner's works were dripping with the experiences and culture of his native Mississippi. A few of his classic works are *As I Lay Dying* and *The Sound and the Fury*. Much of his work was based on the southern past. Few others tried to come to terms with what the past meant to the present, more than Faulkner. In fact, Faulkner said, "the past is never dead, it's not even past." Faulkner's themes tended to deal with how a people who thrive on tradition and having a distinctive culture reconcile that with defeat, tragedy, and institutionalized racism. The question for the white South becomes, how proud should we be of our past? Whereas the story of America as a whole is often translated as one unbroken rise to prominence, the South was defeated, subjugated, and maligned. Faulkner, like many southern writers, had a love–hate relationship with the South, as did his characters.

Conclusion

It is a struggle to say how much of the Faulknerian, traditional South remained after modernization and civil rights reform came to the South. Over the twentieth century, things that made America as it looks and functions today influenced the South. Machinery began to make farm labor less dependent on human beings. Corporate agriculture became the norm, as people increasingly had occupations other than farming. In fact, corporations of all kinds came to the South. Old buildings were torn down and replaced with new ones. In most southern towns, Wal-Mart has taken the place of country stores. Black southerners, along with others, worked to fight Jim Crow and the longstanding unequal racial customs of the South. The Civil Rights Movement indeed brought great change no matter how incomplete it might have been. It is a challenge to say what of "The South" was left. America seems to look much the same wherever one goes.

Certainly there are many positive outcomes due to the South abandoning some of its old ways. Black southerners can participate in the political process without fear. For the most part, the South is a multicultural region where people live in harmony with one another. Tourism is a huge industry. Owing to coastline and a favorable climate, the South has become a destination for people all around the world. Still, when one travels throughout the small communities of the South, the remnants of the Lost Cause and the Civil War can still be seen, mostly through various monuments and statues. Southerners, white and black, still prefer to be something distinctive without the corporatized sameness that marks all of America. Southerners tout their food, manners, climate, and history as something special and worthy of singling out as unique within American culture. It is the history part that can be problematic, though. The American road that the South took was one filled with slavery, racism, and defiance of outsiders who insisted that it change. history in the South still has the power to divide. Can the modern South still exist alongside the old Confederate monuments? Should it? The answers to these questions are ever unfolding.

CHAPTER TWELVE

Industrial Revolution

Chapter 12: Key Concepts

- Describe the rise of big business in America. Who were the leaders and how did they help establish monopolies in the country?

- Evaluate the influx of people to the cities during the Industrial Age. What type of effect did this have on the cities?

- Explain the role of boss politics and the party machine in politics during the Industrial Age. Why was the party machine work so effective?

Introduction

The primary mover behind the emergence of the modern era in America was the Industrial Revolution. When the Industrial Revolution arrived in America in the late nineteenth century it came with a force that changed the course of history. A primarily rural country was transformed into an urban, industrial powerhouse that shaped the next century and set the groundwork for America to become the most powerful nation in the world. New companies emerged, as old businesses either changed in order to compete or simply died out. These new companies offered a wider array of manufactured goods and consumer wares that appealed to the American businessman and mainstream customer. Consequently, as America's economic output surged, the standard of living for the average citizen increased as well.

However, life within the cities was not always bustling and optimistic. American cities stretched and strained under the new weight of change. The poor, working classes, and new immigrants suffered as the golden exterior of the American dream gave way to a sometimes broken, corrupt system that sometimes left them behind. Poverty grew as the gap between the wealthy and the poor widened. Although many believed that anyone, regardless of birthplace, education, or financial circumstances could succeed in America through self-discipline, intelligence, and frugality, not everyone found it. Those that found the American dream had a new chance in life. However, countless others were trapped in poverty and the cycle of big business practices. Many of these laborers began to demand rights and fight against the tyrannical rule of corporation owners. Consequently, their actions sometimes culminated in strikes and violence. Their protests, however, were laying the groundwork for the modern labor movement and providing the means for the working class to have a voice.

Roots of the Industrial Revolution

The second Industrial Revolution began in Europe in the latter half of the 1800s with the rise of new inventions and factories. Textiles were the first industry to be transformed, soon followed by transportation and communication. Textile mills flourished in Britain, and by the mid-1800s the mills were producing clothing that working people could afford. The revolution in transportation was equally striking. Railroads multiplied 100-fold so that by 1914 there were 220,000 miles of track in Europe. Railroad expansion required a huge infrastructure as well, and in response bridges, tunnels, stations, and workshops began to spring up throughout Europe. They were part of an even larger structure of public works, including canals, aqueducts, and drains, that transformed Europe into the modern age. Along with these revolutionary changes, the process of communication accelerated with the invention and operation of the telegraph and, eventually, the telephone.

When the Industrial Revolution swept into America in the late nineteenth century the most dynamic changes took place east of the Mississippi River and north of the Ohio River. An industrial triangle developed among Chicago, Boston, and Washington D.C. where new factories were created due to the large coal and iron deposits. Compared to other countries in the world, industrialization in America was dramatic and quick. The United States offered an abundance of untapped raw materials and energy sources. Coal, iron, timber, petroleum, and water provided new means of production and power.

America's transformation into the industrial age was also quick due to the flood of new workers moving into the cities. European immigration was on the rise in the late 1800s, flooding the nation with new families, and disenfranchised small farmers from rural America were moving into the cities looking for opportunity. These groups became a ready supply of potential workers. In addition, the business acumen of talented and ambitious groups of men harnessing the natural resources and the newly arrived workers developed the means of the large-scale production of goods. The demand for these new goods increased in America as people ventured out west, moved up the socioeconomic ladder into the new middle class, or tried to make a profit in the stock market.

The Great Tycoons

The Industrial Age generated new heights of wealth in American society. Prosperous businessmen, nicknamed "the Great Tycoons," boasted immense amounts of power and wealth. They were the force behind the newly burgeoning industries and provided the framework for the rise of corporate business as well as the concept of industrial capitalism. As the railroad industry enlarged into a national market in the late nineteenth century, the spirit of entrepreneurship spread to encompass the accompanying businesses of steel and oil. These oil and steel industrialists pioneered new strategies to control their perspective markets and dominate the American economy. Three of the most dynamic competitors of the day were railroad businessman Jason "Jay" Gould, steel magnate Andrew Carnegie, and oil giant John D. Rockefeller.

Jay Gould

The first transcontinental railroad was completed in 1869 in Promontory Point, Utah, connecting the new West with the nation's economy in the east. During the next two decades railroad track doubled in America and did so again between 1890 and 1900. This dramatic expansion of the railroads created the country's first big business with Pennsylvania Railroad boasting a payroll of $55,000 and capital of more than $400 million. Railroad entrepreneurs became the forerunners of the new wealth in America, and Jay Gould represented the shrewd (and arguably cruel) business tactics of success in the Industrial Age.

Gould's notorious business actions culminated in his leadership of numerous American railroads as either president or director. He also became the voice behind the building of the second transcontinental railroad in the 1880s. As the new tracks were laid competing businesses had to equally expand or sell out. With the competition growing, the federal government got involved by offering subsidies called land grants to railroad companies. Companies received money, land, and grants from federal and state governments in proportion to the amount of track produced. Consequently, this often led to low-quality track that was laid quickly and haphazardly. States and local communities invited the railroad expansion. They recognized that towns along the railroad lines would flourish and bring money to their local economies. Thus, the expansion of the railroad fed itself.

Andrew Carnegie

Andrew Carnegie, April 1905

As railroad expansion spread in America the steel industry became its backbone, and Andrew Carnegie was the leader of this industry. Carnegie was labeled a "self-made man" and became the model for many people seeking the American dream. The self-made man started at the bottom of the financial ladder and, through hard work and wise business sense, worked his way to wealth. His "rags to riches" story began at the age of 12, when the Scottish-born boy moved with his family to New York in 1848. Carnegie quickly obtained a job in a factory, and eventually rose from cleaning bobbins in a textile factory to becoming one of the richest men in America. Carnegie built an empire, Carnegie Steel, and became the leader in the transformation of iron into steel. Carnegie pioneered the use of vertical integration in his empire. Through vertical integration Carnegie bought the iron mines for his steel company, coal mines for the fuel, and railroad companies to transport the steel. He, thus, controlled all aspects of steel production.

Carnegie was a harsh factory owner. He demanded his employees to work 12 hours a day, 7 days a week, with low wages. The factories provided unsafe working conditions with managers often undermining each other for the sake of competition. Through these means, he was able to produce record-making levels of steel at a minimum expense. He continued his shrewd tactics and kept his prices low by cutting secret deals with railroad companies to acquire lower rates than his rivals for transporting his steel. By these means, Carnegie was able to cut the cost of making steel by half and monopolize the market.

Carnegie was known to the public for his philanthropy. In his 1889 essay titled, "The Gospel of Wealth," Carnegie developed the concept that millionaires needed to live "unostentatious lives" and give away large portions of their wealth for the betterment of the poor and society. He practiced this by giving away $350 million before he died. His money was given to support lavish public projects such as the construction of libraries and concert halls, as well as more discreet ventures in helping fund science and providing thousands of organs to churches.

John D. Rockefeller

"I have ways of making money that you know nothing of." John D. Rockefeller, Standard Oil.

Oil, discovered in Pennsylvania in 1859, became another key part of the American economy during the Industrial Age. Oil refineries started to develop and were sold for relatively little money in the 1860s and 1870s allowing for numerous competitors to vie for the

John D. Rockefeller

companies. John D. Rockefeller became the oil giant of the age as he relentlessly bought out failing and competing refineries and improved their efficiency. This method, known as "horizontal integration," became a model of American business for the modern age and the foundation of Rockefeller's company, Standard Oil. Companies throughout America began to buy out their competitors to eliminate competition and create monster businesses.

Rockefeller also used his business acumen to pioneer the business model known as a "trust." In a trust, competing companies relinquished the majority of its stock to a board run by Standard Oil trustees in exchange for a share of the profits. Standard Oil Trust eventually grew to encompass 40 companies under the direction of a 9-member board. This practice allowed Rockefeller to control prices and set production rates, thus leading to a monopoly in the oil business. Soon he controlled 90% of the oil business in the country and became America's first billionaire. Other industries soon began to follow Standard Oil's example and establish trusts to control their markets as well. These tactics created big businesses that reached new levels of power, unchecked by the federal government or the American people.

Rockefeller's methods were not welcomed by everyone. Journalists and politicians criticized Standard Oil, and their voices eventually led to the anti-trust movement. The most famous antitrust journalist of the time was Ida Tarbell. Writing for the popular *McClure's* magazine, Tarbell targeted Standard Oil Trust with its monopolistic tactics and unfair working conditions. Her criticism helped launch the growing demand that powerful trusts in America be broken apart for the sake of competition and fairness.

Ironically, as a great tycoon in America, Rockefeller led a humble, unostentatious life. He was also a philanthropist and gave away $540 million during his lifetime. As a conscientious church-attender, Rockefeller tithed 10% of his income from his first paycheck consistently throughout his life. He also gave millions of dollars to educational development in American schools and colleges. He provided major funding for Atlanta's first college for African-American women, Spelman College. His other donations led to advancements in health causes, the arts, and science.

J.P. Morgan

Although he was not technically part of the "big 3" (railroad, oil, and steel), J.P. Morgan played a central role in the development and restructuring of American industry. Working in the field of finance, Morgan's actions provided the capital backing and investment opportunities to create the industrial giants of the age.

John Pierpont Morgan was the preeminent finance capitalist in the late nineteenth century. Morgan led the nation's largest investment banking firm. He used the practice of consolidation to build the largest banking institution of his day and become America's unofficial central banker. His institution oversaw the buying and selling of securities (stocks, bonds, etc.) to wealthy Americans and foreign investors to underwrite the growing industrial businesses.

Morgan hated competition and whenever possible he consolidated with competing businesses instead of contending against them. In the 1890s, Morgan rescued ruined railroad companies and reorganized them into conglomerations that placed the majority of the nation's railroads into the hands of only a few directors. He also oversaw the mergers of several small steel companies, and in 1901, Morgan bought Carnegie Steel for $480 million (roughly $9.6 billion today). He merged Carnegie Steel with its competitors to create U.S. Steel, the largest corporation in the world at that time.

Morgan's tactics, as well as those of Gould, Carnegie, and Rockefeller produced the basis of the modern business model, but also created a backlash of social criticism against their unethical, monopolistic, and exploitative methods to amass large amounts of wealth. They became known as "robber barons" and set the standard for the amassing of wealth in America. And their rise to financial power helped build the dream that any person could achieve prosperity through hard work and wise business acumen. However, they also caught the attention of social reformers seeking to expose the corruption and political power of the tycoons. These reformers demanded more federal regulations over business and helped develop this in the coming years.

Rise of the Cities

Birth of the Gilded Age

As the rapid rise of industry stimulated wealth and productivity in America, people from all over the world immigrated to the country to obtain success. These newcomers were joined by scores of American farmers who also moved to the cities to find jobs and opportunity. The promise that drove them was one of American success and wealth, in other words the American Dream. However not everyone achieved their dreams; many were met with the stark realities of harsh living conditions. Author Mark Twain released a book in 1873 titled *The Gilded Age* which captured the contrast between those that found success and those who barely scraped out a living. Twain argued that the get-rich quick era in America was only surface deep. Beneath the layer of golden opportunity was a cheap base of poverty built on the backs of the working class in America.

New Arrivals to the City

America was primarily a rural nation throughout the nineteenth century. Agriculture provided the base for much of the population, as small farmers cultivated subsistent farms. However, with the advent of the Industrial Revolution, new techniques and mechanized

Immigrants just arrived from Foreign Countries—Immigrant Building, Ellis Island, New York Harbor

tools were created that affected a number of these farmers. Some farmers adopted the new tools, such as threshers and harvesters, and were able to create larger farms with considerable crops to sell. This new form of agribusiness generated more wealth for these farmers and established many of them on the path of corporate farming. However many other rural families were not able to compete with the larger farms and had to find an alternative form of work, and thus they moved to the cities. They became part of the larger swell of people seeking work in the industrial work force.

African-Americans moved to the cities seeking opportunities. Black men and women began to move from the south to northern states during the Industrial Age to find work and escape the poverty, racism, and violence associated with the Jim Crow laws in the South. Between 1890 and 1920 over 300,000 blacks migrated to the north, thus beginning what is known as the Great Migration. Between 1890 and 1970, seven million black men and women moved north and created new population demographics.

The greatest source of population growth in the cities during this period was immigrants. Men and women from Europe, especially southern and eastern European countries, poured into America seeking wealth and land. These immigrants were escaping poverty, warfare, and political and religious persecution. They wanted the economic opportunities and upward mobility afforded in the United States and associated this with the acquisition of land. With the passage of the Homestead Act in 1862, immigrant families poured into America to acquire the 160 acres of land promised by the government to those who settled the land for 5 years. These families came from countries such as Russia, Italy, Greece, and Austria-Hungary in Europe as well as Asian nations in Japan and China. Eventually, between 1860 and 1920, 28 million immigrants moved to America. Many of these immigrants came through Ellis Island in New York City or Angel Island in San Francisco.

City Life for the Working Class

Physical Implications

With the flood of millions of people moving into America at a rapid pace the cities could not keep up. Living quarters were scarce and many of the new arrivals had no choice but to live in tenements in areas of towns that came to be known as slums. The most common form of housing was tenements, which were usually made of two to three dimly lit and poorly ventilated rooms. The dingy rooms offered little outside light, no toilet, bath, or running water, and cramped conditions. Sometimes several families lived in the same small spaces. Owing to demand, rents were usually high in these apartments. As crowding increased, disease, abuse, and despair multiplied within the harsh realities of city life.

Chronic outbreaks of disease periodically spread through the cities. Drinking water was often contaminated, as primitive and overwhelmed sewage systems were not able to manage the massive volume of people. This led to the growth of bacteria and outbreaks of typhoid fever and cholera. With the chronic lack of hygiene, little knowledge of sanitation requirements, and cramped conditions, the outbreaks spread rapidly and sometimes became epidemics.

Five cents a spot—unauthorized immigration lodgings in a Bayard Street tenement [New York]

Crowding within the cities and tenements had other physical implications as well. Owing to the dense population in the slums, crime rates spiked. Offenses ranged from minor pickpocketing to violent murder and, as these areas of the city did not have the police force needed to provide protection, criminals were not usually caught. The anonymity found in the cramped urban environment fed criminal activities since there was often no form of accountability.

Fires were another threat. While buildings were erected quickly and regularly due to high demand, the use of subpar materials and haphazard building practices led to unsafe conditions. Once fires broke out, they spread quickly through the substandard buildings and were hard to extinguish. Fire departments were not adequately supplied or trained to handle these massive fires. One of the most famous examples was the Chicago Fire of 1871, which destroyed 3 square miles and left 18,000 homeless.

Psychological Implications

The cramped conditions and hopelessness found among the working class sometimes produced a rise in alcoholism and abuse. It was not uncommon for disillusioned men to succumb to alcohol as a means of escape. Domestic violence was often the result. Women and children became the victims in these situations and soon began to respond. These women formed support groups to provide answers to their predicaments, with some of them calling for the abolition of alcohol. One such group evolved into the Women's Christian Temperance Union (WCTU), formed in 1874, with the end goal of prohibition of alcohol. Women also suffered as they sometimes had to resort to desperate means for income. Those who were not able to find work sometimes turned to prostitution. Although women were forced into prostitution for a variety of different reasons, the bottom line was usually the need for survival.

Work in the Factories

Working Conditions

Newly arrived immigrants provided the backbone of the American labor force and populated the pool of workers in the newly formed factories of the Industrial Age. These dangerous jobs provided unskilled work to the recent immigrants in conditions that were often unsafe and demanding. Working 12–14 hours a day, six days a week, in poorly lit and inadequately ventilated buildings, the workers were placed in an atmosphere conducive to injury. It was not uncommon for men and women to get hurt while working with the large equipment on the job site. For example, the process of purifying iron placed workers in temperatures well over 100°F. Moreover, the loss of limb due to manipulation of dangerous machines and continual exposure to pollution and dust led to major health issues. However, in an age without workman's compensation or unemployment benefits, most workers were reluctant to leave their jobs. Security in the workforce was not guaranteed and most laborers were unwilling to challenge the working conditions of the factories for fear of losing their jobs.

The rapid rise of infrastructure in the cities provided another avenue of employment for many immigrants, albeit often in unsafe conditions. Workers risked life and limb to build the newly erected skyscrapers and bridges, subways, and paved roads to supplement the growth of the urban landscape. One of the most famous engineering projects of this period, the Brooklyn Bridge, captures the height and depth of city life. The Bridge, built between 1869 and 1883, required 300 workers toiling around the clock to complete it. Laborers worked six days a week for $2 a day, and in the course of the construction, 20 workers died.

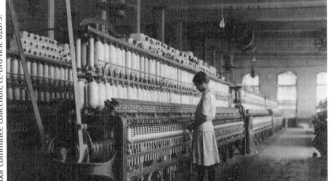

Fourteen-year old spinner in a Brazos Valley Cotton Mill at West. Violation of the law. Matty Lott runs six sides

Child Labor

As the demand for workers grew, as well as the rate of poverty, many poor families sent their children to work or demanded them to move out of the home at an early age to save money. Subsequently, child labor increased decade by decade from the end of the nineteenth and into the early twentieth century. By 1900, children made up anywhere from 18% to 20% of the work force, of which approximately 1.8 million were between ages 5 and 10. This statistic cannot be completely trusted, however, because often children working in the mills, factories, or living on the streets were not accurately counted.

Children worked in many areas, including factories, mills, farms, coal mines, and on the streets. Business managers were eager to hire children. They could pay them low wages, and their small bodies reached the narrow places in the machines or went deeper into the

Manuel, the young shrimp-picker, five years old, and a mountain of child-labor oyster shells behind him. Biloxi, Mississippi

mines than adults. Because most of society viewed children as miniature adults there was no form of protection available to them in the labor force. Poor children often worked more than one job over the course of a year. Many were employed in seasonal work with their families, such as harvesting crops in the fall, and relocating to the cities during the winter months to work in the factories.

Children usually began work around the age of 12 years old; however some boys, as young as 6, set out into the work force earlier and became newsboys or bootblacks. These boys usually worked under an adult contractor and were homeless, as they had been orphaned or cast off by their families who could not afford to feed them any longer. Homeless children sometimes found help when cities set up lodging houses for the boys.

Female Labor

Women also made up a significant amount of the labor force during the Industrial Age. Women's working patterns varied considerably, according to race, ethnicity, as well as marital status. White, married women rarely worked outside the home. Once a woman achieved marriage, it was expected that she would stay home to raise the children and establish a comfortable home. However, these women often found ways to help the family's income through domestic activities such as the canning and selling of garden foods, fashioning crafts to sell, or laundering and ironing clothing for pay.

Necktie workshop in a Division Street tenement

African-American women worked for lower pay and had a higher percentage of married women in the work force than whites. Because of the wage disparity between the races, black men did not earn the same income as their counterparts, thus black married women often had to work to sustain the family's income. Black women worked in many areas, including domestic jobs, factories, and heavy labor.

Sweatshop workers endured crowded conditions and often dangerous work. Most were young women who worked in settings ranging from factories, small rooms, and tenements. Girls usually began work at the age of 12, honing their skills, until they became virtual seamstress machines. These women were generally paid by the amount of pieces they generated; the more clothing produced, the higher the income. Although they usually worked 12 hours a day, 6 days a week earning one to two dollars a day, they often chose to work even longer hours.

Work spaces in the sweatshops usually had very little ventilation and inaccessible exits. It was not uncommon for women to be locked in the room by managers to prevent unwarranted breaks. These dangerous conditions often sparked catastrophe. One of the most famous industrial disasters took place in the garment district in Manhattan, New York. The Triangle Shirtwaist Factory fire erupted in 1911 and led to the death of 145 workers, including girls as young as 14 years old. This largely preventable fire was due to the overcrowded workspaces, inaccessible exits, and rotten safety equipment. The young women who tried to escape the burning inferno died in appalling ways, including being burned alive.

Not all women's jobs, however, were dangerous during the Industrial Age. New positions were created as the business world developed allowing women to move beyond domestic services. Occupational opportunities grew in manufacturing industries, clerical duties, and sales positions in newly formed stores. The burst of industry created a new consumer culture that provided jobs for women at various levels. In addition, women began to attend college at a higher rate during this period creating more job opportunities in skilled areas.

City Landscape

American cities during the Industrial Age were not only made of slums and factories. Cities also offered cultural diversity, entertainment, and new technologies such as electric lights and trolleys. Most cities did not develop along comprehensive city plans but expanded quickly in response to the demands of new growth. Central business districts, including banks, department stores, and corporate offices emerged as well as transit systems that carried thousands of people to jobs and stores from residential neighborhoods. The new trains and trolleys allowed commuters easy travel to the city and helped begin the development of the suburbs. Tall office buildings also began to dot the city horizon.

The need for public services, such as transportation, facilities, and accommodations brought a plethora of engineers and architects to the urban landscape seeking to respond to the demands. New residential apartments for the wealthy and middle classes, with the latest plumbing and electricity, were built. Sewage systems were updated in the wealthier parts of the city to bring clean water and flushing toilets to the urban population. And parks, electric lamps, and cable cars soon dotted the landscape. Montgomery, Alabama became the first city to install a fully electrified streetcar system in 1886, while New York City provided the popular Central Park to its inhabitants in 1873. Cities also expanded public school systems, built libraries, and opened new shops for interested buyers. However, not all city dwellers benefited from the new perks provided within the cities. Parks were situated among the more affluent parts of the city and most tenements did not participate in receiving the advancements of clean water and better sewers. Subways provided transportation to the middle-class commuter and not the poor immigrant.

Middle Class City Life

The newly formed middle-class families began to develop and settle the suburbs during the Industrial Age. These families could afford to buy a house and pay the cost of commuting to the city. In contrast to the crowded conditions and busy atmospheres of the city, suburbs offered cleanliness, quietness, and greenery. These communities tended to settle along similar ethnic and religious backgrounds and fostered the new development of middle-class tastes and values. Middle-class families had fewer children and higher incomes. They purchased a greater array of consumer products, including the newly created Ivory Soap and refreshing Coca-Cola, as well as bigger recreational items, such as bicycles and cars.

Middle-class culture also included time for leisure activities. Bike riding, playing games in the streets, walking to local parks, attending organized spectator sports, and frequenting amusement parks set this social group apart from the lower-income groups living in the slums. Women, influenced by the mass advertising in magazines and newspapers, spent more time on their personal appearance and purchased the latest make-up and fashionable clothing. These women often focused more of their attention on creating a moral and nurturing environment for their husbands and children, thus creating the framework of middle-class values.

Some women, however, used their free time to increase their involvement in clubs dedicated to charity and social reform. Clubs such as the WCTU that promoted prohibition and the National American Woman Suffrage Association (NAWSA) that sought voting rights, provided women with a voice in the political world of men. The efforts of both of these groups affected change in the nation. The WCTU led the way toward the Prohibition of the 1920s and the influence of NAWSA spread across America to obtain suffrage rights for women in the states of Colorado (1893) and Idaho (1896), and led eventually to the nation with the passage of the Nineteenth Amendment (1920).

Wealthy

The Gilded Age created new heights of wealth with lavish displays of prosperity. Opulent mansions in elite districts, exclusive summer retreats, and extravagant dinner parties were the elements of the "conspicuous consumption" of the wealthy. Powerful families competed with each other in their elaborate lifestyles to see who could throw the most extravagant balls, weddings, and parties.

One of the most famous celebrations, the Vanderbilt Ball, highlighted the opening of shipping and railroad tycoon Cornelius Vanderbilt's $3 million mansion on upper Fifth Avenue in Manhattan. The party, estimated at $250,000, was attended by the wealthiest, most aristocratic families in America. Newspapers covered the extravagant party and revealed the breadth of wealth discrepancy in the nation. In an age when the average salary was $700 a year, the conspicuous consumption of the wealthy created a stark contrast between the "haves" and the "have nots" of the working class in America.

Inventions and Consumer Culture

The Industrial Revolution created a society built on the mass production and distribution of goods in America. The period also generated a distinctive surge in inventions as creative individuals designed new items and flooded the U.S. Patent Office with applications. These new inventions, coupled with national advertising and mass production, formed the base of the consumer culture in America.

Revolution in Communications

As railroad expansion continued across America, the need for communication between cities grew and culminated in a revolution. This transformation in communications began with the development of Samuel F.B. Morse's electric telegraph and the Morse code in 1838. Telegraph lines soon were seen alongside railroad tracks, connecting the nation by electrical wire. These coded messages were transmitted quicker than previous forms of communication and transformed business by providing instantaneous connection. Business mogul Jay Gould seized onto this growth of telegraph lines and took control of Western Union through stock manipulation. Western Union soon became the largest company within the telegraph market. By the end of the century, millions of messages were being sent across America and carried around the world, and led to the creation of the first truly world market.

Alexander Graham Bell, a Scottish-born scientist, also helped to revolutionize communications in America during this period. Heavily influenced by the physical impairment of both his mother and wife (they were deaf), Bell worked countless hours trying to find a way to teach the deaf to speak. Through his work he developed a way to transmit voice over wire, thus creating the telephone in 1876. His invention was displayed at the Philadelphia Centennial Exposition in 1876. Although many people and businesses were hesitant at first

Thomas Edison

to use Bell's invention, eventually the telephone revolutionized communications around the world. He created the Bell Telephone Company in 1879, and in 1880, Bell pioneered "long lines" (long-distance telephone service). In 1885, he created the American Telephone and Telegraph Co. (AT&T), which acquired Bell Telephone Co. and became the primary phone company in America. Through his work, Americans were able to communicate not only locally but across the nation in a private and quick manner.

Large-Scale Production

Large-scale production also increased with new inventions allowing Americans' easier access to food and goods. Gustavus Swift and Philip Armour transformed the meat-packing industry, as they developed the process of mass distribution of meats to retailers and consumers. This revolution in meat led to the growth of commercial cattle ranching in the west. Henry John Heinz transformed the food processing industry along a similar vein as Swift. He adopted efficient methods of canning and bottling his sauces, pickles, and condiments and began buying large amounts of vegetables from local farmers, thus also encouraging the growth of agribusiness in the Midwest. Other food processers used similar methods and developed new food businesses, such as Quaker Oats, Campbell Soup, and Borden.

Consumer Culture

America developed a national market through the growth of railroads and communications that connected the people and created a new unified country. People all over America began to be exposed to the latest consumer goods and technological advancements, and the demand for these goods created the first large-scale consumer culture. New inventions and new forms of advertising spurred on the demand for these contemporary items.

Inventions skyrocketed and new patents were being turned out daily to make life easier for middle-class Americans. Isaac Singer patented the first practical and efficient sewing machine in 1851, thus allowing clothing to be made more cheaply and at home. Singer's sewing machine soon became the staple of the textile industry in America, as clothing manufacturers created new styles and cheaper garments for the middle-class shopper. Other inventions tempted the American consumer as well and made shopping easier. Items such as the cash register, invented in 1879, made shopping easier while new luxury items like the Kodak camera (1888) offered exciting new possibilities to the new middle class. Industries began producing the newly patented items in mass bulk leading to lower prices. National advertising in magazines and newspapers created within the country the ubiquitous American customer.

One inventor, more than any other, dramatically changed the home of the average American during the late 1800s. Thomas Edison transformed the world of inventions acquiring over 1,000 patents. He invented the phonograph, developed the use of the filament in the light bulb, and created the motion picture camera, among others. He also pioneered the use of electricity as an energy source. This sparked a revolution in the cities as electricity became an essential part of American urban life powering trolley cars, lighting office buildings and homes, and providing energy to factories. Although rural America was slower to join the use of electricity because most businesses did not find it lucrative to run electrical lines to outlying farms, Edison's inventions helped lay the road toward the modern age.

Theories That Shaped the Industrial Age

Historical periods are shaped by the worldviews of the people who lived during the time. Concepts and principles emerge as societies face the challenges and successes of their age. Many of the practices and beliefs of the Industrial Age were also shaped by certain theories and principles. These principles tried to explain the business tactics of the tycoons, the plight of the poor, and the promise of the American dream.

Laissez-Faire

The philosophy of laissez-faire (French for "leave alone" or hands off) espouses the argument that the government should not impose restraints on business or the economy by means of laws and regulations. Laissez-faire advocates support the notion that businesses should be allowed to grow without government regulations, taxes, or laws. Hence, there were no forms of taxation, environmental regulations, or work-place safety laws in place. Although the monopolies grew unchecked by outside forces, voices emerged within the American society that demanded businesses provide better working conditions, shorter work weeks, and higher pay for their employees. These advocates also observed that with the rise of monopolies through mergers, competition in American business was actually shrinking, thus contradicting the law of competition vital to the economy.

Social Darwinism

Another concept that guided the worldviews of Americans during the Industrial Age was Social Darwinism. This theory reshaped the definitions of success and failure in society. As some businesses grew into giant monopolies, crushing their competitors or simply buying them out, this theory gave validation to their tactics. The business owners felt justified in their elite status, giving rise to the term the "nouveau riche," and became the conspicuous consumers of the age. The nouveau riche, or new rich, grew wealthy within the framework of Industrial Age practices and flaunted their upper-class lifestyles within society.

However, many smaller businesses and workers did not meet the level of success that their wealthy counterparts did and struggled to scrape together a living in America. These immigrants, factory workers, and unskilled laborers lived hidden under the golden exterior associated with the Gilded Age. Many people sought for an answer as to why some groups of people succeeded and others failed, and they found answers in the theory of Social Darwinism.

Social Darwinism was based on the teachings of Charles Darwin. He developed the theory of natural selection in his work, *On the Origin of Species*, published in 1859. In this work, Darwin theorized that in the struggle for survival those species that adapted most successfully to their environment survived (survival of the fittest), while the weaker species died out. Using Darwin's work as a starting point, British philosopher and sociologist Herbert Spencer and American William Graham Sumner developed the concept of Social Darwinism. This theory created the belief that the wealthy and powerful people were the "most fit" people in society, endowed with innate intelligence, adaptability, and strength. These traits enabled them to continue to survive, achieve success in the business world, and triumph over their competitors.

In contrast, the theory taught that the weak, poor, and unsuccessful were "unfit" and, therefore destined to pitiable lives because they were not able to adapt or survive. Their poverty was the result of personal or moral failures, such as laziness, drunkenness, or lack of ingenuity. Therefore, the deprived classes must be consigned to lives of failure and misery, and eventually be allowed to die off to advance the progression of society. According to Social Darwinism, there is no justification in helping the poor because they settled into destitution due to natural selection, and nothing could be done to save them.

Horatio Alger Phenomenon

Another perspective arose during the Industrial Age as a means of explaining the industrial capitalism that shaped the period. This view lent support to Andrew Carnegie's ideal of the self-made man. The movement began among numerous businessmen and literary writers and captured the idea that any person had the opportunity to achieve success in America.

Horatio Alger was a former minister and avid writer who used his stories to attest that anyone, regardless of birthplace, family, or education, could climb the ladder of success. Alger wrote more than 100 young adult books during this period and influenced a whole genre of American literature with his ideas. Beginning with his book, *Ragged Dick,* Alger penned stories that focused on young boys, trapped in a life of poverty, working their way out of dire circumstances to achieve a good life. These boys, through self-discipline and hard work, saved money, avoided liquor, and stayed out of debt to achieve the American dream. Alger sold millions of books and influenced other writers and media during the period to portray the ideal of the self-made man. His ideas reinforced the concept that the American dream was open to anyone.

Gilded Age Politics

Politics during the Industrial Age played little part in the daily life of the average American. Owing to the laissez-faire attitude adopted by government officials during this period, politicians did little to fix the major problems in American society. In general, the electorate was evenly divided between the two major parties with remarkably close presidential elections. Five of the elections between 1876 and 1892 were decided by a 1–3% vote margin, and two presidents (Hayes in 1876 and Harrison in 1888) won the electoral vote while losing the popular vote. It is also a striking observation that no incumbent president won reelection. Although this era of government is known for being nonintrusive and small, especially at the federal level, voter turnout was astoundingly high.

During this period little serious legislation was passed. The primary difference within the parties was the issue of civil service reform. Most presidents practiced the spoils system, awarding their supporters with jobs after the election. Political corruption was the norm as party bosses ran the big cities and politicians bribed city, state, and national officials. In response to the corruption, groups began to form in the late 1800s that demanded the end of the spoils system. The schism between these reformers and the proponents of the spoils system was so intense that it played a role in the assassination of a president.

Presidential Elections

James Garfield was considered a dark-horse candidate in the election of 1800. Garfield, a Republican, moved into the candidacy when the divisions in the party over civil service reform reached a divisive point. Within the Republican Party three groups emerged that either ridiculed civil service reform (Stalwarts), desired some (Half-Breeds,) or endorsed the end of the spoils system altogether (Mugwumps). Garfield was chosen as the candidate by the Republican convention, as he sought to avoid party factionalism.

Garfield won the election, with vice presidential candidate Chester Arthur, against former Union general and Democrat, Winfield Hancock. After his victory, Garfield tried to pacify some of the party bosses. However the schism within the Republican Party was too strong. On July 2, 1881, while Garfield was waiting to catch a train in Washington D.C., he was shot from behind by Charles Guiteau. A disappointed office seeker, Guiteau was allied with the Stalwarts. Garfield died on September 19, 1881, and Republican factionalism was condemned.

Arthur, a former member of the Republican political machine in New York, did not want to be associated with the death of Garfield and radicalism of Guiteau. Soon after his inauguration, Arthur became a strong proponent and enforcer of civil service reform. He oversaw the passage of the Pendleton Civil Service Act, passed in 1883, that established a permanent Civil Service Commission, placing 10% of federal jobs under the merit system. These jobs, which amounted to 14,000 at this time, required exams before employment was rewarded. The Act also prohibited federal job holders from contributing to political campaigns.

Boss Politics

Gilded Age politics was filled with political corruption and party machines. Big businesses often worked closely with public officials to control legislation. They often made handsome donations to the political parties to sway legislation and prevent certain laws from passing they deemed harmful to their interests. Within this framework these political machines, run by party bosses, became the dominant form of power.

Most often associated with the Democratic party of the late nineteenth century, political machines existed in more than 80% of America's largest cities. These machines worked to mobilize large blocs of working class and immigrant voters to cast their votes for them in exchange for goods and services. American cities were filled with large immigrant communities and any politician who could assemble their vote could win public office. New immigrants needed a place to live and work. They also needed an advocate for their interests. Thus, political bosses sent people, usually from the same ethnic background, to connect with and provide these benefits to the family. For example, new immigrants received groceries, a place to live, or help to stop a conviction, and in return they voted for the candidates of the party boss. As long as the needy voted the right way and the politicians remained in power, the immigrants were provided help.

Another aspect of the party machine was the development of mutually beneficial relationships between big businesses and city leaders. Boss Tweed of Tammany Hall, in New York City, epitomized this symbiotic relationship. William Marcy Tweed, a Democrat, ran the city through the club known as Tammany Hall. He worked between the city government and local businesses to strike deals and pocket money. Tweed dominated the city with his extravagant use of public funds on projects that provided him with kickbacks. His machine also sought out immigrants, factory workers, disenchanted homesteaders returning to the city, and even dead relatives for votes, in return for food, work, and living quarters. Eventually Tweed's activities led him to jail. However, the political machines continued to run many large cities well into the twentieth century.

William Marcy "Boss" Tweed

"Stone Wall Do Not a Prison Make"—Old Song. "No prison is big enough to hold the Boss"

Nativism

With the sharp increase in newly arriving immigrants, a movement began among certain Americans who felt the country was quickly losing its identity. This movement called nativism attracted a faction of society that sought to restrict immigration and keep America pure, for its "native born." Nativism was not new to the American populace, as it had developed in previous decades when immigration had peaked. Thus, with the spike in immigration in the late nineteenth century, nativism rebounded. Its advocates decried the crime and filth in the immigrant sectors of the cities as well as the growth of labor strikes associated with radical, foreign ideas. These nativists joined other groups and called for stricter immigration laws, and Congress responded.

In 1882, Congress passed two pieces of legislation, placing limits on immigration for the first time in American history. The Immigration Act of 1882 placed a head tax of 50 cents on each immigrant entering the country as well as barred any "convict, lunatic, idiot, or any person unable to take care of himself or herself without becoming a public charge." In the same year, Congress also passed the Chinese Exclusion Act banning Chinese immigration for 10 years. A couple of years later, the government established immigration depots in most major ports to filter through the new arrivals and deny entrance to those who were sick, had criminal backgrounds, espoused radical political beliefs, or had little money or skill. In like manner, in 1894, several Harvard graduates founded the Immigration Restriction League to establish literacy tests for immigrants to ascertain whether they could read or write in any language. Although President Cleveland vetoed the laws proposed by the League, the nativist movement continued to influence the immigration debate and helped establish limits throughout the next several decades.

Labor Unions and Strikes

During the Industrial Age, labor strikes became increasingly common as disenfranchised and abused workers sought to ameliorate their working conditions. In response, labor unions began to form and provided the voice for change. These labor unions created a voice for the workers as well as a means to obtain the changes desired by the workforce. At first the unions grew slowly and without much success. However, events in the 1870s and 1880s led to an enormous jump in union membership, more active participation in strikes, and opened the door for the involvement of radical groups.

Great Railroad Strike

An economic panic hit America in 1873 and spurred a depression that lasted several years. The depression that followed led to an unemployment rate of approximately 50% (about 3 million people), cut wages for those still employed, and closed banks and businesses throughout America. The reactions of both workers and the unemployed erupted into one of the most volatile periods of labor history.

In the summer of 1877 B&O (Baltimore and Ohio) Railroad announced another wage cut to employees prompting angry workers in West Virginia, whose wages had already decreased from $70 a month to $30 a month, to walk off the job. These strikers, who argued that they could no longer afford to feed their families, started a strike that swept throughout America. The Great Railroad Strike spread through Pittsburgh, Chicago, and across the country to San Francisco as 100,000 other railroad workers joined them in. The strike continued to spread, and an estimated 500,000 workers from other companies, including steelworkers, longshoremen, and industrial workers, also quit their posts. The Great Railroad Strike virtually brought all rail traffic in America to a halt.

In response to the strike, states called out local militias in an effort to force the workers back to their jobs. Not all militias were willing to use aggressive tactics against the strikers to force them back to work. However, when militias chose to use force, violence among the strikers spread. The most famous incident took place in Pittsburgh when the militia opened fire on strikers and killed 20 of them. Angry workers retaliated by destroying two miles of rail track, incurring damages of close to $2 million. By the end of the day, the violence escalated leading to 20 more workers killed.

In response to the national economic impact of stalled railroad traffic, as well as the local eruptions of violence, nine governors called for federal troops to quell the insurrections in their states. President Rutherford B. Hayes reluctantly called out the army to address the strikes. However, the violence of the strike had run its course. Although troops did not use violence against the strikers, they did force the reopening of rail traffic, protected "scabs" as they worked, and maintained peace along the railways. The dramatic rise and violence of the Great Railroad Strike spurred fear in many industrialists. The upper classes as well as the authorities began to associate the labor unions with violence and referred to the strikers, as well as the working class in general, as the "dangerous classes."

Labor Unions

One of the immediate responses to the Great Railroad Strike was the growth of the labor unions, specifically in the Knights of Labor. The Knights were founded in 1869 by Uriah Stephens. Stephens sought to form a union of "universal brotherhood" from all working classes, regardless of skill, sex, race, or nationality. During the 1880s they grew to become the major labor force under the leadership of Terence V. Powderly.

Powderly's approach advocated reforms that included public ownership of the railroads, an income tax, equal pay for women workers, and the abolition of child labor. In theory, the Knights opposed strikes, and preferred the use of boycott and arbitration. However, one of the most effective strikes was led by the Knights in 1885, when workers from three railroads controlled by Jay Gould walked off the job. This strike was so successful that members began to rely more on the use of the strike than the tactics desired by Powderly.

The Knights of Labor were not the only union to offer workers a voice in the late nineteenth century. Other trade unions sought to focus more on workplace issues, including the American Federation of Labor (AFL). Samuel Gompers founded the AFL in 1886 along the lines of "pure and simple unionism." He promoted the organization of skilled workers, like machinists, into unions because they provided more bargaining power. These strikes focused on more immediate objectives such as higher pay and better working conditions.

The Anarchist Riot in Chicago—A Dynamite Bomb exploding among the police [McCormick Strike, Haymarket Square]

Haymarket Square Riot

Radical anarchists and socialists offered a different vision for workers during the Industrial Age. These groups, populated by recent immigrants from socialist nations, believed current methods of reform by labor unions were too slow to bring change to the labor force, and advocated social revolution instead.

One group of supporters set May 1, 1886 as the date for a nation-wide strike demanding an 8-hour work day. The demonstration, set in Chicago, was led by anarchists. Forty-five thousand workers paraded peacefully down Michigan Avenue. Trouble arrived two days later when strikers from nearby McCormick Harvesting Company attacked replacements brought in to work at the plant during the strike. Police arrived and opened fire, killing and wounding several people. In response, the anarchist leaders called for a rally in Haymarket Square for the evening of May 4. Two to three thousand people gathered in the Square, listening to the anarchist speakers, when police arrived and demanded the crowd disperse. Suddenly a bomb exploded in the middle of the police ranks. Gunfire erupted in response, and at the end of the chaos seven policemen were dead.

The Haymarket riot set off a wave of increased fear and rage toward the labor movements, immigrants, and, in general, the working class. Chicago authorities arrested hundreds of radicals for the Haymarket bombing, and eventually eight anarchists went on trial. From the beginning of the trial these men declared their innocence surrounding the bombing, but the judge seemed not interested in innocence or guilt. It soon became evident that these men were on trial for their radical beliefs, not their actions. Although there was no evidence linking the men to the bombing, the judge and jury found the men guilty and imposed the death penalty. As a result, four of them were hanged, one committed suicide, and the other three served time in prison. In 1893, after a thorough investigation, the governor of Illinois pardoned the three men still in prison and condemned the actions of the judge as a travesty of justice.

Pullman Strike

Another economic panic swept through America in 1893 and agitated labor relations to such a degree that it created the Pullman Strike. Pullman Inc., owned and operated by George Pullman, built railroad passenger cars in factories across America. In the early 1880s Pullman designed a model town on the outskirts of Chicago to appeal to his workers and provide them with a city of their own. Model towns were erected by business owners to provide close proximity for workers as well as an economic investment for the owner.

The town of Pullman offered the best parks, shops, and housing in a clean atmosphere catering to comfortable living. Because the town of Pullman was superior to neighboring cities, George Pullman charged approximately 10–20% higher rents than surrounding communities. When the economic panic led to a depression, Pullman cut wages in his company, but refused to reduce rent prices in his model town. Pullman continued to subtract the cost of rent from the workers' paycheck, often resulting in less wages. Simultaneously, Pullman stockholders continued to make a profit as well as the company.

In response to Pullman's business tactics, the railroad workers went on strike in the spring of 1894. Led by the American Railway Union (ARU) and its leader, Eugene Debs, the strike grew and soon encompassed 90% of the Pullman work force. Pullman responded by shutting down the plant and refused any forms of arbitration. However, the strike continued to grow and soon included more than 15 railroad companies, affecting 27 states. The strikers focused on peaceful resistance and targeted the dismantling of Pullman cars from running railroads by stopping trains carrying the cars and uncoupling them as a means of protest. Their actions paralyzed the nation's railway system, shutting down transportation, and the movement of goods.

Eventually, due to public and governmental pressure President Grover Cleveland called out the army to put down the strike. On July 5, nearly 8,000 troops marched into Chicago. In the chaos that ensued, 25 workers were shot, 60 were wounded, and more than $340,000 worth of property was destroyed. Debs was arrested and the ARU was defeated, thus ending the strike. After the violent end to the strike, Pullman reopened his factory. He hired new workers to replace many of the strikers, and left 1,600 workers without jobs or ability to relocate. The use of federal troops against American citizens marked a new phase in labor relations as business owners and employees tried to find amenable means of negotiation. This process shaped the relationship between workers and owners for the years to come.

Results of the Industrial Revolution

The roads carved by the Industrial Revolution laid the groundwork for the country's modern age. New ideas regarding large monopolies, laissez-faire capitalism, and labor relations formed the framework of business for years to come. Many of the business practices that developed, such as mergers and vertical integration, were adopted by upcoming entrepreneurs. Simultaneously, the financial decisions and individual creativities of the big business moguls shaped the economy of the country.

However, not everyone found the American dream. The corruption underlying the creation of the monopolistic companies and the crooked deals that shaded the political world guaranteed that certain groups of people were destined to stay in poverty. This division between the classes sparked labor disputes encouraging some to demand not only worker's rights, but revolution in the American government as well. The nation was at a tipping point regarding its future political development. The needs of the working poor spurred the creation of advocates focused on creating social reforms. America was laying the foundations for a new industrial age.

CHAPTER THIRTEEN

The West and Imperialism

Chapter 13: Key Concepts

⊙ What was the lure for Americans to move West in the years following the American Civil War? What did they hope to gain by moving to this area and what would they have encountered?

⊙ Evaluate the relationship between settlers to the West and American Indians. How did the interests of each group conflict with the other? Describe the outcome.

⊙ What was the argument both for and against American expansion beyond its ocean borders? Discuss the debate and the assertions of each side within the arguments for and against imperialism.

Since the first Europeans arrived on the North American continent, settlers sought new horizons by heading West. Even today, wide-open landscapes represent unencumbered freedom to many Americans. The march began as soon as the Jamestown colonists started to expand. The wave of migration accelerated as news of gold and silver strikes reverberated across the country. After the Civil War, even greater numbers of people pushed beyond the Mississippi River in hopes of new opportunities. The United States, as a nation, also looked West, beyond the bounds of the Pacific Ocean. As the nineteenth century came to a close, the desire to become influential in two spheres, the Atlantic and Pacific, proved irresistible to politicians and entrepreneurs alike. The lure of the West included hopes of great fortune for the settler, business interests, and the nation as a whole.

"Go West"

Even before Horace Greeley was credited with saying, "Go West young man, and grow up with the country," the idea to develop western territory existed as part of the American psyche. The term "manifest destiny," coined by journalist John L. Sullivan in 1845, suggested that Americans had an obligation to bring civilization to the unsettled areas of the West by moving there. When European-Americans arrived, providence (i.e., God) would watch over their efforts. Wealth by various means awaited those who left their communities back East. Land, gold, silver, or business enterprises were not only available, but plentiful for the enterprising individual who dared pack up and relocate. In the California Gold Rush of 1849, over 300,000 migrants came on the rumor of riches. If not a prospector, lush farming land was available in Oregon country, Texas, or any number of other promised locations.

In the middle of the Civil War, President Lincoln promised free land to anyone willing to take possession and work to improve it. The 1862 Homestead Act attracted over 1.6 million applicants occupying more than 270 million acres of public land. In addition to farming, citizens used the land for mining, ranching, and businesses, all seeking their fortune via westward migration. The main obstacle to beginning a new life in the West was the population who already inhabited the territory. Since early colonization, Native-Americans continued to be pushed off their homelands. Despite efforts to reclaim land taken by white settlers, the onslaught of European-Americans continued to threaten Native homeland, sometimes creating retaliation in response. Whites used those examples as evidence of Native savagery, and through treaty and warfare, the U.S. government attempted to relegate Indians (as they were called at the time) to regions white settlers did not want. But each time a new area became the target of migration, treaties required renegotiation to allow the influx of whites.

The events that brought massive numbers of white Americans into new areas of the West quickly were gold and silver strikes. In Nevada, Montana, Colorado, and the Dakotas, barren land, ceded to Native-American tribes, became the object of demand for whites when

Transcontinental Railroad—The meeting of East and West connected the United States that advanced commerce and sped travel. Railroad lines became the choice of Americans seeking to advance their fortunes in the West in the late nineteenth century.

Mexican Vaqueros—Much of what Americans learned about cattle ranching came from Mexicans who had been handling livestock on the range for centuries before the migration of settlers from the east. Even the attire American cowboys are known for came from the vaqueros.

a precious metal was discovered on it. For example, the Fort Laramie Treaty of 1868 expressly forbade the intrusion of whites to the Black Hills area. However, when gold was discovered there, the federal government allowed people access to one of the biggest strikes in American history. The Great Sioux War that ensued and the annihilation of a portion of the 7th Cavalry including its leader, Col. George Armstrong Custer, worked to the favor of the whites when the government annexed the Black Hills.

Further south along the Great Plains, prosperity came, not in the ground but by grazing cattle on the soil. Settlers to the large state of Texas, learning from the Tejanos (Spanish for Texan) bred cattle long before European Americans began to arrive. After the Civil War, raising beef offered opportunity to those who could raise enough money to buy steers and acquire land to graze them. For those who did not have capitol, jobs driving cattle to market provided employment. The development of trails to drive livestock to railroad centers so that the animals could be transported to the slaughterhouses of Chicago, made all the work of raising and herding profitable. Along those trails, cattle drives employed cowboys of many different backgrounds. At least one quarter was African-American. Even more were Hispanic. Much of the attire and many of the techniques of "cow-poking" were the invention and development of "vaqueros" (Portuguese for mounted herder). These were traditions brought over from the Iberian Peninsula during the days of early colonization. As with mining, by the late nineteenth century, livestock herding grew to the point that consolidation drove many smaller operators out of business and ranching became a corporate enterprise.

The territory of the West remains as vast as it was when settlers came in the nineteenth century. The railroad was the mode of transportation developed to ease the challenges of distance. Since its invention in the early nineteenth century, the goal of a transcontinental route had been a priority. Business interests and government realized the dream of a train ride across country in 1869 with the laying of a ceremonial golden spike at Promontory

Point, Utah. From there other coast to coast routes followed, taking the spoils of the West to the East (gold, cattle) and individuals in the other direction, in search of a new life. Any time word leaked out about a gold strike, opportunists came in droves to find fortune. Most sought it in the streams, where the precious metal lay in the water among the rocks, available just to sift out with a "placer cradle." Placer mining required few financial resources and often yielded only fragments of a vein's full potential. Corporations quickly replaced placer miners and used capital-intensive machineries such as hydraulics and stampers to remove the mountains that contained the gold or silver. Like with cattle, the individual prospector soon became obsolete.

All over the West, prospectors discovered precious metals like gold, silver, copper, and lead. Following the rush of miners seeking to unearth gold near Sacramento, California in 1848, periodic discoveries were made throughout the West. Silver brought prospectors to seek their fortune in the Comstock Lode in Nevada, gold in the Black Hills and Wyoming. By the dawn of the twentieth century, people flocked to Alaska as word of a strike swept the nation.

Towns like Deadwood, South Dakota and Bodie, California profited and suffered from the influx of miners. Both quickly emerged from camps with a few inhabitants to established towns. Most of the residents were men. They worked the mines in the daylight hours and sought diversion at night, either in the saloons, brothels, or gambling houses. Violence was prevalent. Law followed order in these towns where city officials often chose to tax rather than ban activities of vice. Much the same situation existed in cattle towns like Dodge City and Abilene, Kansas. Miners and cowboys lost their wealth as easy as they gained it in these towns, where the real beneficiaries were those offering alcohol, prostitutes, and card games. Today, Deadwood survives as a tourist and gambling destination.

For women in these early towns, life offered few choices. They either became service personnel, washing or feeding the cowboys and miners, or they sold sex. Since almost all the men in these towns were either single or without their wives, business was brisk. Unscrupulous brothel owners lured women to these boom towns under the pretense of some other occupation then forced them into prostitution. Suicide was high among these women, as many saw no way out of their circumstances. A few women owned houses of prostitution, but mostly men controlled the sex trade.

Existence in the boom towns of the West depended on the ability to handle the coarseness of activities that came with daily life. Both miners and cowboys faced hardship

Cowboy statue—In the stockyards of Fort Worth, Texas a commemoration of the work done by cow handlers who at times, turned the work of steering cattle to market into sport, which is still practiced today.

Historical Cowboy—The work of a cowboy was much less about freedom and riding the range and more about constantly keeping cattle moving while working for wages. Long drives ended at railheads where many let off steam by spending their wages in activities of vice.

Deadwood, South Dakota— Located in a gulch in the Black Hills of South Dakota, Deadwood came into existence after the discovery of gold there. It quickly grew after word got out. Vice and lawlessness grew with it. Wild Bill Hickok was killed there during a card game in August 1876.

in their jobs, but prospectors were particularly known to be rough customers. Their livelihood required them to rip from the earth its treasures and in doing so they dared other individuals to try and take it from them. Miners fought each other regularly over slights, real, or imagined. In towns before law was established, these men meted out individual (sometimes collective) justice as they saw fit to further their ambitions.

Before the end of the nineteenth century, mining, cattle ranching, and logging grew in scale to the point that massive capital was needed to continue expansion. Both cowboys and miners began to work for corporations as wage laborers. With both, early individual efforts could only grow to a limited degree. Larger interests were needed so that an economy of scale could continue to maximize profits. Hearst, Haggis, Tevis, and Co. became one of the biggest mining operations in the country. Its growth began when prospector George Hearst invested in ownership of mining interests and used his skill to determine which sites held promise. Hearst's astute judgment of a vein's potential helped his company gain prominence and ultimately dominance in the mining industry. His company mined gold in Lead, near Deadwood until 2002.

Corporate mining and ranching companies expanded operations well beyond the capacity of individual efforts from the earlier era. Unconcerned about environmental damage, corporations created huge craters as they dug into the earth while also washing away mountains to get at the ore. With individual miners and cow hands serving as employees, many chose to unionize for better wages and safer working conditions. By the end of the nineteenth century, the individualism associated with those early entrepreneurs in the West was gone. Most workers made a living in the same way as factory workers in the East, as wage earners.

One pursuit that could still attract a person who valued the freedom of his or her labor was farming. Americans came West looking for a plot of land to clear and develop for various crops. But here too, many came into contact with corporate interests. Conflict arose over the land. Large-scale ranchers began using barbed wire to keep migrating farmers from squatting on their land. Sometimes, these fences obstructed paths to public land. Homesteading farmers believed that the land should remain part of the open range so everyone would have access to

Historical Miner—The possibility of 'wealth beyond counting' lured many men to areas where mineral strikes were rumored. Most either were unsuccessful or spent what they mined, leaving them to either give up mining as a profession or follow the next rumor to another town.

sometimes limited resources, like water. Likewise, ranchers resented fences that kept their cattle from grazing on land as the steers were being driven to market. Some used fencing protection laws to claim and shutoff land they did not own. The conflict resulted in numerous "fence cutting" wars from Texas to Montana. By the end of the nineteenth century, laws regulating how fences could be erected, as well as access (a gate in good working order) every three miles, reduced the number of conflicts.

Even in the best of conditions, farming could be extremely hard work. Many who came West hoped God would reward their efforts with good yields. Since the 1840s, the idea of Manifest Destiny employed faith as a protection from the many unknowns of western homesteading. As the nineteenth century progressed, technological advances made farming easier. The singing plow developed by John Deere allowed seed to be planted deeper, thus making the plant stronger as it reached the surface. Cyrus McCormick's mechanical reaper assisted the harvesting of crops like wheat, saving farmers from having to constantly bend over to scythe stalks. Some land proved to be hard to tend no matter what machinery was used. On the plains of Kansas and Nebraska, where trees were short in supply, farmers had to use sod for housing until the profits from the crops made the purchase of less vermin infected building materials possible.

Nebraska Land for Sale— Advertisements such as this attracted numerous people from the east looking for a new start, which is what the West offered.

Historical Western Farm—For the many who came west, land was the prize commodity. Following the Homestead Act, settlers came west to establish their own farms. Some were successful but others did not anticipate the poor soil, harsh winters or lack of trees for building.

Life on the farm could be a lonely existence. Homesteaders claimed as much land as they could possibly farm, limiting daily connections with neighbors. The only time contact with anyone other than family would be possible was at church on Sunday or sporadic trips to the nearest town for the purchase of supplies or to sell the harvest. Some farmers did try to maintain contact with other landholders for social but more importantly, political associations. Organizations like the "Grange," or the "National Grange of the Order of Patrons of Husbandry" as it was officially known, started back East but quickly spread to include western farmers. The Grange championed railroad regulation to keep their transportation costs down. They also backed numerous social issues of the time like temperance and women's suffrage. Perhaps their most lasting initiative was local cooperatives that allowed farmers to collectively store grain in warehouses for later sale. In the 1880s, they wielded powerful political influence because of their large membership that included farmers from all parts of the country.

Migrants came from many parts of both the United States and beyond to try their hand at farming in the West. Northern Europeans flocked to the lands near the Canadian border from Minnesota to Montana. They understood the climate since it resembled the temperatures from which they came. Former slaves, called Exodusters, left the plantation fields in the South to run their own farms as freedmen. Before the Civil War, members of the Church of Jesus Christ of Latter Day Saints, commonly called the Mormons, migrated to the Great Salt Lake region to establish their own farms and community in order to be free of religious persecution. Leaving the United States in 1844, the nation would catch back up to them after winning the Mexican War and claiming the territory into which they had settled. Spanish speaking people once part of Mexico dealt with the change of national status as they continued to work their lands, now part of the United States. Along the railroads and in mining and cattle towns, Chinese immigrants worked as cheap labor in jobs that provided needed services, like restaurants and laundries, as well as railroad construction. Some welcomed the Chinese, but violence against these immigrants erupted periodically over their willingness to work for less while taking jobs from other Americans. In 1882, the Chinese Exclusion Act denied them immigration to the United States, the only group to which such an act has ever been specifically legislated.

The American Indian

The advance of Euro-Americans to the West extended the same problem that began in Jamestown. To whom did the land belong? Overcrowding in the East and subsequent acquisitions of territory made further conflict inevitable. When President Andrew Jackson forced the removal of Native-Americans to Oklahoma, it was to give them land that no one wanted. By the mid-nineteenth century, attitudes about the Great Plains had changed and settlers began moving there in greater numbers. The "Indian problem" grew in scope as more Native-Americans were pushed further west.

The influx of settlers meant the creation of new territories prompting some changes to policies toward Native Americans. From the Louisiana Purchase to the Mexican War and settlement of the Oregon Territory, the United States of America amassed a huge swath of land that spanned the continent. Curious and seeking opportunity, those living in the East headed west, and in doing so, began the process of turning what they regarded as vacant land into territories. Once 60,000 American inhabitants settled a territory, the areas could petition for statehood. But the Native-Americans inhabiting those lands proved to be the same kind of impediment their eastern counterparts had been since early settlement. The U.S. government established policy for Indians within the new boundaries of the nation, but the rules changed often to accommodate eastern migrants.

As the number of settlers grew in the West, conflict with Native-Americans often erupted in armed confrontation. Even before the Civil War concluded, but especially after, the government called its army west to protect the new settlers. Outposts like Fort Phil Kearney in Wyoming were strategically built along the Bozeman Trail to protect miners and farmers on their way to Oregon. Not happy with white encroachment, Native warriors attacked wagon trains along the trail. The government response was to construct more forts for protection and staff them with personnel able to clear Indian resistance. Among those charged with keeping migrants safe were the 9th, 10th, 24th, and 25th cavalry also known as the Buffalo Soldiers. This was a nickname for some all-black regiments who served the American cause of expansion with valor.

Even before the end of the Civil War, confrontations between the federal government and varying tribes sparked a series of Indian Wars that lasted until

Wagon Train—Before the railroad reached across the county, many settlers headed west in a convoy of wagons lead by an expert in travel. Journeys had occur during the summer months to get over the Rocky Mountains. The Oregon Trail as well as Sante Fe and others were the superhighways of the time these wagon trains took.

1890. The opening round in the conflict took place at Sand Creek, Colorado in 1864. After driving Confederates from the Arizona Territory, Colonel John Chivington conducted a raid with remnants of his Union command against an encampment with mostly women and children. Chivington believed Native-Americans to be dangerous and inferior beings. A Methodist minister by training, he saw it as his duty to God to eradicate Native-Americans. "I have come to kill Indians, and believe it is right and honorable to use any means under God's heaven to kill Indians," Chivington remarked. His attitudes toward Native-Americans were not considered unusual or particularly offensive at the time.

Like Colonel Chivington, many Civil War leaders came West to assume commands against a new enemy. Famed Union generals, such as William Tecumseh Sherman and Phillip Sheridan, believed that Native-Americans who stood in the way of progress had to be removed or destroyed. Sherman had little respect for his new adversary. He remarked that "the more Indians we can kill this year, the fewer we will need to kill the next, because the more I see of the Indians the more convinced I become that they must either all be killed or be maintained as a species of pauper. Their attempt at civilization is ridiculous." In his argument, Sherman made known his harsh and unforgiving policy toward all hostile Native Americans. Writing to his friend and boss, President Ulysses S. Grant, Sherman remarked "we must act with vindictive earnestness against the Sioux, even to their extermination, men, women and children." As an architect of post-Civil War Indian strategy, General Sherman argued for a policy that facilitated economic development in the West, and this primarily included the expansion of the railroad. Any disruption to progress he regarded as unacceptable and had to be met with overwhelming force. Native-Americans stood as the primary obstacle.

Phillip Sheridan was another Union general turned Indian fighter. He has often been credited with saying "the only good Indian is a dead Indian." Though not an accurate quote, Sheridan's philosophy was not far from it. Sheridan first conquered Native-American resistance in Texas and then amassed a command over the Great Plains that allowed him to employ his strategy against the Indians with the same fervor that he demonstrated during the Civil War. He endorsed making war on the primary food source for Indians, the bison. Referring to buffalo hunters, Sheridan asserted, "these men have done more to settle the vexed Indian question than the entire regular army has done in the last 30 years. They are destroying the Indians' commissary." Before contact with Europeans, an estimated 60 million bison roamed the North American continent. Killing them deprived Natives of the meat, hides, and bones (for weapon and tool making) on which they depended. By the end of the nineteenth century, less than 1,000 buffalo remained.

The practice of ill treatment of Indians was common place. Forcing tribes to relocate to reservations gained currency as the government negotiated new treaties during the Indian Wars. In 1867, Congress formed the Indian Peace Commission to investigate the reason for continued warfare on the plains. Convened in St. Louis, Missouri, the group found Congress itself responsible for much of the problem. Citing broken provisions and an ongoing need for renegotiation, the Commission tried to settle conflict between settlers and Indians once and for all with a number of new treaties. President Grant endorsed the findings of the Peace Commission but his subordinates, including Sherman (who was on the commission) and Sheridan, did not.

The Indian Peace Commission resulted in a series of new treaties, designed to be more humane to Native-Americans that would limit the options of tribes to live in their traditional ways. The Medicine Lodge Treaties and the Fort Laramie Treaty of 1868 required tribes to give up vast amounts of land in exchange for smaller, well-defined areas (reservations) that, at the time, no white settlers wanted. The deal created "unassigned lands" that opened settlement throughout the central plains from the Dakota Territory south to Texas. All non-native migrants had to do was to avoid the reservations. Conversely, Natives were expected to confine themselves to the assigned areas. However, as with previous treaty enforcement, violations quickly occurred.

The Lakota Sioux considered the Black Hills, located in present-day South Dakota, as sacred. Congress ceded the territory as part of the Fort Laramie Treaty after a number of skirmishes between Oglala Lakota chief Red Cloud and the Army. However, by 1874, the discovery of gold enticed prospectors to intrude. Soldiers made early attempts to keep the miners out of the Black Hills, honoring the provisions of the treaty. When news spread, thanks to an expedition by Colonel George Armstrong Custer, more hopeful prospectors came, rendering the treaty practically void. After members of the Lakota tribe attacked the miners, the Army used the retaliation as an excuse to seize the Black Hills.

The discovery of gold in the Black Hills elevated tensions that were already high between Native-Americans and the U.S. government. Custer was a rising military star after establishing himself during the Civil War as the youngest major general in the Union Army at 23. Following his 1874 expedition, Custer led a portion of the 7th Cavalry as part of a military force charged with finding wayward Indian groups and bringing them back to the reservations. On June 25, 1876, Custer split his forces, leaving himself with a little over 200 men. He charged a village on the banks of the Bighorn River, employing the same kind of battle strategy that had won him accolades during the Civil War. However, his small band met a force led by the legendary Crazy Horse and a contingent of warriors twenty times larger than his own. As Custer's portion of the 7th Cavalry found itself surrounded, a desperate battle ensued that resulted in the death of Custer and all his men. Often referred to as "Custer's Last Stand," recent archeology at the battlefield site has revealed Custer's men attempted to retreat but were overwhelmed.

The success of Native-Americans at Little Bighorn shocked the nation. News reached many back east as they celebrated the centennial of the United States. Calls for retaliation were immediate and swift. But with the fighting force severely reduced, the Army did not return to the field until much later in the year. The victory at Little Big Horn, however, proved to be the zenith of Native-Americans in their struggle to remain free from governmental control. Some of the warriors against Custer returned to the reservation. The following year, Sitting Bull escaped to Canada while Crazy Horse surrendered to the U.S. government.

One Native-American leader sought to lead his entire tribe out of the United States. Continued encroachment by settlers and demands by the military convinced Chief Joseph that living within the borders of the United States was no longer reasonable. The Nez Perce eluded cavalry for three months as they attempted to flee to Canada. Their journey of almost 1,200 miles ended just 40 miles from the border when they were intercepted by General Nelson Miles in Montana Territory in 1877. Chief Joseph proclaimed, "I will fight no more, forever" after seeing his tribe exhausted and hungry from their attempted flight. Authorities confined the remainder of his band to a reservation in Oklahoma.

Periodically, relations worsened to the point that episodes of resistance became front page news from the West. One Chiricahua Apache leader symbolized the dilemma facing the Army in making the frontier safe for white settlers. Geronimo, a variation on his given name of Goyahkla, refused to adhere to demands that he live permanently on a reservation. He and his followers fought against both Mexican authorities who had killed his mother, wife, and children, and an American government that tried to resettle his people in reservations. Geronimo and those loyal to him objected to the broken promises made by the government. He continually eluded the American military, but finally in 1886, Geronimo was apprehended and imprisoned. For the rest of his life (another 23 years) authorities confined him to army bases and prisons in the South and Midwest. When Geronimo died at Fort Sill, Oklahoma in 1909, his last statement exemplified why he was so feared. He said, "I should have never surrendered. I should have fought until I was the last man alive."

While the conflict had been ongoing since the arrival of the first European settlers, the Indian Wars accelerated in the years following the Civil War. Looking back in 1894, the Census Bureau estimated that almost 50,000 Native-Americans had been killed as the result of conflicts compared to around 20,000 Anglos (whites). Forcing Indians further west resulted in numerous treaties, including renegotiated ones. The object of those agreements always required Indian removal from land wanted by new settlers to the region. Indians were required to move to less- hospitable land, where they were guaranteed to live forever. Each time Indian groups were relocated, promised provisions seldom came or, when they did, proved inadequate.

Throughout the 1880s, the fight with various tribes of the West began to lessen as many Native leaders were captured. Most were confined to reservations, even though Chief Joseph made a personal plea to President Rutherford B. Hayes for more humane treatment. Oglala Lakota war leader Red Cloud lived out his life on the Pine Ridge Reservation in South Dakota. He died at the age of 88. Lakota spiritual leader Sitting Bull, who had successfully escaped to Canada returned after a four-year exile, also spent the rest of his life at Pine Ridge. Chiricahua Apache leader Geronimo spent most of his old age in Oklahoma.

Several Indian prophets claimed to have visions that told them soon the land would be restored to them, Natives would forever leave the reservations, and their white enemies would no longer be a concern. In 1889, a Paiute prophet named Wovoka began the Ghost Dance—a variation of the circle ritual that had been practiced by numerous tribes for centuries. The difference in this ceremony was the sudden popularity of the dance and the inability of agency officials to understand and control the activities of their residents. At Pine Ridge, additional troops were called in to handle the situation. In mid-December, Sitting Bull, who resided at Pine Ridge, was killed after refusing to be taken from his home. It was a time of escalating confusion and tension.

The standoff reached a climax on December 29, 1890 after Natives at Pine Ridge were ordered to surrender any weapons to the military. Reports vary, but one account stated that Black Coyote, a Miniconjou Lakota who may have been deaf and did not speak English, refused to give up his rifle. Two soldiers grabbed Black Coyote. His gun then fired perhaps by accident. Immediately, the rest of the troops began firing on the entire group of Native Americans who were encamped by Wounded Knee Creek. Over 150 Lakota men, women, and children were killed or mortally wounded. Twenty-five soldiers also died. The Natives were buried in trenches near the site of the massacre. Over the years, people have viewed Wounded Knee as a needless slaughter of the Lakota while symbolizing all the mistreatment of Native Americans. It has also been viewed as the capstone of the Indian Wars. No other armed resistance took place by Natives until a siege, staged by members of the American Indian Movement in 1973, occurred at the same site of the 1890 confrontation. The later event took place to protest some of the same issues that Natives had been contesting throughout the nineteenth century, including the bad faith of the American government in fulfilling treaty provisions and corruption among agency officials.

Following the passage of the Dawes Act in 1877, official policy sought to Americanize Indians. Colonel Richard Henry Pratt conveyed it most succinctly when he wrote, "kill the Indian, save the man." He concluded that Native-Americans could be civilized and trained to leave behind their communal lifestyle. To that end, Pratt founded the Carlisle Indian Industrial School, a boarding school in Pennsylvania for Native-Americans to teach them the ways of the dominant culture in the United States. With the Dawes Act came another redistribution of "unassigned lands." Since the presidency of Andrew Jackson, Oklahoma had been the destination of various Native groups to allow ongoing growth within the nation. However, by 1889, the land formerly labeled as "Indian Territory" became desirable to the point that government officials devised a method for settlers to claim portions for their own use. As part of the Indian Appropriation Act of 1889, Congress allowed settlers, "boomers" as they were called, to claim land beginning from April 22. Some did not wait for the official opening. Instead they sneaked into the territory, gaining the nickname of "sooner."

The Myth of the West

For those who went to the West, but more so for those who did not, the allure of the region held a fascination. One time scout Buffalo Bill Cody saw opportunity in taking western motifs and characters and displaying them in a traveling show. For 30 years that spanned the end of the nineteenth century into the twentieth, Cody organized a version of life in the West complete with a few of its most famous names. Sitting Bull toured for a time, as did frontier scout Calamity Jane. But the main focus of the show was to represent life in various part of the West. Cowboys roped steers, sharpshooters like Annie Oakley demonstrated their skill with a rifle, and performers even reenacted historical events like the Battle of Little Bighorn. The shows idealized and sensationalized life in the "Old West." Buffalo Bill's extravaganza toured the eastern United States as well as Europe and was very popular. So much so, that in advance of the show's arrival, advertisement posters only included

Buffalo Bill Postcard—Buffalo Bill Cody may be the single most important figure to craft our understanding of the West. His Wild West Shows sought to preserve what was going on in the region but also sensationalized people and events leading to later Hollywood movies.

Tombstone, Arizona—The town of Tombstone, Arizona is less than 50 miles from the Mexican border, a boomtown that sprung up after a silver strike. However, it has become immortalized over a thirty second gunfight in October of 1881 between two factions in the town vying for control.

a picture of a buffalo with Cody's likeness set inside. The only text read, "I am coming."

The myth of the West permeated American society even as the region developed. By 1890, the Census Bureau declared the frontier closed. Historian Frederick Jackson Turner thought and wrote about what this meant for the past and future of America. His "Significance of the Frontier in American History" posited that much of the American character could be exemplified by the frontier spirit of Americans moving west. Individualism, creativity, and the desire to tame the wilderness demonstrated the resourcefulness of Americans, thereby explaining their greatness. Jackson offered his frontier thesis at the Chicago Exposition in 1893. Among the examples of greatness came a warning. With the frontier closed, where were Americans to explore and tame, in order to fulfill the need Turner outlined in his thesis that defined the American personality?

Perhaps the frontier was closed, but myth and legend were also creating new avenues for the expression of American character. A few stories and real-life people became well known. One of the most retold and celebrated episodes in the "Old West" came on a late October day in 1881. The town of Tombstone, Arizona sprang up just a few years earlier after Ed Schieffelin discovered silver on a ridge just 30 miles from the Mexican border. Like any boom town, migrants flocked to the makeshift and lawless camp. Among those who had come to prospect were the Earp brothers, Virgil, Morgan, and Wyatt, all lawmen in other western towns. While in Tombstone, the Earps involved themselves more in gambling houses than mines and quickly developed a rivalry with other migrants. The matter was settled with a short but renowned gunfight. The story of the "Gunfight at the OK Corral" epitomized the lawlessness and quick gunplay of the West, while making legends of the Earp Brothers. The truth of the situation turned out quite different than the story. Whatever the case, Wyatt Earp ended up in most versions as the good guy who protected his town and established order. His actions, as well of that of his friend John Henry "Doc" Holliday, have been portrayed in a multitude of books and films since the gunfight.

Into the Pacific and the Caribbean

The conquest of the contiguous states and territories to the west gave Americans pause as to what new opportunities would be available for them in the future. With the United States enclosed by borders with Canada and Mexico, expansion required an off shore option. Fortunately, new lands lay in wait for exploration. In 1867, much to the ridicule of many, Secretary of State William Seward negotiated the purchase of Alaska from Russia. For $7.2 million, the United States acquired over 400 million acres that calculates to about 2 cents per acre. It became the outlet Americans needed when settlement options declined in what Alaskans came to call the "lower 48." Much like the Dakota Territory and California, gold was the reason that people flocked to Alaska in the late nineteenth century. Discovered in 1896, over 100,000 prospectors came, including Wyatt Earp. Few made fortunes in their trek to the Klondike, but as the twentieth century dawned, Alaska provided one last frontier for the kind of adventurous American who Frederick Jackson Turner had earlier lionized.

After the creation of California as a state in 1850, commercial interests began to look at the Pacific Ocean as a highway to the Far East for trade and influence. Goods from that part of the world had fascinated westerners for centuries, and by the late nineteenth century, U.S. commerce had grown to the point that Americans had something to trade. Americans now faced some important questions. Should the United States take numerous islands in the Pacific for economic and strategic purposes? The example had already been set by the colonial empires of Europe who controlled lands all over the world. France, Great Britain, Spain, Portugal, Holland, even an emerging Germany were all involved in colonialism. By following suit, the United States simply furthered its own economy and ability to compete on a global scale. The argument for imperialism replaced westward expansion once the frontier was closed, giving Americans new places to look for growth.

The Anti-Imperialist League rose to voice opposition to American acquisition of lands beyond the boundary of the ocean. Membership included such diverse personalities as writers Mark Twain and Henry James, industrialist Andrew Carnegie, labor leader Samuel Gompers, and even former president Grover Cleveland. They believed that the legitimacy of the American system came from the Lockean philosophy of "consent of the governed," and the United States had no legal right as well as no moral authority to take control of people who had not sought to join the Union. The League asserted that to acquire territory by force fundamentally differed from the principles upon which the nation was founded. Though members remained very vocal about their opposition to American foreign policy with regard to colonization around the world, their concerns went unheeded.

One of the first places the United States looked for new territory was Cuba. Thomas Jefferson was the first American president to eye the island, saying it would be a "most interesting addition". Before the Civil War, southerners saw Cuba, 90 miles from Florida, as a good possibility for the expansion of slavery. The Ostend Manifesto of 1854 suggested the United States to take the nation by force if the Spanish refused to sell. During the Grant presidency, Cubans sought to establish their independence in what became known as the Ten Years War. The United States House of Representatives voted to recognize the new republic, but Grant refused, instead making offers through the U.S. Minister to Spain to buy Cuba. The United States also supported a Cuban rebellion in the early 1870s, sending private citizens including some former Confederates to ferment dissent. Those American revolutionaries supported the Cuban rebellion by running munitions to Havana. This assistance continued until the Spanish captured the most notorious blockade running ship once used by the Confederacy called the Virginius. After executing crew members as pirates, the United States threatened war. A negotiated settlement that included reparations and Spain's return of the Virginius temporarily settled the dispute.

One significant obstacle to American expansion had long been the state of the American Navy. As the United States developed into a world power, strategists like Alfred Thayer Mahan asserted that the United States needed a strong naval fleet to further its goal and compete on the larger stage. As an admiral, Mahan used the model of the British to demonstrate the need of a large and technologically advanced navy. His writings on sea power greatly influenced and facilitated an expansionist mood in the United States. Mahanism, as the doctrine came to be called, provided the vehicle by which the United States could arrive and take its place as a leader of the world's destiny into the twentieth century.

American imperialists set their sights on a number of islands in the Pacific as a way to grow the nation. As commercial interests grew on the Hawaiian Islands, American business took a more active part in its operations. In 1887, a new constitution was drafted that reduced the kingdom in power and influence, opening Hawaii to takeover by the United States. Though President Grover Cleveland was partial to the monarchy in place, his successor, William McKinley, was not. A provisional government replaced the kingdom of Queen Lili'oukalani in 1893, and the United States annexed the islands five years later. Hawaii served the strategic as well as economic needs of the United States, as it was located roughly halfway between North America and Asia.

The Spanish-American War

The majority of island possessions that came under American control was a result of the long-threatened war with Spain. While the dispute centered around Cuba, a number of other territories also became part of the United States in the treaty following the war. Following the Virginius Incident, the drum beat more softly but still steadily for an end to Spanish control of Cuba. Spanish colonies in the western hemisphere were anathema to the Monroe Doctrine, and while Spain had already lost most of its claim to the New World,

Cuba, and Puerto Rico remained a leftover of European colonization. In the 1890s, support for an independent Cuba began to grow again.

The American press were especially interested in the unfolding events in Cuba—particularly two publishers in New York City who had a competitive rivalry with one another. Joseph Pulitzer and William Randolph Hearst both took over newspapers out west (Pulitzer in Kansas City, Hearst in San Francisco) before acquiring tabloids in the nation's largest market with the goal of establishing the nation's premier publication. Pulitzer 's *New York World* and Hearst's *New York Journal* came to focus on growing turmoil in Cuba that in turn sparked readers' interest and sold papers. One example was the plight of a young damsel in distress who found herself under the unwanted control of unscrupulous Spanish soldiers. The debate remains unsettled to this day about her intentions, but Evangelina Cosio y Cisneros' story filled the pages of the *Journal*, as Hearst employed a reporter to devise a plot to rescue her from her captors, in essence the struggle of Cuba in a microcosm. In the end, the rescue of Cisneros proved to be easy but was reported in the paper as death defying. Expecting war, Hearst also sent the famed western artist Frederic Remington to Cuba in order to sketch the battles for the publication. When Remington wired Hearst that there was nothing to draw, Hearst replied, "You furnish the pictures, I'll furnish the war." The efforts of Hearst and Pulitzer to influence the outcome of activities came to be called "yellow journalism" primarily because of the jaundiced approach the two editors took to reporting news.

Trade in sugar and other commodities in Cuba gave the United States a heightened interest in the island. President William McKinley's administration negotiated with Spain to allow an autonomous government to take control of the island, but fearing retaliation, McKinley ordered the battleship the USS Maine to sail to Cuba to protect American interests. After a month in Havana harbor, the Maine exploded killing 267 sailors. For months, controversy surrounded the origin of the explosion. Did the Spanish try to rid themselves of an American presence? Did Cuban revolutionaries plant a bomb to look as though the Spanish did it? Was someone who wanted a

Battleship Maine—The remains of the Battleship Maine, an American vessel anchored in Havana Harbor in February of 1898 when it blew up. Jingoist Americans charged the Spanish with sabotage but later inquiry found that a boiler on the ship overloaded and caused the explosion.

Library of Congress, Prints & Photographs Division, LC-USZ62-19254

war at all costs willing to sacrifice American lives to get it? In the end, and with numerous investigations trying to determine the cause of the blast, forensic experts concluded that the Maine suffered from a malfunction in the ship's boiler and the explosion was an accident. Nonetheless, the timing of the incident gave hyper-patriotic Americans, called "jingoists," an opportunity to point the finger of blame at the Spanish. For pro-war Americans, "Remember the Maine" became the battle cry.

McKinley sought a peaceful solution, but the tide of war was too great. In the two months that followed after the sinking of the Maine, congressmen and newspaper editors alike argued war with the Spanish was the only honorable course. Quickly, the war plan against Spain not only included Cuba but other Spanish possessions as well. In less than a week after the United States declared war, American ships attacked halfway around the world. The fleet in the Pacific sailed toward the Spanish territory of the Philippines—where another independence movement had been trying to throw off Spanish control. In less than a day, the naval squadron under the command of Admiral George Dewey defeated the Spanish fleet. By the end of the summer, the United States took complete control of the Philippines. Filipinos who sought to establish an independent nation were bitterly disappointed. Their leader, Emilio Aguinaldo, once the guest of Dewey and the American forces, now fought his former host in a bitterly contested attempt to throw off what Aguinaldo considered a new oppressor. Ultimately, over 4,500 Americans became casualties as they tried to quell the insurrection staged by Aguinaldo's forces. That same summer of 1898, the American Navy also took control of the former Spanish colony of Guam.

In Cuba, naval forces blockaded the island as American troops prepared for an invasion. Assistant Secretary of the Navy, Theodore Roosevelt, who put Admiral Dewey on alert for his attack in Manila Harbor, quit the War Department to volunteer for active service in a unit he helped organize. The first U.S. Volunteer Cavalry, or "The Rough Riders," consisted of Roosevelt's college buddies from Harvard and cowboys he met while a rancher in North Dakota. The attack force was comprised of other units as well, including four regiments of African-American soldiers. Under the command of General William Shafter, troops landed at Daiquiri, with a battle plan to attack Santiago. Several consequential battles were fought outside Santiago, including El Caney and San Juan Heights, but the greatest number of American casualties came from Yellow Fever. The disease killed almost 9 out of every 10 soldiers who died in Cuba. Within 10 weeks, the contest was decided with the Americans victorious over the Spanish. The United States also took the smaller island of Puerto Rico from the Spanish as part of the same military action.

Signed in December of 1898, The Treaty of Paris formally ceded Cuba, Puerto Rico, the Philippines, and Guam to the United States in exchange for $20 million. The United States stood ready to begin the twentieth century as a world power, and also an imperial one. Debate continued among Americans as to the justice of controlling those who did not speak English and who knew little of American customs, but most considered the intervention of the United States as a benevolent gesture that put native peoples on the path to self-determination. The Spanish-American War also did much to more fully reunite the United States after the Civil War, offering a unity of purpose against a common foe. Former Confederate cavalry officer Joe Wheeler even referred to his Spanish opponents as "Yankees."

A World Power

Emboldened by success, one veteran used his experience in the Spanish-American War to become president of the United States. Theodore Roosevelt, Lieutenant Colonel of the Rough Riders, wrote extensively about what he called his "crowded hour" during the Battle of San Juan Hill. His popularity upon his return home propelled him to the governorship of New York in the fall of 1898. Two years later, he found himself on the Republican presidential ticket with incumbent William McKinley. Then fate played a hand in TR's career, as an assassin took the life of President McKinley during a visit to the Pan-American Exposition in Buffalo, New York. At 42 years of age, Theodore Roosevelt became the youngest chief executive in the history of the United States.

Roosevelt believed in furthering the power of the nation that he now lead. The powerful nations of Europe, Britain, France, and Germany looked with anticipation toward China. Business interests coveted the unique products created by the Chinese that Europeans had sought for centuries when they hauled porcelain, fabrics, and spices back over the Silk Road during the Renaissance. Now, Americans had a more direct route. In addition, millions of Chinese might enjoy American products if they had an opportunity to buy them. The possibility of trade kept the pressure on the colonizing nations to establish a presence in the Far East. The only problem lay in the fact that no one nation had the upper hand in making China their possession. As a compromise, Secretary of State John Hay suggested an "Open Door Policy" in which the United States proposed to allow all colonial powers the right to trade openly with China.

For some Americans, China offered one of the "corners of the earth" that they, as Christians, were expected to seek out for conversion. Both Catholic and Protestants spent large amounts of money and time preparing missionaries to go to China. The number of missionaries grew steadily after the Civil War, with more than 60% being women. By the turn of the century, westerners totaled over 2,500 with around 1,000 Americans included. Missionaries faced famine, plague, and war. With the number of Christians continuing to rise, an 1899 backlash led by the nativist group, the Society of Righteous and Harmonious Fists (Boxers) arose against foreigners who sought to convert the Chinese from their ancient ways. One hundred eighty nine missionaries were killed by the Boxers who held beliefs concerning their own invincibility, similar to that of the Native-American ghost dance. Thousands of Chinese Christians died, also. An eight nation alliance was required to stop the violence against Christians which opened China even further to western influence. Ten years after the Boxer Rebellion, overthrow of the Qing Dynasty lead to the establishment of China's first republic.

Social Darwinism was one of the things that inspired conquest of foreign lands and missionary work like that in China. Since Charles Darwin's theory about the adaptive traits of animals in order to survive, the concept was applied to society through the writings of Herbert Spencer. He argued that western Caucasians produced the most intellectually advanced societies because of their adaptability, which guaranteed their success. The self-affirming premise gave westerners an argument of their own superiority thus allowing them to rationalize their treatment of people with lesser technology. Westerners began to see it as their duty to "civilize" all other groups in which the came into contact, applying to Native-Americans as well as Cubans and Filipinos, even the Chinese.

Monroe Doctrine/Roosevelt Corollary

During the nineteenth century, American foreign policy began to consider the Monroe Doctrine inviolable. Two-time Secretary of State James G. Blaine organized a Pan-American Conference with the goal being an association for greater trade with Latin America. As a hedge against the McKinley Tariff of 1890, Blaine proposed freer trade with Central and South-American nations as a market for American goods and to provide leadership in the Western Hemisphere. The Pan-American Conference achieved little, especially when events that caused conflict took over.

In Chile, an incident involving Americans threatened war between the two countries when a brawl erupted between sailors from the U.S.S. Baltimore and local Chileans. The fight outside a bar in Valparaiso resulted in the death of two Americans and the imprisonment of 17 others. News of the outcome reached an outraged President Benjamin Harrison who threatened an attack if reparations were not made. The Baltimore Incident resolved when Chile issued a formal apology and paid the United States $75,000. American intervention into Latin America continued for the next 30 years.

At one time or another during the presidencies of Roosevelt, Taft, and Wilson, each sent troops into Cuba to maintain order under the auspices of the Roosevelt Corollary. Much of that self-imposed responsibility came from legislation created after the Spanish American War when Cuba became a protectorate of the United States. The Platt Amendment gave the American government the authority to regulate activity in Cuba, which the United States exercised repeatedly.

Library of Congress, Prints & Photographs Division, Detroit Publishing Company Collection, LC-DIG-det-4a24682.

Panama Canal—The United States sought a more convenient travel route from east coast to west by encouraging the Panamanians to revolt against Colombia, then seeking an agreement to build a canal. The project was completed in 1914.

The most substantial intervention in the affairs of the western hemisphere came with the desire to build a canal in Central America that reduced ocean-going voyages from the Atlantic to the Pacific. Throughout the nineteenth century, proposals came and went over the best place to build a massive ditch to avoid sailing around the southernmost tip of South America. A number of routes were considered, but in the 1880s, the French began construction in the Colombian province of Panama. Construction challenges and yellow fever forced abandonment of the project, but by the early twentieth century, Theodore Roosevelt took up the challenge. Two problems arose. First, Panamanians were revolting against the government of Colombia, which Roosevelt condemned. Secondly, the Colombian government failed to ratify the treaty, leading Roosevelt to use the first problem to solve the second. He changed positions on the Panamanian Revolution, instead backing their independence and subsequently getting their approval to build. Construction took 10 years to complete and when the canal opened in 1914, the United States administered and operated it until the end of the twentieth century.

Roosevelt's opponents criticized his methods of obtaining the canal as well as his use of gunboat diplomacy to demonstrate American military might. Repeatedly, U.S. forces bolstered the Roosevelt Corollary even to the point, during the later part of his presidency, of sailing a portion of the American fleet around the world to demonstrate the power of the American Navy. The ships were painted white as a sign that "The Great White Fleet," as it was called, came in peace. In reality, the display announced the arrival of the United States as a substantial player in world affairs, rivaling the Old World of Europe as a force to heed in the new century.

Roosevelt offered numerous contradictions when it came to international relations. His use of the military suggested he was a warmonger, but he also won the Nobel Peace Prize for his successful effort to barter an end to the Russo-Japanese War. The Treaty of Portsmouth resolved the conflict between the Russians and the Japanese while also advancing the presence of the United States as a partner in matters concerning the Pacific.

As the nation turned from Civil War to expansion, the end of the nineteenth century created a substantial period of growth to the shores of the Pacific and beyond for Americans who continued their restless pursuit of self-determination within the context of a growing nation. Meeting every obstacle as a surmountable challenge, they subdued the vast expanses of the West, and most everyone there, as well as lands beyond their borders. Along the way, these Americans discovered an awakening authority to broker events in both the Atlantic and Pacific region. A new nation emerged that had only decades before had been locked in a civil conflict. Perhaps, Americans knew this was just the beginning of their road to world preeminence.

CHAPTER FOURTEEN

Progressivism

Chapter 14: Key Concepts

○ What events and institutions of American life in the 19th century gave rise to Progressivism?

○ Assess the success of the federal government in using a Progressive strategy to solve the pressing social ills of late 19th and early 20th century? Did the approach work? What problems were solved? What problems were not?

○ What were the causes of American entry into World War I? Were those causes justified? Did the United States successfully attain its goal with the outcome of WWI?

The explosive growth of the United States in the late nineteenth century, created troubling problems for a nation emerging as economic and military power in the world. While Americans proved to be adept at converting to an industrial society, not everyone enjoyed the wealth and ease that came with prosperity. The debate raged between an unfettered capitalist economy and a growing tide of socialism that had already swept Europe. For Americans were aware of the perils of each, a progressive approach offered the best way to stem the excesses of industrialism while advancing its growth. Progressivism laid the groundwork for the next generation when the calamity of the Great Depression would seek even greater answers from the federal government, building upon what Progressives started at the turn of the twentieth century. Progressivism became a more acceptable road to reform than did the Populist and radicals that demanded change.

Political Economics

American constitutional government had originally been intended as an unobtrusive instrument, designed to stay out of the way of the lives of most Americans so that they could follow their own livelihoods. Periodically, citizens directed the activity of government with their vote. With the exception of war, the job of the government was to allow as much freedom and independence as possible. However, conditions changed and the United States became a more industrialized and interconnected society. Disparities emerged, leaving some Americans without assistance in handling corrupt practices that arose. Who would help these Americans? A growing number of people recognized systemic problems growing out of American capitalism but lacked any meaningful recourse for change. While good for the "captains of industry," working conditions for those employed was hazardous with no protections in place. As conditions worsened, the only entity large enough to control and regulate American companies was its own government, the same one that had previously taken a "hands off" approach to the private affairs of its citizens, which included work.

The first important change came in the structure of the federal government itself. Since Andrew Jackson's presidency, loyalty exceeded qualifications in attaining a job at the national level. The spoils system repaid campaign supporters for

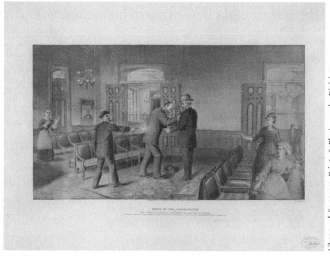

Garfield Assassination—The assassination of President James A. Garfield four months after he became the chief executive shocked the nation. The reason for the attack became a rallying cry for change. Charles Guiteau shot Garfield when he did not receive a government job for his efforts to help get Garfield elected.

helping get a president elected. Abraham Lincoln very plainly commented about the rush of office seekers coming to see him that there were "too many pigs for the teats," meaning more people looked for jobs that they felt earned for getting him elected than positions for them. The issue came to full public attention following the election of 1880. After James Garfield came to the presidency, Charles Guiteau believed that he deserved an ambassadorship for speaking on behalf of the Garfield Campaign. Brushed aside, Guiteau formed a plot to kill the president, which he attempted as Garfield walked through the train station in Washington, DC in the summer of 1881. Shooting the president twice, Garfield sustained mortal injuries that would claim his life three months later.

Outrage replaced shock as the nation demanded reform in the spoils system. The new president, Chester Alan Arthur championed civil service reform, even though he had risen to a position of prominence in the Republican Party through patronage. The Civil Service Act of 1883 began the process of protecting federal jobs from political changes and was seen as a good step toward making government ethical, the same government that Progressives increasingly saw as the instrument for uprooting corruption elsewhere in American society.

Reaction to Laissez-Faire

As the industrial revolution gained momentum in late nineteenth century American life, treatment of workers became an important issue. Over half a million industrial accidents, including around 30,000 deaths, occurred each year. Laissez-faire philosophy emphasized the autonomy of business to conduct its affairs in any way it saw fit. However, the rising danger of the workplace, created a demand of intervention to improve working conditions, which included safety but also higher wages and shorter hours.

Jacob Riis—Jacob Riis used photography to show the terrible conditions in New York's tenements. The images he captured brought attention to the plight of workers in sweatshops and factories.

Though workers knew the factory environment firsthand, the rest of America learned of the deplorable circumstances through the writings of a group of journalists, collectively known as muckrakers. These reporters brought to light the long hours, low pay, and dangerous situations in numerous industries with the hope of serving as a catalyst for change. Theodore Roosevelt, coined the name for these crusading writers, saying that they had uncovered and exposed the unseemly manner in which products were made in America. Though his characterization of reporters raking the muck (a reference to waste or filth) was not a positive one, he read their findings with interest. Ida Tarbell outlined the unethical practices of John D. Rockefeller's Standard Oil Company. Lincoln Steffens revealed political corruption.

Photographers also played a significant part in revealing the ills of capitalism to the American public. The images captured by Jacob Riis of New York City's tenements and the families who lived in them gave the public visual evidence of the deplorable conditions some industrial workers were forced to endure in order to make a living.

Workers championed their own cause with a growing membership in unions, but their efforts splintered between craft unions, such as the American Federation of Labor (AFL) and more radical efforts like the International Workers of the World (IWW). Under Samuel Gompers, the AFL, sought only skilled workers and as a result, left out many other factory hands. The IWW, though open to all workers, alienated some because of extreme tactics to gain attention for the struggle of its workers. The Wobblies, as they were called, also maintained connections to socialist, Marxist, even anarchist philosophies that put them on the far left of the political spectrum. Their slogan of "an injury to one is an injury to all" counted on the collective effort needed to gain the attention of management and make substantive change for the workers. The number of IWW members never got to the point that strikes called by the leadership could cripple production and bring management to the bargaining table consistently, but they did gain attention.

Since the Industrial Revolution began in Europe, issues of treatment were a longer standing problem abroad than in the United States. In the universities of Germany, scholars examined the plight of workers, theorizing how best to protect them from harsh treatment. Ultimately, the solution coalesced around government as the only institution with the mandate to protect its citizens and the power to regulate business for the well being of its workers. New Zealand became the first nation to implement progressive reforms, leaving the United States to follow at the turn of the twentieth century.

Numerous strikes by unions often failed to galvanize public support for the plight of the workers with government consistently on the side of management to keep the flow of goods heading to the consumer. Labor strife became synonymous at times with class conflict as organizations like the Wobblies emphasized the income gap between workers and management. In the last half of the nineteenth century, almost every major strike ended with the federal government playing a hand in forcing strikers to go back to work or helping management hire replacements, all in the name of economic continuity. But in the first dozen years of the twentieth century, two events signaled a change in the way the federal government saw itself in the ongoing struggle of the workplace.

Early in the presidency of Theodore Roosevelt, a strike by anthracite coal miners in northeastern Pennsylvania threatened to deny families of a vital source of heat for the winter. TR clearly understood the impact of the impasse and sought to mediate the dispute. Workers wanted higher wages, shorter hours, and recognition of their union. Previous U.S. presidents had called out the National Guard to restore order and production in times of large-scale strikes, but with a national catastrophe facing Americans, Roosevelt chose a different path. He put together a commission to arbitrate between mine owners and representatives of the workers. Initially, management balked at the impertinence of the workers and refused to negotiate. The coming winter however, pressurized the situation, so a quick solution took on greater importance and the president threatened nationalization if the owners refused to bargain. TR, with the help of finance capitalist J. Pierpont Morgan resolved the strike and got workers back to mining the type of coal preferred for home heating. In the end, the miners did not get all they wanted. Instead of the 8-hour day they sought, the agreement called for a 9-hour day, down from 10. Owners paid higher wages but not as much as the union sought. Although management still refused to recognize the United Mine Workers Association, arbitration was a tacit acknowledgement of the union as a representative of the workers. The incident marked a significant turning point by the federal government in labor relations.

Nine years later, a tragic incident demonstrated how deplorable conditions could be for workers. The Triangle Shirtwaist Company occupied the top three floors of the Asch Building in the garment district of New York City. Constructing women's blouses, called shirtwaists, on row after row of sewing machines, mostly immigrant women constituted the workforce. Twelve hour days at wages below the current equivalent of minimum wage were standard. Conditions at Triangle and other factories like it, gained a nickname. Workers referred to them as "sweatshops." On Saturday afternoon, March 25, 1911, fire broke out at Triangle. Doors to the fire escape had been locked by the owners earlier in an effort to curtail breaks by workers. Elevators carried a few to safety but in the heat of the fire, the elevators quickly broke down. The stranded had two choices, face the fire or jump to their certain deaths from the windows. The owners survived by reaching the roof of the building but 146 workers did not, in what is still the worst industrial accident ever in New York City.

Library of Congress, Prints & Photographs Division, LC-USZ62-34985

Triangle Shirtwaist Fire—The worst industrial accident in the history of New York, the Triangle Shirtwaist Fire killed 146 people, mostly women. It demonstrated the dangers of the factory and brought about over 60 laws the provide a safer work environment.

The Triangle Shirtwaist Fire brought the conditions for factory workers to the public consciousness. The tragedy spurred numerous new regulations for the workplace including maximum working hours, factory conditions and fire precautions. Those reforms came mainly at the state level. No federal effort to structure American manufacturing developed immediately, but as the problem gained increasing attention, adjustments began. In many ways, the investigation of workplace conditions exemplified the philosophy of the Progressive movement.

Unlike the radicals of the era, Progressives sought small adjustments within the system as opposed to a substantial overhaul as the means to improve society. Over the years, federal guidelines would be established to protect workers against events like the Triangle Fire. For example, in Muller v. Oregon, the Supreme Court unanimously ruled that long hours, like the ones seamstresses worked at Triangle were unreasonable, and set the hours per workday for women at 10. Though the decision raised questions about equal protection (men still had no limits on their workday), the decision fit the Progressive agenda of using government to solve social problems.

Business did not accept the increased attention to working conditions without attempting to push back. Frederick Winslow Taylor became famous for his research into industrial efficiency. His "time and motion studies" looked at human activity on the shop floor as a type of machine, whose motions could be streamlined for maximum productivity. *The Principles of Scientific Management* outlined Taylor's philosophy and gained great acclaim for the practice of industrial engineering as a means to increase the output of America's factories.

Beyond fighting unionism in factories and increasing efficiency from each worker, companies used their growing clout as advertisers to stifle the national discussion on the state of the industrial workplace. Internal public relations departments emerged to argue the company's side in any issue seen by management as unfair. Some went so far as to drop their advertising in magazines that included muckraking articles. The National Association of Manufacturers denounced many Progressive reforms as economically dangerous. After a quarter of a century building a successful business model, most organizations did not welcome comment or critique from laborers or media on how the product got made.

The Social Gospel

Modernist Christianity played a significant role in the reconsideration of worker treatment in the Progressive era. In 1894, the British journalist William T. Stead wrote a muckraking book that linked industrial reform, exposure of political corruption and evangelism. It was called *If Christ Came to Chicago*. In the book, Stead made the case that Christian values demanded societal reform. Stead's "government by journalism" opened the door to discussion of individual responsibility in industrial wrongs that needed to be righted.

Christian theologian Walter Rauschenbush exemplified the Social Gospel movement as a wing of Progressivism. He argued that belief in Christianity for personal salvation was selfish and ignored the greater problem of a society that needed the service Jesus advocated in his ministry. Forming a group called the Brotherhood of the Kingdom, Rauschenbusch personally served his fellow man in some of the most poverty-ridden locations in urban America, including Hell's Kitchen in New York City.

Service in the areas that needed it most also drove Jane Addams to seek means to help the less fortunate. With her personal inheritance, Addams financed a settlement house in Chicago. Addams and fellow seminarian Ellen Gates Starr converted a run-down mansion into a community center for numerous immigrant populations, providing a plethora of social and cultural services. Addams created Hull House to offer whatever the neighborhood needed, including practical and academic educational opportunities. Child care, language training, and food services were all supplied while social scientists studied the population, seeking to understand the root causes of poverty and disenfranchisement. Hull House served up to 2,000 people per week, housing some, training others, with the goal of better equipping all who came there to improve their life. Hull House served as a model and across America, over 400 settlement houses emerged with the same mission as the one created by Jane Addams. The settlement house movement lasted over 100 years with Hull House closing in 2012. It is now a museum.

Not all Christians endorsed the solutions offered by Walter Rauschenbusch and Jane Addams, or even agreed that their faith required societal responsibility. Ministers, like former baseball player turned evangelist Billy Sunday, saw some Progressive reforms as socialistic and at odds with his conservative, individualistic interpretation of Christianity. However, he did agree with Progressive initiatives concerning temperance, child labor, and women's suffrage. Likewise, some Progressives offered solutions to problems that the Church argued was anti-Christian and beyond the scope of society to change. Margaret Sanger argued for the right women to determine how many children they should have. She popularized the idea of birth control but was met by stern opposition from the Church and traditionalists alike who believed that the husband, as head of the household, determined the size of the family. Reducing family size reduced hardship she believed, saying "ignorance breeds poverty and poverty breeds ignorance." Forced to flee from the United States for a time over her controversial writings, Sanger nonetheless, helped validate contraception as a means to control family size and reduce poverty.

Vice loomed as the unfortunate outgrowth of poverty, a problem Billy Sunday and Margaret Sanger could agree upon. Their ideas on how to curb vice differed dramatically though. The Social Purity Movement sought to curtail ills such as spousal abuse and child labor by attacking what they felt were the root causes of family disfunction, alcohol consumption and prostitution. Most churches agreed that, as sin, these practices weakened the family unit. In the nineteenth century most advocates of social purity would not have classified themselves as Progressives. However, like Progressives, they believed that the solution to these problems came as legislation against the continuance of alcohol consumption. The Women's Christian Temperance Society and the Anti-Saloon League entreated the federal government to pass legislation outlawing such vice. As Progressives looked for allies to bring about a more stable American society, ending prostitution but more significantly prohibiting the use of alcohol became a goal that Progressives accepted.

Progressivism took as many different forms as participants at the turn of the twentieth century, all seeking to work within the society as a means to reform. American philosopher John Dewey wrote on many aspects of the American system but centered much of his advocacy on the developing education system in the United States. Saying that learning had a particularly democratizing affect, Dewey stressed the value of education as a way to, not only recognize change in American society but also steer it toward more desirable goals, and to do so required experimentation. A pragmatic approach, Dewey argued, after careful observation, could yield new and exciting ways in which the problems that confronted Americans could be explored and overcome.

Through the efforts of John Dewey and others, a system for public education emerged, to provide a base for learning and offered alternatives to factory work for future generations. What began as primary schools supported by a community or a church, evolved into larger enterprises, creating a graduated organization for children and adolescents to gain reading, writing, and mathematical skills. Scheduled around the farming calendar, schools operated in the winter, usually for three to four

Early American Public School—Primary schools had mostly been a community effort until the turn of the 20th century when states began to see the value of a public education. Schools generally ran during the winter in a one room facility that housed all grades that ranged up to the eight grade.

months. Originally, education was a matter for the community to decide, with each setting the rules and the calendar. As Progressives began to stress the need for a more formal system, states took over the responsibility, allotting funds and setting standards, a system which continues to this day in the United States.

Mandatory education for children also served to keep them out of the factories. Child labor had been practiced since the earliest days of the industrial revolution, on the farm too, for that matter. But many Progressives felt entry into a factory at the age of eight or nine, hampered that child from further advancement in society. As challenges to child labor wound their way through the courts, schools provided a positive alternative to idleness and/or labor. One of the most powerful tools to persuade Americans that child labor robbed children of their future can be seen in the work of Lewis Hine, as an investigator for the National Child

Lewis Hine Cotton Mill—Photographer Lewis Hine exposed the use of children in southern cotton mills with his documentary photographs in the early 20th century. It took twenty years, but his images helped to end the practice of child labor, coming at the same time as state requirements to make education mandatory.

Labor Committee. He went from mill to mill documenting the plight of young workers. His efforts also included photographs of children at their work stations. The photographs helped sway popular opinion against child labor, however fully barring school age children from the workplace would not happen until 1941.

A main tenet of the Progressive movement was to work on behalf of those who could not fully advocate for themselves, in pursuit of a more equitable society. Children served as a prime example, but even some adult groups joined with Progressives to seek ends to unfair treatment. For generations, women demonstrated for the right to vote and for equal legal status to men. As women's groups began to advocate strongly for the right to vote, they joined with many Progressives who found commonality in many of the same issues. The National Woman Suffrage Association under Carrie Chapman Catt took a conciliatory approach to gaining the right to vote while the National Women's Party with Alice Paul as head, engaged in more militant behavior, like disrupting male attended sporting events. The goal of the two groups were the same, their tactics were not.

One area in which Progressives saw only modest reform was civil rights. As president, Theodore Roosevelt invited Booker T. Washington to the White House for dinner, causing a tremendous backlash by mostly southerners. TR was sympathetic to African-American calls for change being advocated by Washington, but more forcefully by W.E.B. DuBois, who differed significantly with Washington over the methods and timing of equality. A few Progressives joined with DuBois and other African-Americans, as part of the Niagara Movement to be found as the National Association for the Advancement of Colored People in 1909. The NAACP became central organization for African-Americans to seek voting rights and an end to segregation in the United States.

Some Progressives went to an extreme when theorizing solutions for American society. Contemplating the work of his cousin Charles Darwin, Englishman Frances Galton advanced the word "eugenics"as a pseudo-scientific approach to the creation of human beings. He asserted that undesirable traits could be bred out of mankind (as well as desirable traits be promoted) through selective breeding. Taken seriously during the era, eugenics attempted to take choices about having children out of the hands of individuals and putting those decisions with the state to create a better class of people in the next generation. In the United States, some individuals were sterilized to keep them from having children, often without their knowledge or consent. Occurrences of forced sterilization continued in the United States until the 1970s. Used almost exclusively on minorities and the poor, courts eventually ruled the practice unconstitutional. Eugenics was not a part of the Progressive movement. Instead, it was a radical fringe attempt to engineer society.

In the growing concern for the ill effects of industrialism, some Progressives began to question the destructive use of natural resources in the United States. Naturalists, such as Ralph Waldo Emerson and John Muir had written about the virtues of the wild and keeping areas away from commercialization. As those lands grew more threatened, Progressives saw legislation as the best means to keep unique natural landscapes from being exploited.

Theodore Roosevelt, a conservationist himself, agreed with some of the motives of those who sought to preserve unique areas of the United States from encroachment. However, TR's view centered around efficient use of natural resources instead of complete protection. During his presidency, he allowed some public works projects to be built to serve various populations (such as the Hetch-Hetchy Dam at Yosemite for San Francisco's water supply), while declaring over 230 million acres protected by the federal government (which included the Grand Canyon).

Governmental Action

If government was the means to a solution for many of the problems facing American society at the turn of the twentieth century, the ways in which governments from the municipal level to Washington, DC pivoted to streamline these changes became significant to the process. Since Progressives were never uniform in their priorities for change, coalitions both large and small focused on various issues for reform. Some worked at the local level, some the state, and some sought grand change throughout the nation.

One hotbed of activity was Wisconsin. Under the leadership of representative/governor/senator "Fighting Bob" La Follette, the "Wisconsin Idea" offered a method to study issues and propose solutions. Especially during his time as governor of Wisconsin, La Follette looked to the University of Wisconsin's faculty as his "brain trust" to examine social suffering. From there, he would use his power as an elected official to enact laws for more equal treatment of workers in Wisconsin. During his tenure, with the assistance of his advisors, La Follette enacted legislation to regulate railroad rates (to assist farmers), set a minimum wage (for factory workers), created the first workman's compensation system in the nation (for injured factory workers), among many other reforms. He also favored the direct election of U.S. senators (for more open government), women's suffrage, and a graduated income tax. La Follette sought the presidency, several times as a Progressive Party candidate, the most successful time in 1924 when he won his home state of Wisconsin and garnered almost 17% of the vote nationally.

As an example of the disunity among Progressives, Robert La Follette championed many reforms but his strain of Progressivism differed sharply from other leaders in the movement. For example, La Follette's first candidacy for president pitted him directly against the other titan of the Progressive camp, Theodore Roosevelt. When the United States joined the Allies in World War I, La Follette vehemently opposed American entry. For his stand, other senators denounced him, questioning his patriotism. Unwilling to be cowered, La Follette argued for his right of free speech, even in time of war, making his case that allying with other governments, such a Britain and France, gave tacit approval to all their actions and policies, which Bob La Follette believed tarnished the reputation of the United States. The debate switched the focus from that which La Follette had build his career upon and that for which he was most passionate, the rights of workers and the greater spread of democracy against concentrations of power and wealth.

Other states and cities served as launchpads for unique Progressive changes. In Cleveland, Ohio Mayor Tom Johnson created a municipal power company to compete with private companies and bring down the price of electricity for Cleveland consumers. Numerous western states enacted initiative, referendum, and recall processes to give voters more power in electoral politics. An initiative provides the framework for a citizen, with enough accompanying voter signatures, to propose legislation be put on the ballot, for the entire voting populace, not the legislature to decide. Likewise, when the legislature wanted popular input, to see what the will of the people is on a particular issue, they put a proposal on the ballot for voter approval. Even though voters elect officials for prescribed periods of time, an office holder thought not to be competent during their tenure, could be petitioned by ballot proposal for removal from office, ahead of the end of their term. These measures, though not in every state, have been used repeatedly to bring issues up for public consideration and hasten public interaction beyond election time.

Nationwide, Progressivism came to the forefront with the presidency of Theodore Roosevelt. As with his intervention in the anthracite coal strike, TR brought a very different view of governmental power than that of his predecessors. Roosevelt's ancestry would hardly have indicated his support for Progressive reform. Born into a wealthy New York family, his contemporaries thought office holding unworthy of their strata. But TR understood the "noble obligation" he had as a person of means. Unfortunately, his first term as president did not come from an electorate mandating change. Roosevelt's activism was thought to be too radical for the Republican establishment, so the party found him a place where he could do little harm, the vice presidency. But McKinley's benefactor and friend Mark Hanna knew the danger of putting TR on the ticket. He vigorously worked to keep it from happening, but eventually told the president "Your duty to the country is to live for four years from next March." Unfortunately, William McKinley could not fulfill that duty. Just six months into his second term, an assassin mortally wounded McKinley leaving the presidency to Theodore Roosevelt. Hanna understood that Roosevelt had a very different agenda from the pro-business McKinley and tried to tie TR to McKinley's unfinished legislative program. Roosevelt had different ideas, even if he had no "elected" mandate upon which to offer his plan.

Although an "accidental" president as other vice-presidents who came to the office were called, Theodore Roosevelt proved to be a very different kind of individual. Active and well-read, TR authored almost three dozen books. Reportedly, he read on average, one book per day. One of those readings proved especially influential. After digesting Upton Sinclair's *The Jungle*, a muckraking expose of the meat-packing industry, TR could not eat his breakfast sausage. The president ordered an immediate investigation into the unregulated practices of companies that handle meat. The result was the Meat Inspection Act and the Pure Food and Drug Act, as well as the agency to oversee governmental scrutiny, today known as the Food and Drug Administration. In much the same kind of way, TR's reading Frank Norris' book, *The Octopus: A Story of California*, about the unfair pricing practices of railroads to the detriment of farmers, Roosevelt shepherded through Congress the Hepburn Act, to regulate the railroad industry. The chain of events exemplified the variety of ways a problem could come to public attention and how legislation could immediately be used to protect consumers via federal action.

Uncertain of his authority to proceed differently from his predecessor, for whom he served as replacement, TR sought the presidency in his own right in 1904, putting forth his agenda under the title of "The Square Deal." In his campaign, he clearly said that he did not want to end capitalism, just curb the excesses. Exemplified in the title, Roosevelt wanted to make the economy fair and even, thus the "square," for everyone. The four pillars of the square deal involved business regulation, consumer protection, environmental conservation, and labor/management relations. In some cases using existing laws and agencies, like the Sherman Anti-Trust Act and the Interstate Commerce Commission, and in others like the newly created Hepburn Act, TR sought to make American commerce fair and square for everyone.

As part of the problem with businesses and their power to dictate pricing in the marketplace, President Roosevelt saw too many companies acting in collusion to keep prices artificially high. In fact, many companies that should regard each other as competitors openly acted in concert through an apparatus called a "trust." Basically, a trust operated as a super structure with all the major companies within an industry granting authority to the trust to determine prices. Headed by the management of the top two or three companies, a trust controlled the amount of product available to the market and forced smaller companies to abide by pricing structures to assure that no renegade manufacturer undercut the "big boys" and gained a greater share of the market. Though the Sherman Anti-Trust Act had been created to prevent such manipulation, the law had instead been used on labor unions to keep worker groups from growing.

During Theodore Roosevelt's presidency, he broke up 43 trusts, establishing the government's legitimacy to act in the public interest to facilitate competition. His hand-picked successor, William Howard Taft, oversaw even more anti-trust suits, 99, although many of those began during the Roosevelt Administration. Trust-busting became a means by which Progressives could bring down prices for consumers and stimulate competition in the marketplace. When the Taft Administration broke up the American Tobacco Company, controlled by James B. Duke with R.J. Reynolds as a subservient participant, the move allowed Reynolds to grow his business in a way that participation in the trust would never have allowed and gave him the ability to grow his company to the point of eclipsing Duke's.

William Howard Taft, even with a greater number of trust breakups than Roosevelt, did not embrace the mantle of Progressive in the aggressive way that TR did. Uncertain of winning the 1904 election, Roosevelt vowed to consider McKinley's

William Howard Taft—After pledging not to run again if he won in 1904, Theodore Roosevelt handpicked his successor, William Howard Taft. When Taft did not handle the job as TR expected, Roosevelt ended their friendship by running against Taft in 1912.

Library of Congress, Prints & Photographs Division, Detroit Publishing Company Collection, LC-D429-48019.

second, unfulfilled term as his first and observing the unwritten rule of only two terms per president, TR vowed to not run again in 1908, picking Secretary of War, Taft as his heir apparent. But, in retirement, Roosevelt could not withhold his criticism of Taft's actions as president. Chiding Taft on trying to break up U.S. Steel, saying Taft could not tell the difference between a good trust and a bad trust, as well as other decisions made by Taft, the relationship soured. Roosevelt publicly called Taft a "fathead with the brains of a guinea pig" which wounded the sitting president. As his presidency progressed, Taft returned to a more pro-business approach, with even his foreign policy being influenced by the power of big business. TR felt betrayed by Taft's actions as president. A confrontation became inevitable.

The election of 1912 provided the setting for Theodore Roosevelt to disavow himself from the policies of the Taft Administration. Rationalizing a run for the presidency that he had previous said that he would not seek, TR clarified that he only meant "consecutive" terms. Roosevelt challenged Taft in every available primary for the nomination. Primaries were a brand new political operation and a Progressive reform to allow more openness in the selection of a party candidate for president. However, in this, the first ever election with primaries, the results were nonbinding. Roosevelt went to the convention with wins in 9 of the 13 states that held primaries. Taft won two and Bob La Follette won two. TR owned a clear lead in the delegate count but was denied the nomination because the Republican leadership favored Taft delegates to Roosevelt's. TR and his followers bolted the convention, reconvening six weeks later at the same hall in Chicago under the banner of the newly formed Progressive Party. The mascot for the party became the bull moose when a reporter asked Roosevelt if he was in shape for the campaign. TR answered, "I'm as fit as a bull moose."

Unique among campaigns for the president, 1912 is the only time in American history where a former president, a current president and a future president vied for the office. In addition to Roosevelt and Taft, Democrats selected former Princeton University president and governor of New Jersey, Woodrow Wilson as their standard bearer. Plus, Socialist Party candidate Eugene Victor Debs ran. A union leader who helped organize the International Workers of the World and the American Railway Union, Debs came to the attention of Americans first for his involvement in several famous strikes. By 1912, he embraced socialism and in the election received over 900,000 votes out of 14.8 million votes cast. During the campaign, Roosevelt was shot while delivering a speech in Milwaukee, Wisconsin, from which he recovered, but on the election day, no one won a majority of those almost 15 million votes. Combined, TR and Taft polled 50% but with the ballots split between them, Woodrow Wilson won the election with 42% of the vote.

During the campaign, TR, Taft, and Wilson offered Progressive solutions to the problems facing the American public. While Wilson campaigned on a platform of less government intervention under the banner of "the New Freedom," his administration operated quite the opposite. Wilson's Progressive strategy for a more equitable economy differed only slightly from his two Republican challengers. Instead of taking trusts to court in order to break them up, Wilson created the Federal Trade Commission to regulate trade practices in the United States. During his first term, he also sought the same kind of structure to control banking with the Federal Reserve System. In much the same way as TR though, the Federal Reserve was created to act as the arbiter between privately owned banks and their customers, with the government stepping in on the behalf of the public for their representation and benefit. In addition, Wilson sought to bring down the tariff for imported goods for the first time since the Civil War to increase competition, which favored buyers.

Woodrow Wilson vowed to make the changes he sought permanent, not subject to future court challenges or revocation of laws. Not since Reconstruction had an amendment to the Constitution been passed but during Wilson's presidency four amendments to the Constitution were passed, all borne out of Progressive ideals. The first was the 16th Amendment, allowing for the creation of an income tax that would not be apportioned to the states but would instead go to the federal treasury. Originally proposed in 1909 while Taft was president, the amendment took three years to be ratified by the required three-quarters of states in the union. The 16th Amendment was a way to recoup revenue lost by the reduction of the tariff. Progressives supported a graduated income tax as a way to curb the wealth of the rich. Anyone making over $3000 (or as a couple making $4000) was expected to pay a 1% tax on their income. After $20,000, an additional 1% was added with a rise of 1% at benchmark income levels. Additional percentages topped out at 7% for annual earners of $500,000 or more. Believing it fair for everyone to pay according to ability to do so, the 16th Amendment passed to become a permanent revenue source for the federal government instead of a temporary measure used, as it was in the Civil War, to pay for a catastrophic expenditure.

Following the 16th Amendment came another Progressive effort to bring representation closer to the voters. While members of the House of Representatives have always had to gain a majority of voters in their district to represent them, the Senate selection process operated quite differently. In the original Constitution, selected senators came from state legislatures, making the process indirect and taking selection of candidates from the hands of the people. Possible corruption tainted selection and often state legislators could not agree on a candidate, leaving positions open and states underrepresented. The change had been long championed by Progressives as a way to rest more power into the hands of voters. When offered to the states, the 17th Amendment passed in less than a year. By 1918, every member of the U.S. Senate was elected by popular vote.

The vile affects of alcohol, or "demon rum" as opponents liked to call it, had been touted by those wishing it banned. From the late nineteenth century into the twentieth, momentum for ridding the nation of alcohol grew, citing the wasted productivity and excessive violence that came from allowing consumption. Protestant denominations especially considered the use of strong drink a sin. Ultimately, groups like the Anti-Saloon League sought not to ban the drinking of alcohol but to make illegal the distilling and fermenting of spirits. The 18th Amendment reflected that approach. If acquiring liquor, wine, and beer were made difficult then more Americans would be likely to give up the practice of imbibing, or so the logic went. The 18th Amendment stipulated that the states had a time limit, seven years to ratify. It took one year and a month for adoption. The Volstead Act passed Congress quickly to follow the intent of the 18th Amendment and by January of 1920, Prohibition went into effect. While many evangelical Christians hailed Prohibition as the most effective use of government, most Americans refused to give up their consumption of alcohol. During the 1920s, flouting the law became fashionable and by 1933, another amendment to the Constitution came to the states repealing Prohibition. The 21st Amendment passed in less time than the 18th.

The last of the Prohibition Era amendments to be passed centered around the voting rights of women. Since the Seneca Falls Convention of 1848, groups of women lobbied for the right to vote. Some women argued that they should be included as part of the 15th Amendment, which ultimately enfranchised former slaves. However, when discussion of passage turned to the inclusion of women, abolitionist leader Frederick Douglass balked, saying "it's the Negro's hour," in essence making the case that suggesting women were a part of the amendment would so burden down the 15th Amendment as to make it unacceptable to state legislatures. In the meantime, a growing number of states, mostly in the West, granted women the right to vote in state and local elections. But women's groups kept up the pressure. Each day, volunteers stood across from the White House with a sign that read, "Mr. President, how long must women wait for liberty." Sympathetic to female suffrage, Woodrow Wilson asked the leading women's groups demonstrating for the right to vote to help him in the American war effort and he would promote their attempt as soon as hostilities ceased. True to his word, President Wilson called a special session of Congress to pass an amendment. Previous attempts had failed, the last in early 1919 by just one vote. Specifically saying that the right to vote cannot be denied "on account of sex," the 19th Amendment passed in time for women to vote in the presidential election of 1920.

A Progressive War

Woodrow Wilson spent much of his first term as president continuing the Progressive ideals of his era, albeit in his own way. However, two years into his first term, world events began to eclipse his domestic agenda, requiring more of his time to first, keep the United States out of the conflict, then secondly, to mobilize the nation to be the decisive factor in settling it.

The Great War began inauspiciously enough, as a Yugoslav nationalist assassin murdered the future leader of Austria. For 100 years, no major war engulfed Europe and by the twentieth century, a system of alliances gained a balance of powers among the major states. As those alliances shifted, keeping the peace became more precarious until the death of the Austrian heir to the throne, Franz Ferdinand ignited tensions to the point that most of the important powers of Europe chose sides. Germany, Austria-Hungary, and the Ottoman Empire, or the Central Powers, opposed primarily, Russia, France, and Britain, known in the United States as the Allies. With an immigrant population from all of those countries who now claimed American citizenship, Wilson determined the best policy for the United States was one of neutrality. Plus, the summer of 1914 proved to be an especially trying time for the president as his wife Ellen lay dying.

President Wilson spent the first few years of the war trying to maintain a stance of total neutrality. His strived to stay above the fray, with offers to mediate between the combatants. Neither side took Wilson's offer, but rather infringed upon United States' vessels as indifferent to the conflict, resulting in the loss of American lives. The most renowned example came in the May of 1915, when a German U-boat (submarine) sank the British passenger liner, R.M.S. Lusitania in waters just south of Ireland, within a war zone designated by Germany. In addition, the Lusitania had been assigned as an auxiliary military ship and contained munitions at the time of its sinking. Almost 1,200 passengers and crew died including 128 Americans. The sinking aroused much anger in the United States but Wilson resisted the temptation to join the British in the war. Alternately, he forced the Germans into halting submarine warfare, at least for a while. Some historians have cited statements by Winston Churchill as proof that the British sought to sacrifice a passenger liner like the Lusitania to arouse American anger so that the United States would join the Allies. If such was the intention, it did not succeed, on that occasion.

Numerous Americans including former presidential rival and fellow Progressive Theodore Roosevelt, demanded action and faulted Woodrow Wilson for his restraint. TR compared Wilson's actions following the Lusitania to an earlier period in American history when he wrote, "If Lincoln had acted after the firing of Sumter in the way that Wilson did about the sinking of the Lusitania, in one month the North would have been saying they were so glad he kept them out of the war." But gaining the Sussex Pledge from the Germans, not to engage in unrestricted submarine warfare sufficed for Wilson to go into his reelection campaign using the slogan, "he kept us out of war." Roosevelt fumed at the provocation of the Germans and the unresponsiveness of the United States. Working with his former commander in Cuba, Leonard Wood, TR launched a preparedness campaign that originally Wilson opposed. The president continued to stress nonintervention with the United States serving as mediator in the war. After the Lusitania, Wilson reluctantly accepted the need for an enhanced military display, calling for "armed neutrality." However as late as early 1917, Wilson remained hopeful that an American declaration of war could be avoided.

Theodore Roosevelt—The original Progressive in the White House, TR came to the job when McKinley was assassinated. He shocked many Republicans with his attempts to help the working class, but his policies were immensely popular with the electorate.

Still seeing the role of the United States as mediator, a Progressive ideal, President Wilson put forth the idea of negotiation over warfare on a grand scale with the creation of a world body as a means to create stability. Wilson surmised that he could arbitrate conflict within the League of Nations, establishing international law for the purpose of promoting world peace. The society, with the United States as a prominent member, would come together to examine regional conflicts and negotiate resolutions before armed warfare mobilized nations against each other. For the rest of his presidency, Wilson strenuously advocated this plan. It became the cornerstone of Wilsonian foreign policy.

The 1916 election showed a nation sliding inevitably toward war but earnestly trying to keep out of it. Despite Wilson's assertions in the campaign, his recent moves toward preparedness and the increasing desperation on both sides to, in the case of the Allies, drag the United States into the war, and oppositely with the Germans to keep the Americans out, voters remained wary that the Wilson Administration could keep detached for another term. In an incredibly close election, Wilson and the Democrats advanced a Progressive domestic agenda to entice voters. In California, the margin of victory was less than four-tenths of 1%. Had it gone for the Republican Charles Evans Hughes, a sitting presidential bid would have been rebuffed. Other states like Minnesota and New Hampshire were equally close.

Just as Woodrow Wilson took the oath for his second term as president, a frantic Germany made two miscalculations that assured entry into the war by the United States, even with a hesitant chief executive. First, the Germans formally abandoned the Sussex Pledge and resumed unrestricted submarine warfare against the Allies and all who supplied them. During the month of March 1917, six American ships went down in the Atlantic. Next, the United States intercepted the Zimmerman Telegram, a confidential message from Germany to Mexico offering to retake all land lost by the Mexicans in the Mexican-American War of 1846–1848 (which included Texas, California, Nevada, Arizona, Utah, New Mexico and parts of Colorado, Oklahoma, Wyoming, and Kansas). The offer required Mexico to declare war on the United States as a distraction from joining the conflict in Europe. Of course, Germany would have to win the war to fulfill a promise of taking back the American southwest, but the play angered Americans and galvanized support against Germany to the point that a month into his second term, Wilson delivered his argument for a resolution of war before a joint session of Congress. In both houses, the vote passed overwhelmingly.

Immediately, the United States geared up for the conflict. Already, a draft had been authorized and by the summer of 1917, men between the ages of 21 and 31 years who were unmarried or had sufficient income to support families without their presence, received orders to report for military instruction. Camps sprang up all over the United States for the purpose of training and indoctrinating recruits and draftees into military life. Over 2.8 million men were drafted.

Woodrow Wilson—A university professor turned politician, Woodrow Wilson was a southerner who became the president of Princeton University, then governor of New Jersey before running for president. During his two terms, the US passed four Progressive amendments to the Constitution.

Organized as the American Expeditionary Forces (AEF), Wilson named General John J. "Black Jack" Pershing as commander. Pershing insisted troops to be well trained before entry into the front lines, so through the rest of 1917, American presence remained light. Pershing also required that soldiers went into battle under American commanders, avoiding the perception that French and British leadership were mishandling the lives of "our boys". In reality, American officers used many of the same frontal attack strategies as the Allies and fell in the same kinds of numbers. But the Americans proved to be a fresh and unstoppable force along the battle lines of northeastern France.

By the spring of 1918 over one million American troops landed in France. In a forlorn attempt to win the war before the full influx of American soldiers, Germany staged a spring offensive. Once the German invasion was checked, the tide of U.S. troops in Europe reached one million, with only half that number eventually engaging in battle. By August, Pershing brought those overwhelming numbers to bear and the Hundred Days Offensive, staged by the Allies, began to crush German opposition. The forces of the Kaiser fell back as the Americans participated in a steady advance, pushing the Germans out of France. With an average of 10,000 fresh Americans arriving along the front lines every day, successes mounted in hard-fought battles like Chateau-Thierry and Belleau Wood. American soldiers fought alongside French and British troops as well as infantrymen from Canada and Australia. The final push began in September with the Meuse-Argonne Offensive that lasted until the Armistice.

Finally, on the 11th hour of the 11th day of the 11th month, the war was over with the surrender of the Germans. American casualties (killed/wounded/captured) totaled over 360,000. A total of 117,000 died while under arms, around 25,000 from influenza, the rest from battlefield wounds. Although American casualties were significant, the other combatants sustained much higher losses with the British losing one million, France suffering 1.7 million deaths and the Central Powers totaling well over eight million dead. In all, over 18 million people died in the First World War.

For Americans, the loss of lives was tragic, but the condition of returning soldiers shocked many civilian loved ones. Technology in the early twentieth century outpaced battlefield tactics and with no wide-scale war fought in the United States in the last 50 years and in Europe, a century, soldiers came back with accounts of hardships never endured before in battle. Developments like mustard gas, long-range artillery, trench warfare,

Trench Warfare for American Soldiers—The use of trench warfare became widespread by World War I. American soldiers followed the previous tactics of the French and British in using them when the arrived on the battlefield in 1918.

airplanes, barbed wire all combined to create a new type of fighting, complete with new types of injuries. Even with substantial drilling prior to shipping out overseas and training before entering the war zone, American troops had to adjust to the battlefield realities as they found them. The carnage surprised, and at times overwhelmed soldiers, many returning with psychological as well as physical scars. However, the American forces weathered the challenge of turning back the Kaiser's forces and securing victory for the Allies.

Among the many heroes of the war came one that defied logic. Alvin York at first sought to avoid service as a pacifist, his religious teachings being the reason. But once he reconciled his duty to God and country, York, an excellent marksman from his days as a wild game hunter in the mountains of Tennessee, participated in the advance on Germany in a significant way. During the Meuse-Argonne Offensive, York lead a small group that took an entire enemy machine gun nest, killing 20 Germans, capturing 132 more, silencing 32 machine guns. For his efforts, Alvin York received a promotion to sergeant, the French Croix de Guerre (Cross of War) and the American Medal of Honor. Sgt. York became famous in the United States for his valor. A group from Nashville bought him a farm to show the states' gratitude. Resisting the enticement to become a celebrity, York turned down appearance and endorsement offers, returning to the hills of northern Tennessee. Later, during World War II, Alvin York served in an honorary role but his example of American-fighting ingenuity, helped to inspire the next generation of U.S. soldiers.

Sgt. Alvin York—One of the most decorated US Army soldiers of the first World War, Sgt. Alvin York initially opposed the war but went on to lead an attack on a German gun emplacement, killing 20 and taking 132 prisoner, almost singlehandedly.

Library of Congress, Prints & Photographs Division, LC-DIG-ggbain-29128

Once Congress declared war in April 1917, everything changed in the United States. American factories quickly pivoted from consumer goods to war materiel. The War Industries Board coordinated the anticipated needs of the AEF with the production capabilities of companies like Ford Motor Company went from producing automobiles to turning out tanks, airplanes, and individual armored shields that protected soldiers as they moved forward on the front. The labor force changed dramatically also. With men summoned for active duty, women moved into the workforce to fill the role of factory laborers. Also, the need for workers created opportunities for minorities to move up in industrial society from the least skilled jobs. A "great migration" took place during the war years by African-Americans from the South, heading to northern industrial centers, like Chicago and Detroit to take jobs building those tanks and airplanes.

African-Americans also served in the military with distinction during World War I. However, continued racism toward blacks reduced their efforts to mostly support services by the leadership. Some African-Americans fought in segregated units with white officers as their commanders. However, the French welcomed black troops from the United States, offering a place in combat roles, beside their own soldiers. One regiment, the 369th Infantry, nicknamed the "Harlem Hellfighters" became part of the 16th French Division and were fully accepted by the French, In fact, the "Men of Bronze" as they were also called, received the French Croix de Guerre for their heroism during the war.

Back home, the entire nation was reorganized for war. The government encouraged "victory gardens" for families to feed themselves, saving canned food for soldiers. Celebrities and local dignitaries publicized Liberty Bonds to finance the war effort. These actions were not sporadic events, but part of an organized effort by the U.S. government to favorably enhance the public's perception of the war, and their acceptance. President Wilson called for the creation of The Committee on Public Information (CPI) the same month war was declared, as an independent bureau to promote the reasons for engaging in the conflict. He sought out George Creel as the head of the agency. Creel gathered together marketing experts, like Edward Bernays who used motivations theorized from the research of his uncle, Sigmund Freud to tap into people's psyche for approval and participation. Creel also engaged some of the best visual artists of the day like Charles Dana Gibson, N.C. Wyeth, and J.M. Flagg. The CPI flooded the market with war propaganda, and not just in the United States. Offices of the CPI operated throughout the Latin America and Europe, seeking support of American war aims. Printed material numbering in the millions went out to support the American war effort, some of it ending up in Germany.

The CPI marketed the war to the public in a way never seen before. Hundreds of poster designs went up on sign posts and bulletin boards across the nation with pithy statements about patriotism and practical ways to contribute. The most famous poster directly confronted the viewer. John Montgomery Flagg illustrated an elderly man pointing directly forward, the caption reading "I want you for the U.S. Army." Flagg based the image upon previous depictions of a character symbolizing the United States. With a "star spangled" uniform, Americans easily recognized the old man as "Uncle Sam." Flagg's message was unswerving, refusing to allow his fellow citizens the ability to passively sit out the war.

The CPI reached into almost every corner of American life. If Uncle Sam posing a question directly was not enough, the CPI engaged volunteers to go out and personally conduct presentations on the urgency of the war. Known as "four minute men," this public relations army practiced to be succinct but persuasive in their speeches. Often, the presentation was made in theaters during the time it took to change reels in the silent movie era.

Uncle Sam Recruiting—The most famous of the Creel Committee posters enticing men to enlist for service in the American Expeditionary Force during World War I. The character of Uncle Sam became a lasting symbol of the United States since its introduction.

Library of Congress, Prints & Photographs Division, LC-DIG-ppmsc-03521

An estimated 11 million people heard one of the 75,000 volunteers give four-minute speeches all across the country in the effort to bolster support the war.

Woodrow Wilson argued that this war was fought for Progressive goals. The Great War was to be a "war to end all wars." If the United States engaged upon this culminating crusade, Wilson argued, to rid the world of outdated, oppressive imperialism, then there would no longer be need of warfare to settle disputes and as an extension of each nation's foreign policy, war would become outdated. To dissenters, he argued that this war could cure the ills of modern society and broaden opportunities for American style system of human exchange. He encapsulated his vision of the conflict and the peace it would ultimately bring when he pointed out that this war would "make the world safe for democracy."

Not everyone bought the argument, no matter how regularly they heard it or how emphatically it was presented. One group in particular, German-Americans remained ambivalent. In some parts of the United States, German custom remained so strong that families still practiced the ways of the old country and spoke the language of the fatherland in their home. Significant contributions and products by Germans to American culture suddenly seemed unpatriotic in a world where the United States declared war on their ancestral homeland. Some even sought to change the popular vernacular in hopes of erasing the names of German sounding products. For example, to make certain foods still acceptable to the buying public, the name of sauerkraut was changed to "liberty cabbage." Americans could no longer eat frankfurters, unless they were called hot dogs. Hamburgers were intended for a change to "liberty sandwiches," no longer a reminder of the town from which they originated. Just like the British monarch changing the family name because it sounded too German from Saxe-Coburg and Gotha, to Windsor, American institutions with Germanic backgrounds changed to accommodate the realities of war.

Dissent in time of war became a right easily refused by the Wilson Administration. A number of laws quickly passed squelching opposition. The Espionage Act of 1917 kept any American from speaking out against the war, declaring that open dissent equaled disloyalty. The Sedition Act followed a year later broadening the areas in which prosecution could be sought. Among those charged with violation was Wilson's old opponent from the 1912 election, Eugene Victor Debs, whose opposition to the war netted him 10 years. Even after the war, Wilson refused to pardon or commute the sentence of Debs. Tested in the courts subsequently, the Supreme Court found the law to not violate free speech rights of Americans and has since been used to prosecute others from Julius and Ethel Rosenberg (1950) to Edward Snowden (2013). In addition, Congress also passed the Trading with the Enemies Act to keep businesses from aiding an avowed adversary to the United States.

Eugene Victor Debs—Eugene Victor Debs had a long career with the issues that concerned Progressives, however his philosophy leaned in much more of a socialist direction than his counterparts. He lead the American Railway Union and was repeatedly a candidate for president. In 1920, he ran from prison, jailed for his dissent during World War I.

While most Americans accepted the limit on their free speech due to the necessity of war, by 1919, the question arose if these laws were designed to keep dissent permanently outlawed. With no effort to lift restrictions, members of various philosophies and practices inimical to the American system became vulnerable. The rise of the first Marxist government in Russia, which became the Soviet Union, brought considerable fears of proliferation in the United States. Predicting that once workers in one nation seized the means of production, others would quickly follow. Wilson and his Attorney General, A. Mitchell Palmer sought to expel radicals of every stripe. Targeting mostly immigrants, a postwar sweep of those proposing radical solutions and/or overthrow of the United States were deported. Anarchist Emma Goldman and 500 others were banned from the United States. As retaliation against the Attorney General, a mail bomb was sent to his house. Palmer was unhurt but stepped up his hunt for "reds" as Bolsheviks were called, as well as any other undesirables. The public was at first behind the "Palmer's Raids" but began to see the attacks of the "Red Scare" as an infringement upon civil liberties.

Once the war ended, Woodrow Wilson worked incessantly on crafting a peace policy to guide humanity in the aftermath of the most destructive war the world had ever seen. His agenda came to be known as the "Fourteen Points" that defined the number of ways he sought improvement. Going to the Palace of Versailles, just outside Paris in early 1919, Wilson engaged Prime Ministers David Lloyd George of the United Kingdom, Georges Clemenceau of France and Vittorio Emanuele Orlando of Italy to define the official terms of the end of the World War. All were skeptical of Wilson's philosophy, but the President argued, pleaded, and bullied the other leaders into acceptance of his Fourteen Points as the guiding principle to create a treaty. During the conference Orlando walked out of negotiations, Lloyd George wanted reasonable but firm treatment of the Germans, but Clemenceau insisted on handling Germany harshly, in order to render future wars impossible. The Germans were only invited to Versailles to sign the deal with no negotiation.

The direction of the Fourteen Points centered on a massive restructure of power by European nations. Wilson insisted on open treaties "openly arrived at," a provision the Versailles Conference violated when the Big Three (United States, Britain, and France) engaged in secret discussions. In addition to removal of economic barriers and open travel upon the seas, Wilson wanted nations with colonies to empower those colonies as much as possible. He also lobbied for a League of Nations as a forum to settle future disputes. The rest of Wilson's manifesto centered around reorganizing the map of Europe, drawing the lines to more closely enclose ethnic and cultural groups as nations for their own self-determination. Among the changes, Wilson stipulated the reemergence of Poland, a nation whittled away by Prussia, Russia, and Austria, gone from the European map for 125 years.

Wilson believed himself and the United States righteous in the cause of peace. At the end of the conference he said, "at last the world knows America as the savior of the world." Other leaders saw the Fourteen Points in a different light. Upon hearing of them, Clemenceau sneered, "the good Lord only had ten." By the end of the process, Wilson left some of the specifics of the treaty to Clemenceau who demanded Germany to accept full responsibility for the war, disarm, and pay huge war reparations. Observers saw the French enmity toward the Germans as unfortunate, possibly laying the foundation for future conflict between the two.

Bringing the Treaty of Versailles back to the Senate, the body constitutionally charged with ratifying treaties, President Wilson offered it as a "done deal" with the only option, an up or down vote. During his trip, Wilson built no Congressional support for the treaty after he neglected to invite any Republicans. Senators quickly divided up into different camps. "Reservationists," under the leadership of Republican Henry Cabot Lodge were willing to work with the treaty, but wanted input, meaning some changes. "Irreconcilables," among them Progressives Bob La Follette and Hiram Johnson refused to accept Wilson's effort, saying the President overstepped his authority. Among all senators, the most objectionable aspect to the treaty was the idea of handing over sovereignty to a world body like the League of Nations. Lodge attempted to work with the President to gain a compromise but could not build a coalition that provided the necessary two-thirds majority for passage. Meanwhile, Wilson remained adamant. Having won the Nobel Peace Prize, Wilson considered his position above reproach. He decided to bypass the Senate by embarking upon a nationwide campaign to gain popular support for the treaty and pressure senators into accepting his efforts.

The summer of 1919 saw the high and low point of Woodrow Wilson's presidency. Upon returning from Paris, Wilson basked in the confidence that the Treaty provided "peace without victory." After all, during his time in Europe, crowds hailed the American president with cheers of "Viva Wilson." But quickly, he ran into a buzz saw of opposition forcing him to appeal directly the American people to gain support for his work at Versailles. In early September he and his second wife, Edith Bolling Galt Wilson, took a train to the western states, where opposition was most fierce. He delivered dozens of speech daily on the treaty.

Already worn out by the Paris negotiations and the Senate ratification fight, the President's latest crusade proved too much for him. In late-September, Wilson suffered from a series of strokes and returned to Washington, DC immediately. Back at the White House, he suffered another stroke, a massive one that left his left side paralyzed. His wife and doctors kept the severity of his condition from Congress, his cabinet and the public. For the next few months, no one saw the president. Mrs. Wilson carefully screened activities, taking bills that needed the President's signature into him privately, without witness. Some suspected Mrs. Wilson of acting as a replacement, refusing to allow Wilson to be judged incapable of carrying on the job. No one will ever know how much of the decision-making the President's wife handled during that period. Eventually, Wilson regained enough of his strength to finish his term and resume daily activities, but he never was the same again. Reportedly, Woodrow Wilson expressed interest in a third term, but few in the Democratic Party saw renomination as realistic.

As Woodrow Wilson left office, debate raged over the League of Nations. After several votes, the Senate refused to pass the Treaty of Versailles leaving the United States without a resolution to the World War. That chore fell to Wilson's successor, Warren Harding, who campaigned on a platform of a "return to normalcy." Ultimately, the United States concluded a separate treaty with each opponent but flatly refused to join the League of

Nations. Wilson's high-minded ideals and hopes of bringing a lasting peace to the world, went down to defeat, laying the foundation for another devastating world war to be fought 20 years later.

For Americans in 1918, the war and its casualties were not the only hardship to be faced. To this day, the origins of the Spanish Flu are uncertain, but what came to the United States, first starting in early 1918, ramping up the following winter and holding on until 1920, inflicted a significantly higher mortality rate than the war. Worldwide, the influenza epidemic infected over 100 million people with an estimated 10 to 15 million succumbing to it. In the United States, the death rate was five times higher than the war, with an estimated 675,000 killed. The Spanish Flu epidemic did not just prey on children and the elderly as most influenza epidemics did. Healthy adults, especially Native-Americans died from the fast spreading affliction in the winter of 1918–1919.

The Progressive Era became an umbrella for a myriad of changes in society facilitated by the federal government, an instrument largely untapped for assistance by Americans up to that time. Culminating with involvement in the First World War, Progressives remained as varied in their solutions as they did in number, some opposing solutions other Progressives endorsed. The era set the stage for the next wave of economic policy making, the New Deal. Government intervention has remained a controversial topic in American politics, as policy makers debate the necessary balance for government to simultaneously protect its citizens without becoming oppressive. The good intentions and positive aspects of the Progressive Era deepened the conversation concerning what Americans could and should expect from their government.

CHAPTER FIFTEEN

The 1920s

Chapter 15: Key Concepts

- Describe America's foreign policy following World War I and the Treaty of Versailles. Why did America respond in this way?

- Discuss the positive effects of the culture of the 1920s on American society, the economy, and African-Americans.

- Evaluate the cultural challenges of the 1920s. What were the challenges and how did America respond to these challenges?

Introduction

The 1920s catapulted America into the modern age. Nicknamed "The Roaring Twenties" and "The Jazz Age," the decade produced dynamic changes, as flappers danced the Charleston and gangsters controlled high-demand products. The decade was one of economic prosperity, new social mores for women, and innovative forms of music. The radio connected the nation together, and the economy was roaring. Businesses were operating without regulations, the use of credit reached new limits, and the stock market was soaring as buyers purchased on margin, allowing for easy sale of stocks.

However, not all was glittering or promising in the Roaring Twenties. The ease of credit and the lack of business regulations led to an unstable economy with false faith in the soundness of money. Racial tensions erupted as returning soldiers sought jobs, often displacing women and African-Americans. With the rise of the Soviet Union, an encompassing fear of the spread of communism sparked a Red Scare in the country that led to the hunt for "enemies of the state" which often focused on newly arrived immigrants. And workers agitated for better wages due to rising inflation in the postwar years that sparked led to a new wave of strikes. The 1920s was a complicated time in American history filled with new promises and a reminder that the changes in the world came with a price.

The American Political World of the 1920s

Post-war American Diplomacy

With the end of World War I the Treaty of Versailles set in place an uneasy peace and an uncertain sense of security in the world. The Treaty established several changes that helped reshape the world. The Middle East was reformed, new countries in Europe were created, and the Central Powers were harshly punished. Germany felt the brunt of the repercussions of the Treaty. Germany was stripped of all of its colonies and given new boundaries. Its armed forces were dramatically reduced. Similarly, the country was not allowed to revive its large-scale military weaponry, including tanks, an air force, or submarines. Germany was also expected to pay for war damages with heavy reparations that amounted to tens of billions of dollars. And worst of all, it had to accept the War Guilt Clause, admitting full responsibility for starting the war and taking the blame for all the loss and damage that the Allies suffered.

Women of the National League for Limitations of Armament demonstrating in Washington DC in 1922.

Most of the Treaty focused on punishing Germany; however another key aspect of the Treaty of Versailles was the creation of The League of Nations. The purpose of the League was to preserve peace and prevent future wars by pledging respect and protection to each member's territories. President Woodrow

Wilson hoped that countries would join the League as a measure of accountability and commitment to peace.

Wilson arrived at the Peace Conference in Paris at the end of the war promoting his Fourteen Points. The Fourteen Points were proposed by the president as his plan for world peace. The document included several items, including the abolition of secret treaties, a reduction in armaments, and freedom of the seas. However, the plan for the creation of a League of Nations was primary to Wilson's cause. He believed that his ideas should set the framework for the postwar world.

Much to Wilson's dismay the other major Allies at the Peace of Paris Conference vehemently disagreed with his concept of peace and chose not to adopt most of his plan. England and France were too bitter and angry over the German aggression that led to war. Thus, the Conference created a different form of peace treaty than the one Wilson had envisioned. However, it did save an important part of Wilson's Fourteen Points; the Allies agreed to the idea of the League of Nations. Wilson's battered pride found some comfort as the major powers adopted one of the key parts of his postwar plan.

Wilson returned to America from the Peace Conference appeased and determined to convince the U.S. Senate to ratify the Treaty of Versailles and join the newly created League of Nations. His desire for a world of peace and free trade were built upon the premise of a collective global security that would prevent future wars. However, he was met with stiff resistance from the recently elected Republican Congress. Congress was not in the mood for committing America to the new international entity seeking to preserve peace nor for ratifying the Treaty.

Opposition to Wilson's work came from the Republicans after the president made clear his intention to create peace without their help. During the election of 1918, the Republicans won both Houses of Congress and believed their influence should play a role in the peace negotiations. However, the president chose to cater only to Democrats and avoid the bi-partisan support he needed. Dismissing the election results, the president refused to include any Republicans in the American delegation to the Peace Conference in 1919 including former President Taft who supported the League. Consequently, the Republicans felt slighted after they were excluded from the Paris delegation.

In July, 1919 the president submitted the Treaty of Versailles to the Senate for ratification. He quickly faced opposition and criticism as Massachusetts senator, Henry Cabot Lodge, who became Wilson's chief adversary. The two had developed a long-standing hatred for one another, and the arguments surrounding passage of the Treaty only worsened their relationship. As the new Republican majority leader and chairman of the Foreign Relations Committee, Lodge opposed joining the League arguing that American interests would become subservient to the collective decisions of others. Lodge maintained that specific terms as to how America would interact with the League needed to be clarified to guarantee that American foreign relations would not be restricted in the effort to work on behalf of international peace.

Lodge was joined by others who opposed the Treaty. One group of opposition, known as the "Irreconcilables," opposed the League of Nations under any circumstance. This group, composed of 14 Republican and 4 Democratic senators, argued American interests superseded foreign affairs. Others in the Senate, however, were willing to work with Wilson for admission to the League as long as certain amendments would be added. These, led by Lodge, wanted the League to formally acknowledge the Monroe Doctrine, thus reasserting American dominance in the western hemisphere. They insisted on the reassurance that the United States could only be sent into a foreign war with the consent of Congress, arguing that allegiance to the League could violate the U.S. Constitution and possibly commit the country to war against the will of the people. Overall, most of the Senate was leery of the president's actions in forming the Treaty. The Constitution makes the U.S. Senate the ultimate decision-making authority, and Congress wanted their voice heard in the ratification process.

The arguments and opposition facing Wilson compelled him to take his case for the League, and thus the Treaty of Versailles, to the American people. In September 1919, Wilson, still exhausted from the Paris Conference, set out by train on an ambitious cross-country speaking tour to plead his case with the American people. On September 27, while in Pueblo, Colorado, Wilson collapsed and had to return to Washington D.C. After returning to the nation's capital he suffered a massive stroke that left him partially paralyzed. The president spent the next year and a half in his bedroom severely weakened from the stroke and trying to rehabilitate. His hopes for American involvement in the League, as well as his work on gaining passage of the Treaty, were dashed. The Senate rejected the Treaty of Versailles and refused to join the League of Nations.

Foreign Policy

Although it never joined the League of Nations, America exercised some economic and diplomatic influence in the postwar world. Following World War I, most Americans supported an isolationist stance seeking to stay out of any further global conflict. The United States emerged from World War I with a strong economy and enjoyed a decade of economic growth. American banks poured millions of dollars into war-torn European countries in an effort to aid economic recovery, as New York replaced London as the center of world finance. Consequently, American money and culture spread to Europe.

In 1923, Germany suspended its war-reparation installment of $2.5 billion due to its struggling economy. In retaliation for breaking the Treaty of Versailles, France invaded and occupied the German industrial area of the Ruhr Valley. In an attempt to solve the impending calamity and provide aid to strengthen the German economy, a team of American bankers led by Charles Dawes intervened. The Dawes Plan, in place from 1924 until 1929, was a means to lessen the economic hardship of Germany and stimulate economic revival. The plan halved German reparation payments for 1924, increasing payments incrementally for the next 35 years, and provided new American loans to the country. The plan's actions got money flowing again in Germany and forced the French to retreat, thus averting further aggression in Europe.

America found other ways to foster international peace aside from economic aid. In an effort to establish global balance Secretary of State, Charles Evans Hughes crafted the Five-Power Naval Treaty in 1922. This treaty, signed by Britain, France, Japan, Italy, and the

United States, committed them to the proportional reduction of their naval forces. The treaty led to scrapping more than two million tons of warships for the goal of peace. In a similar manner, in 1928, Secretary of State Frank Kellogg and French Foreign Minister Aristide Briand forged a pledge to renounce war and settle international disputes peacefully. Signed by over 50 nations in a solemn ceremony, the Kellogg–Briand Pact sought to constrain movements of war through a mutual commitment to global peace.

While America experimented with various ways to try to guarantee international peace during the 1920s, most of its attention was given to domestic policies. Since the country had no desire to be involved in foreign events that might spark another war, it focused on internal improvements.

The 1920s Politics

The political landscape throughout the 1920s was somewhat quiet and removed from the American public. The Republicans held the presidency throughout the decade and worked from the premise that the best way to help the public was to stay out of business interests and the economy. Businesses were freed from earlier regulations and taxes, thus creating an atmosphere of growth. As politicians rejected the call of government intervention and regulation, held over from the Progressive Era, they contended that private economic endeavors should guide the American economy. Andrew Mellon was the Secretary of the Treasury for all three Republican presidents. Mellon believed that the federal government essentially had three major goals: balance the budget, reduce government spending, and cut taxes. These policies helped spur a decade of economic prosperity.

President Harding

Former businessman and Ohio native Warren Harding ran for president as a Republican in the 1920 election. He won in a landslide victory against his opponents, Democrat James Cox and Socialist Eugene Debs, as he called for a "return to normalcy." Harding's words rang with a promising tone to the millions of women who voted for the first time after passage of the 19th Amendment. After the havoc and toil from World War I, Harding stated that "America's present need is not heroics, but healing; not nostrums, but normalcy; not revolution, but restoration." His call to return to the years prior to the war was a welcome message for the overwhelming majority of Americans, and they rewarded him with the White House. Harding pushed through measures that helped American enterprise, kept high tariffs to protect businesses, and instituted tax cuts on higher incomes. Harding also personally championed civil liberties for African-Americans.

Harding's administration, however, was not without scandals. He had a group of advisors made up of several cabinet members, politicians, and industry leaders that were known as the "Ohio gang." These were friends of Harding from his days in Ohio who, many speculated, obtained their jobs as a reward for their faithfulness. They became synonymous with corrupt deals, such as selling government jobs and providing pardons and/or protection from prosecution to those they favored. Several other members within Harding's administration were critical of the Ohio gang and the influence they had with the president, but Harding continued to entertain the gang. He regularly played poker with them, winning them the nickname the "poker cabinet." Harding's fondness for his friends, however, eventually tied him to one of the biggest political scandals in U.S. history.

In 1922, Secretary of the Interior and Ohio gang member, Albert Fall, made the front pages of the newspapers when he was accused of accepting bribes of more than $400,000. The allegations stated that Fall was secretly leasing federal oil reserves in Teapot Dome, Wyoming to private oil companies. In return for access to the oil reserves, Fall was charged with receiving large cash gifts and no-interest loans. Fall was found guilty of bribery and became the first Cabinet member convicted of a felony while holding the post. Harding was devastated by the revelation and fallout of the scandal, and his reputation was tarnished by the association. The Teapot Dome scandal brought his presidency into question and also took an enormous toll on his health. The scandalous actions bore witness to a new term, "Teapot Dome," that became synonymous with political corruption in the American vocabulary. During the summer of 1923, Harding and his wife traveled throughout the country, becoming the first president to visit Alaska, in an effort to share his policies and repair damage to his reputation. While Harding was in San Francisco, he suffered a massive heart attack and abruptly died on August 2. Vice President, Calvin Coolidge, became the new president and sought to maintain much of Harding's policies.

President Coolidge

As the 30th president of the United States, Coolidge was thoroughly conservative, as he kept the federal government limited in scope. Coolidge provided tax cuts for corporations and wealthy individuals, thus reducing government tax revenue by half and limiting government spending. He was a strong promoter of American business, captured in his familiar phrase that "the business of America is business." Nicknamed "Silent Cal" because of his taciturn nature, Coolidge avoided controversy and sought to restore dignity to the presidency after Harding's scandalous term.

During the election of 1924, Coolidge used the phrase "Coolidge prosperity" to reemphasize the economic prosperity of Republican administrations. He ran against Democrat John Davis and third-party Progressive Robert LaFollette. The Wisconsin Progressive was a member of the waning Progressive Party and vowed to resurrect its platform of the pre-World War era. He focused on the need to support labor unions, the necessity of the regulation of business, and called for protection of civil liberties. The American people, however, opted to continue the policies of the current decade and gave Coolidge a sound victory.

Cultural Phenomena in the 1920s

The 1920s created a distinct American culture. As the economy roared during the decade, many Americans benefited from it. The middle class grew substantially and the number of millionaires in the country increased 400% compared to the previous decade. This new availability of disposable income sparked a consumer revolution. These buyers eagerly sought out the latest inventions and trends, and mass advertisement encouraged the belief that every American had a right to prosperity.

Similarly, city life bustled anew with neon lights, the broad scope of available electricity, and new opportunities for adventure. More people moved into the cities than ever before, and for the first time in American history the majority of its people were town dwellers instead of rural farmers. This division in society created friction between the innovative ideas and modern beliefs of urbanites and the conservative values of thrift and self-denial of the country folk. In a similar manner, the birth of the "new woman" challenged traditional values and opened the door for the modern age of women's rights.

The nation found ways to unite, however, around media. The radio united Americans together as never before as they listened to the same news stories, soap operas, and music. With the rebirth of African-American culture, and consequently the rise of Jazz music, many Americans found ways to connect in the ever-changing environment of the 1920s.

The Birth of Mass Culture

The 1920s witnessed a consumer revolution, as American wealth expanded as never before. The nation's total wealth more than doubled throughout the decade allowing for higher standards of living, and for the first time, individuals with disposable income. These Americans were more than willing to spend their money on the newest and most alluring goods highlighted in the national advertisement campaign of companies. Work weeks substantially shortened for most members of the middle and working class, thus creating "leisure time" for many as well as the opportunity to spend. Consequently, from coast to coast Americans bought the same goods, producing for the first time a mass culture in the nation.

New inventions, such as automatic wrist watches, electric irons, pop-up toasters, and instant cameras, beckoned eager shoppers in mail-order catalogs and department stores. Men and women all across the country eagerly shopped for the same goods and helped build a new American culture. This consumer revolution generated the belief that one's personal worth was measured by material possessions. As advertisements stimulated the desire for new products, they also told the story that traditional values of thrift and saving were obsolete. In order to be popular, secure, and successful, Americans needed to compete with their neighbors. Consequently, in the attempt to reach success many Americans began to purchase items on credit.

Credit became the vehicle of purchasing power for many American consumers throughout the decade. Credit was advertised as the easiest way to obtain the possessions that every American needed and deserved. Many department stores and businesses offered generous lines of credit. Everything from furniture and appliances to single-family homes were bought on installment plans, thus creating large amounts of consumer debt. There are estimates that consumer debt more than doubled during the 1920s.

Automobile Culture

The 1920s put America on wheels. Henry Ford was cheered as an American hero with his mass production of the Model T and became the greatest example of American ingenuity of his time. Millions of cars were produced throughout the decade as Ford perfected the use of the assembly line to create the highest number of vehicles with the lowest cost. By 1925, one car rolled off the assembly line every 10 seconds.

Youngsters and their Model "T" near Pacolet, South Carolina

His efforts made him a billionaire but also reduced workers to near robots in the factories. The assembly line became the standard for almost every factory in the early 20th century. This style of business reduced work to its simplest, most repetitive task, and helped establish the use of specialized divisions and professional managers in the factory system. Ford's use of the line allowed for mass production of the automobile, reducing the price of a car throughout the 1920s from $800 to $300. Located in Detroit, Michigan, Ford sought to be close to steel, oil, glass, and rubber plants and employed hundreds of thousands of Americans.

As the dominance and demand of the automobile grew throughout the 1920s, it stimulated economic growth in other areas. The need for more infrastructure, gas stations, and mechanics and garages spurred the creation of jobs. Cities began to grow and, with the new ease of travel, Americans journeyed out by car. As people traveled away from home, the need for eateries, overnight motels, and service stations also grew, thus expanding private businesses. Mom and pop gas stations and family-owned restaurants spurred new types of industry. The restaurant industry was born as more people dined out than ever before in American history.

As these new entities began to emerge, the federal government also got involved and spent more money on road development than anything else. An estimated one billion dollars was spent on infrastructure during the decade, employing large numbers of Americans. Roads, tunnels, and bridges were built to accommodate the new travelers. In all, by the end of the decade, one out of every four Americans was employed in some format within the automobile culture.

Cars also altered American lifestyles. When the decade ended, there was one car on the road for every five Americans. These cars offered new opportunities to Americans. Since distance was no longer an issue for those with automobiles, some people made choices to move further away from the city thus creating suburbs. Americans had more choices for their work, as they now had the option to live further away from their jobs. They could choose where to shop, what church to attend, and what to do with leisure time.

Urban Life and American Culture

American culture changed dramatically during the 1920s. People caught the new movies at the theaters while many at home were entertained with radio and music programs. Sports heroes emerged from small towns and captured the imaginations of Americans all over the nation. New forms of dance and entertainment beckoned men and women to throw off their Victorian notions of propriety and embrace a new age.

Media

The radio played a key role in creating the American culture of the 1920s. Approximately, 60% of all households acquired a radio throughout the decade, thus connecting the country together for the first time. Families came together to hear local and national news, enjoy the same soap operas and comedies, sway to the newest styles of music, and become informed of the latest election results. Radio shows, such as the comedic *Amos and Andy* or the detective-based *The Shadow,* drew listeners of all ages. In a similar manner, farmers loyally listened to the seasonal weather reports, businessmen relied on the insight gained into the financial market, and baseball fans followed the excitement of the World Series. This led to the creation of a mass culture creating new topics for conversation.

Advertising also played a role in creating this culture by crafting shared tastes in foods and other commodities. These advertisers promoted their brands, such as Rice Krispies cereal, Peter Pan peanut butter, Oscar Meyer hot dogs, and others. Advertisers catered their commercials to target audiences and created the longing and demand for newly developed products.

American culture continued to grow as thousands of movie theaters were built in cities throughout the nation. Delighted movie-goers celebrated the adventures of the heroes and heroines of the big screen, as they laughed with the antics of Charlie Chaplin and swooned over Rudolph Valentino's love scenes. Hollywood, California became the center of the film industry and created the first movie stars. Although the decade began with black-and-white, silent films, the "talkies" soon triumphed with the release of the musical film, *The Jazz Singer*, in 1927. Many Americans became enraptured with the lives and habits of the screen stars and emulated their dress and styles.

Spectator Sports

The 1920s also experienced an explosion in spectator sports. Although baseball was first professionalized in 1869, it became America's favorite past-time in the 1920s, as working class men connected with the raw strength of the sport. George Herman "Babe" Ruth epitomized the hopes of the working man and changed the sport of baseball forever. As he set home-run records (60 home-runs in one season) and grabbed World Series titles while playing for the New York Yankees, Ruth continued to capture the American imagination with his rowdy and carefree lifestyle.

Americans also celebrated the rise of Jack Dempsey. Dempsey went from winning quick money by boxing in saloons as a teenager to becoming one of the most well-known heavy-weight champions in the nation. He won the heavy-weight title in 1919 and defended it for the next five years. Sports heroes such as Dempsey and Ruth captured the spirit of the decade and represented the triumph of the hard-working American.

Professional football also organized during the 1920s. Football had been the sport of the educated throughout the late nineteenth and early twentieth centuries. Developed within the collegiate system, colleges created teams and built large stadiums, in the old Greek and Roman Coliseum models, to attract large audiences. In the early 1920s, as popularity of the sport grew, the need for organization within professional football teams began to intensify. In response, the American Professional Football Association was formed in 1920, and became the forerunner to the National Football League in 1922. The APFA's first president was former college football player and Olympian, Jim Thorpe.

Dance and Music

New styles of music and dance carved out another sphere of American culture and gave birth to the phrase, "The Roaring Twenties." As young people flocked to dance halls to listen to the innovative styles of music, they created new dances that pushed the limits of the propriety of the Victorian era. These new dances, such as the Charleston and Lindy Hop, required partners to move unreservedly without the stiff and prudish constraints of the earlier age. Other more subtle and mature styles of dance, including the foxtrot, waltz, and tango, set partners into more intimate styles of movement. Although many older Americans denounced these dances as immoral and deplorable, dance clubs sprung up all over the country and attracted large audiences. These halls not only provided the latest styles of music and dance, but also sponsored contests for the best dancers. As styles morphed throughout the decade and challenged the social mores of the country, music changed as well, testing and expanded American culture.

The birth of Jazz captured the hearts and ears of Americans during the 1920s. "The Jazz Age" decade flouted the new styles of African-American musicians using syncopated rhythms and improvised solos. Jazz musicians, such as Louis Armstrong and Duke Ellington, appealed to the younger generation and provided an emotional connection to music. The music became a form of expression as artists played and sang away their "blues" or celebrated life with their energetic compositions. Not everyone appreciated or accepted jazz music, however. Some Americans denounced it as the "devil's music" and tried to find ways to ban it in their towns. By the end of the century, several dozen communities throughout the country prohibited jazz music from its dance halls.

Harlem Renaissance

African-American culture continued to evolve throughout the 1920s with the celebration of a new movement. As black soldiers returned from World War I, many of them joined the Great Migration of the previous years. Throughout the war poor, blacks from the

Library of Congress, Prints & Photographs Division, FSA/OWI Collection, LC-USW3-023956-C.

Duke Ellington's trumpet section

South poured into the northern states looking for work and freedom from the violence and strict racial system of the South. After the war, these families were joined by returning black soldiers and new waves of immigrants from the West Indies that settled in the upper Manhattan borough of Harlem, New York. As New York City's black population increased over 100% throughout the 1920s, there was a new birth of African-American culture.

Harlem became the home to thousands of black men and women during the 1920s, including intellectuals, artists, social leaders, and musicians. This movement created some of the greatest black leaders of the twentieth century. The Harlem Renaissance generated a new confidence and hope among black Americans that spilled over into cultural and political activities. These men and women challenged cultural norms by creating new forms of music and night life as well as tackling issues such as racial pride, black identity, and the need for equality.

Americans, both white and black, flocked to Harlem to listen and dance to the jazz musicians at clubs in the district. The most famous location was The Cotton Club, and it was operated by a New York gangster in the heart of Harlem. It hosted the most widely known jazz singers of the time and brought recognition to some of the artists of the Harlem Renaissance. Jazz artists, such as Louis Armstrong, Duke Ellington, and Bessie Smith, defined the future of jazz both in America and abroad and created a musical phenomenon.

The Harlem Renaissance also engaged the racial tensions of the decade. Black leaders came forward to challenge the racial status quo and bring attention to the plight of African-Americans in the country as well as highlight their contributions. W.E.B. DuBois and the National Association for the Advancement of Colored People (NAACP) aggressively pursued passage of federal antilynching laws to quell the mob violence permeating the South.

Jamaican-born Marcus Garvey took a different approach to the racial hostility of the age. Garvey appealed to poor blacks disillusioned with the political inequalities of the nation and encouraged them to rediscover their African heritages. Garvey regularly mounted soapboxes and gave speeches advocating African pride and the need to maintain racial purity by avoiding interracial marriage. He denounced the NAACP for its connection with white contributors and admonished black Americans to gain economic independence and become active in politics. Garvey created the Universal Negro Improvement Association headquartered in Harlem. He resurrected the Back to Africa movement from the early nineteenth century, advocating for the migration of black Americans back to Africa and attracted thousands of supporters. Although he was a charismatic speaker and garnered a substantial following, Garvey was eventually found participating in illegal activities and was deported in 1927.

Other African-American leaders emerged to counter the Jim Crow laws and racism of the age. The most prolific writer of the Harlem Renaissance was poet Langston Hughes. Hughes expressed black themes and heritage throughout his works as he wrote in the rhythmic styles of jazz. His first poem, *The Weary Blues*, won first prize in a literary contest exposing his talent to America and expressing "the black man's soul." Alain Locke's anthology, "The New Negro," helped popularize the term used to describe the new self-confidence and assertiveness of African-Americans in the post-war era. The New Negro was someone who believed in racial pride and celebrating black achievement. The movement highlighted other black artists, such as author Zora Neale Hurston, who became the most successful black female writer of the first half of the twentieth century.

The New Woman

Women experienced huge changes during the 1920s. As the older notions of propriety were challenged in the post-war era, women experienced a revolution and created the model of the "new woman." These women were more independent, had disposable incomes, and dressed in more provocative styles. They also voted and confronted the traditional modes of work as they carved out a contemporary view of women.

As soldiers returned from World War I, working women went back to their homes and resumed domestic lives. However, some women experienced a form of liberation during their working years and sought to continue the change into the 1920s. Approximately, 25% of American women worked during the decade, challenging old notions of gender roles. Women continued to hold the majority of the service workforce jobs, such as nursing, teaching, and social work. New alternatives emerged for the working woman in positions as secretaries, sales clerks, stenographers, and office clerks. As more women entered the work force, they soon had their own disposable income. The ubiquitous advertisements of the age began to cater to the new target audience of young women by encouraging them to buy the newest clothes, accessories, and cosmetics made trendy by movie stars and magazine models. At the same time, new types of appliances were advertised that made house work easier, thus creating more free time for the home-maker to find ways to pass time and spend money.

Challenging the social mores of the period, some women in the cities developed a more brazen definition of the new woman, known as the "flapper." Flappers wore bobbed hair, make-up, and clothing that revealed bare arms and legs. These women danced to jazz music, frequented

Man seated at piano, surrounded by group of glamorous girls, Washington, D.C

Library of Congress, Prints & Photographs Division, LC-USZ62-93721

Charleston at the capitol

speak-easies where they drank illegally and smoked, and engaged in sexual activities. They rode bicycles, drove cars, played sports, and defiantly tested societal mores. Zelda Fitzgerald became the icon of the new woman and was dubbed by her husband, F. Scott Fitzgerald, the "first American flapper." Her lifestyle became a model for young women throughout the nation as they emulated her relaxed morals.

Women gained political rights during the 1920s. With the passage of the 19th Amendment in 1920, women were granted the right to vote. For the first time, women gained the attention of politicians as they sought their votes. Feminists had been pressuring Congress to pass legislation for decades. As more states began to grant women suffrage Congress was persuaded to establish a new constitutional amendment. Thus, the 19th Amendment was born. The amendment guaranteed all women the right to vote, and women exercised this right for the first time during the election of 1920.

The 1920s Iconic Individuals

The 1920s created new national heroes for the country as sports stars, Hollywood heart-throbs, and African-American cultural leaders emerged at the fore-front of the American imagination. The decade also introduced a few other iconic individuals that stole the attention of the public and sparked new national conversations.

Charles Lindbergh

The Age of Flight began in the 1920s. Although flight had been around for years, during World War I airplanes became associated with the destruction of the war and aerial dog-fights. This image changed, however, as the new decade reshaped the airplane industry by focusing on the perks of quick transportation of both people and goods. Thanks to the heroics and success of Charles Lindbergh, the age of flight was reformed.

Flying nonstop across the Atlantic Ocean became the dream of numerous airplane enthusiasts during the early part of the 1920s. Lindbergh became the first person to fly solo nonstop across the Atlantic Ocean in 1927. He piloted his plane, *Spirit of St. Louis*, from Long Island to Paris in 33.5 hours, landing in the midst of a throng of people. During his flight Lindbergh used primitive tools, including a paper map. He often looked out the window in order to navigate. He succeeded, and Lindbergh became an instant hero, gaining the nickname, "Lucky Lindy." He returned home to become one of the most popular individuals of the twentieth century. His feat represented not only ingenuity and bravery but also came to encompass the spirit and initiative of the American people—and they adored him.

Five years after his record-breaking flight, Lindbergh experienced disaster when he lost his infant son. On March 1, 1932, 20-month old, Charles Lindbergh Jr., was kidnapped from his home and held for ransom. The kidnapper sent a note, riddled with spelling mistakes, demanding $50,000 in exchange for the whereabouts of the child. The kidnapping became a national phenomenon, as various government agencies vowed to help locate the child and news reporters sensationalized the story. Six weeks after the kidnapping, the child was found dead in the woods. Police tracked the ransom money to a German immigrant named Bruno Richard Haupt-

Charles Lindbergh, wearing helmet with goggles up, in open cockpit of airplane at Lambert Field, St. Louis, Missouri

Library of Congress, Prints & Photographs Division, LC-USZ62-68852

mann in 1934. Hauptmann was found guilty and executed in 1936. The Lindbergh family sought to find solace by moving temporarily to England, while in America Congress was persuaded to pass the "Lindbergh Law," making kidnapping a federal crime.

Leopold and Loeb

What became known as the "crime of the century" was committed by 19-year-old Nathan Leopold, and his counterpart, 18-year-old Richard Loeb. Both teenagers were believers in Friedrich Nietzsche's philosophical tenet known as the Ubermenschen (ultrahuman; superhuman). This philosophy espouses the idea that within society there are individuals who are destined to rise above the populace owing to their high levels of intelligence. These "supermen" are not bound by the laws of society, and because of their high aptitudes, they can rise above definitions of good and evil.

Leopold and Loeb were friends in college when they began to partake in small crimes "just for the thrill of it." Eventually they decided to execute the perfect crime. On May 21, 1924 the two teenagers kidnapped 14-year-old Bobby Franks, killed him, and proceeded to demand money from the family. Franks was a friend and relative of Loeb, thus he made an easy target when the young men happened upon him while he was walking home from school. Leopold and Loeb lured Franks into their rental car, struck him in the head several times and, eventually, suffocated him. They dumped Franks' body in a drainage pipe in a marshy area and returned home to resume normal activities.

Although Leopold and Loeb believed they had planned the perfect crime they left behind several clues as to their identities. The police soon tracked them down and both were arrested. The teens' families hired Clarence Darrow to represent them at the trial. Consequently, the "crime of the century" became the "trial of the century." Darrow decided to plead "guilty" on behalf of both defendants, to spare them the death penalty, and spent his time seeking to influence the judge that Leopold and Loeb were victims of circumstantial powers beyond their control. The defense used psychiatrists to explain how the teens were products of their emotional and sexual insecurities as well as the philosophy of Nietzsche. After Darrow's 12-hour closing argument in which he attacked capital punishment as having its "roots back to the beast and the jungle," the judge sentenced Leopold and Loeb to life in prison plus 99 years for kidnapping and murder.

Cultural Challenges in the 1920s

Cultural disputes rocked the country throughout the 1920s. Americans began to argue with each other concerning the merits of creationism as opposed to evolution after the ban of evolutionary theory in the classroom was defied. In a similar manner, Darwinism helped spark a new intellectual movement known as Eugenics, which swept through the social and scientific world. Other cultural conflicts also arose as discontented intellectuals and artists created a subculture of rebellion in the face of American consumerism. And racial clashes erupted as returning soldiers competed with employed African-Americans for jobs.

Prohibition

The 1920s is famously known as the Prohibition Era. When Prohibition became law at 12:01 a.m. on January 16, 1920, many Americans proclaimed that the nation would be alcohol-free forever. The newly passed 18th Amendment banned the manufacturing, storage, and sale of intoxicating liquors in the country. Weeks before the implementation of the new law, customers flocked to local stores, hotels, and saloons to stock up on alcohol. These buyers carried liquor away in cars, baby buggies, and children's wagons while newspapers and magazines provided articles on how to make alcohol at home. The evidence soon became clear that although alcohol was banned in America, the Americans would find ways to skirt the law.

Throughout the early twentieth century, the Temperance Movement had been growing. The campaign highlighted the values of health, morality, and thriftiness as well as the domestic violence and lost paychecks associated with alcohol. Passage of the amendment was secured with the promise to protect American families and raise the moral code of the nation. These advocates argued against the voices of those who feared the increase in power within the federal government. In conjunction with the 18th Amendment, Congress passed the Volstead Act as the enforcing statute. This act established criminal penalties for violations of the law as well as defined the makeup of what constituted "intoxicating liquors." Prohibition agents sought to destroy all illegal alcohol within the nation. Although the government funded only a few thousand agents, they regularly raided popular nightclubs and known bootleggers' hideouts to catch them with their stash.

Lack of government funds as well as weak enforcement of the law helped create an atmosphere of defiance and resistance within the country. Men and women found numerous ways to break the law, including the organization of smuggling rings, the creation of bootleggers, and the infamous and widespread corruption of public officials who could be bribed to look the other way. During Prohibition, respectable, middle- and upper-class women began to visit speak-easies, transport illegal alcohol, and drink openly violating the earlier social norms and challenging the role of women in society. Ironically, rather than establishing an increase in American virtue as promised by temperance crusaders, crime rates within the country during the Prohibition era skyrocketed along with the demand for alcohol. As demand grew, organized crime syndicates established powerful empires that moved bootlegged liquor within major American cities.

New York City Deputy Police Commissioner John A. Leach, right, watching agents pour liquor into sewer following a raid during the height of prohibition

Library of Congress, Prints & Photographs Division, NYWT&S Collection, LC-USZ62-123257.

Battles between organized gangs raged throughout the country as mob leaders fought over territories and goods. Al Capone became the most famous gang leader of the era with his Chicago bootlegging empire. Capone grossed more than $60 million a year in his enterprise that encompassed prostitution, bootlegging, narcotics, robbery, and murder. Capone's gang consistently tried to expand their territory by gunning down rival gang members. The St. Valentine's Day Massacre of 1929 captured the intensity of the wars when Capone's men, posing as cops and pretending to arrest seven rival gang members, lined them up, and murdered them with machine guns. Prohibition agents continued to try to track Capone and other mobsters throughout the 1920s. The police finally caught up with Capone and arrested him in 1929 for a short stint in prison. After his release, he was arrested again and sent to prison for tax evasion in 1931.

The reaction to Prohibition by the American population tested the status quo of the culture. Contrary to the effort to increase morality and protect families by outlawing alcohol, it became socially acceptable to commit crimes within the social world. Men, women, and even teenagers, joined the clusters of bootleggers and drinkers, openly breaking the law. Crime also increased due to the unyielding rise of gang violence. When the Great Depression began in the early 1930s arguments renewed that Prohibition was hurting the American economy as well as affecting the morality of the day. Thus, when Franklin D. Roosevelt was elected in 1932, he immediately asked Congress to repeal the 18th Amendment. The 21st Amendment, passed in 1933, ended America's experiment with Prohibition.

Red Scare

With the overthrow of Czar Nicholas of Russia in 1917, and consequent rise of the communist Soviet Union, many Americans began to fear the spread of radical forms of governments. New waves of labor strikes in the early part of the decade fueled the fear that communists were conspiring to start a revolution in the United States by means of a working class rebellion. These fears grew into the movement known as the Red Scare, as Americans hunted for communist agitators and spies. The Red Scare began after a series of eight separate bombings that took place in key American cities during June, 1919. These bombs, of extraordinary capacity, rocked places such as New York, Boston, and Washington D.C. The bombings were traced back to an extreme group of anarchists based in the United States led by Luigi Galleani, a radical anarchist who advocated violence as the means to overthrow governments. When one of the bombs exploded at the home of Attorney General, A. Mitchell Palmer, the call for retribution and justice strengthened.

Palmer began a special investigative force, soon to become the Federal Bureau of Investigations headed by J. Edgar Hoover, to find revolutionaries in the country. During the years 1919–1920, a series of raids were organized on the headquarters of radical organizations, including anarchist and communist groups, focusing on foreign residents and immigrants. Thousands of immigrants were detained and hundreds were deported. As immigrants were being rounded up in the country, many Americans sanctioned the government's actions. However, when a pair of Italian immigrants were arrested and tried for murder, some Americans believed the justice system had gone too far.

Sacco and Vanzetti

Nicola Sacco and Bartolomeo Vanzetti were Italian immigrants who arrived in the United States in 1908. The men became part of a militant anarchist group that preached and practiced revolutionary violence, located in Massachusetts. This political group rejected the concept of the state as well as private property and formed their own subculture, offering their followers everything from anarchist newspapers and schools to theater groups.

In May 1920, Sacco and Vanzetti were arrested and charged with the robbery and murder of a shoe company paymaster and his guard in South Braintree, Massachusetts. Overseeing the trial, and openly prejudiced against radical immigrants, was Judge Webster Thayer. Although the evidence tying the men to the crime was inconclusive, it soon became clear they Sacco and Vanzetti were not on trial for their actions; they were on trial for their radical beliefs and Italian heritage. The influences of the anti-radical atmosphere within the country played a decided role in the outcome of the trial.

When the trial in 1921 ended, both the jury and Judge Thayer were convinced that both men were found guilty, and they were sentenced to death. In the years following the verdict, protests erupted throughout the immigrant community and spread to the international world as people spoke out against the American justice system and their biases. Although both men sought to appeal their verdict they were denied, even though it was evident that personal prejudices influenced the guilty conviction. Thus, on August 23, 1927, Sacco and Vanzetti were electrocuted. Their deaths sparked division and violence in America as well as European uproar against American policies. The dynamics surrounding the Red Scare filtered through various levels of the American governmental system and helped launch an anti-immigrant, antiradical sentiment in the country throughout the decade.

Bartolomeo Vanzetti (left) and Nicola Sacco, manacled together surrounded by heavy guard and onlookers, about to enter the courthouse at Dedham, Massachusetts where they will receive the death sentence for murder they committed seven years ago

Renewals of Nativism

As massive waves of immigrants surged into the country after World War I, some Americans began to warn that the country was losing its culture and purity. The fears associated with the radical beliefs of some immigrants, coupled with the government crackdown on these people, renewed calls for reform.

After the war, large-scale immigration grew again, including the poor, Jews, Catholics, and political radicals from many Southern and Eastern European countries. With America seeking to reorganize its work force in the postwar years as well as assimilate its soldiers into society, many people began to call for limits on immigration. Included in this call was the underlying fear of revolutionaries infiltrating the country and seeking to overthrow the government. As a result of these influences, nativism began to resurge in the country. This movement desired to keep American culture pure for the "native" Americans. They pressured the government to respond with limitations on immigration.

In response, Congress passed the National Origins Act of 1924. This limited the number of immigrants allowed into the United States from particular countries, based on the total number of people of each nationality residing in America. Using the 1890 census as its base, the law stated that only 2% of each nationality's current population in America was allowed entrance into the nation. Consequently, the law decreased the number of immigrants allowed into the country by almost 80%. Mostly affected were the newer immigrants from Southern and Eastern Europe, while Western European immigrant numbers grew because of their long residency in America.

However, the western hemisphere was not restricted as heavily as other parts of the world. Throughout the early twentieth century, surges of Hispanic migration took place as individuals and families from Mexico crossed into America. Many of the people in these groups were seeking refuge from the ongoing Mexican Revolution as well as escaping economic disasters and turmoil. The majority of these immigrants went to work in the railroad industry. Between 1910 and 1920, almost one million legal Mexican immigrants were hired by railroads for construction and maintenance. Other Hispanic immigrants went to work in the agricultural sector in the southwest.

Revival of the Ku Klux Klan

As the country wrestled with the rise of nativism and the surge of new immigrants, the anti-foreign attitude that developed helped resurrect the Ku Klux Klan. The Klan was founded in 1866 as a means for white southerners to resist the Republican Party's Reconstruction plans and subjugate the newly freed slaves. Throughout the latter part of the century, the Klan reasserted Democratic control in the South and maintained strict control over black men and women. However, during the 1920s the Klan reinvigorated its platform and expanded its power.

Klan membership soared from 3 to 4 million during the 1920s as men and women across the nation joined the nativist movement to promote "100% Americanism." With the 1915 release of D.W. Griffith's blockbuster film, *Birth of a Nation,* the Klan was celebrated for its actions as necessary and heroic in an attempt to keep America pure and moral. Klan activities spread beyond the South and organized into a network of local societies across America.

Klan members claimed the need to defend and protect the family as well as uphold morality in the community. Opposed to blacks, Catholics, Jews, and immigrants, the members also focused their attention on adulterers and domestic abusers. Women joined in the effort to promote prohibition, establish strong public schools, and encourage traditional family morals. Klansmen became so powerful during the decade that they won public office in seven states and lynched almost 200 black individuals. At its height, in 1925, the Klan demonstrated their strength when they met at the nation's capital. Approximately, 50,000 Klansmen rallied and marched down the streets of Washington, D.C.

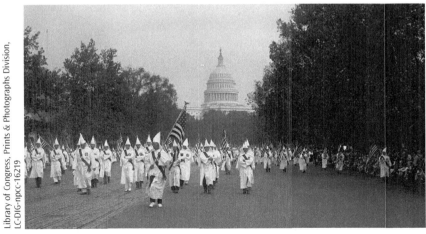

Library of Congress, Prints & Photographs Division, LC-DIG-npcc-16219

Ku Klux Klan parade, 9/13/26

Scopes Trial

In the postwar era, many Americans sought a "return to normalcy" by renewing their Christian faith. In the Midwest and South, many Americans turned to Fundamentalist Christianity as a means of comfort. These conservative groups stressed an exact interpretation of the Bible that included the insistence that the miracles within the text, including the creation story, were literally true. Fundamentalists defended these traditional and supernatural beliefs against modern attempts to reinterpret them.

Clarence Darrow at the Scopes evolution trial, Dayton, Tennessee, July 1925

As a consequence, when Charles Darwin's ideas concerning the theory of evolution and creation of man started to spread in academic fields, Fundamentalists challenged these theories. Several southern states passed legislation in the early 1920s making it illegal to teach evolution in the classroom. However, these actions were met with resistance when civil liberty groups, including the American Civil Liberties Union (ACLU), joined with like-minded scientists and pushed to defy the newly established laws. As a result, a Tennessee high school biology teacher became the focus of a national dispute.

John Scopes, a young biology teacher in Dayton, Tennessee, chose to test the state's ban against teaching evolution in the schools when the ACLU offered legal support to any teacher willing to challenge the constitutionality of the law. In 1925, Scopes intentionally violated the law by teaching evolutionary theory to his students. He was subsequently arrested and put on trial.

The Scopes case, nicknamed the "Monkey Trial," began on July 10, 1925 and proceeded throughout the sweltering summer months. Within a few days of it beginning, hordes of spectators, journalists, and advocates for both sides of the creation argument arrived. It soon became evident that the trial was not only about the guilt of Scopes or the constitutionality of the Tennessee law. Broadly speaking, the trial represented a clash of worldviews within the American population. Traditional, biblical beliefs, held by most Americans, were being questioned with new scientific theories that excluded the uniqueness of a God-centered creation.

Thousands of people came to the small town of Dayton to be a part of the excitement while selling concessions, Bibles, and stuffed monkeys. The trial soon became a media circus, and Americans eagerly surrounded their radios nightly to listen to the events as they unfolded. Two of the most popular lawyers of the day were involved in the case. Clarence Darrow joined the defense on behalf of the ACLU. He was a brilliant defense lawyer from Chicago and an agnostic. Three-time Democratic presidential candidate William Jennings Bryan represented the prosecution. Bryan was a recognized Fundamentalist and popular with many rural Americans. He was an outspoken objector to Darwinism, however, not on the basis of science. Bryan felt a new belief system regarding the origin of man would undermine morality and virtue. He argued that human ethics were dependent on religion, and when mankind replaces God with something else, spiritual values and inherent ethical behavior are lost. Some in attendance at the trial were hostile toward Darrow, including most of the journalists. Journalist H.L. Mencken continually berated Bryan in his articles and represented him as Darwin's "missing link;" ape-like and backward in his literal belief in creation.

When the presiding judge declared that scientific evidence supporting evolution was inadmissible, Darrow found another way to dispute the Tennessee law. He chose to call Bryan as his sole witness and thoroughly examined him in an effort to discredit his literal interpretation of the Bible. Bryan was subjected to ridicule, forced to make contradictions in his statements, and lost his chance at a closing argument due to Darrow's tactics.

After a quick deliberation on July 21, the jury found Scopes guilty and fined him $100. Although Bryan won the case, he was not viewed as the victor. His religious beliefs were undermined through his humiliation. The Monkey Trial became an argument that went beyond challenging state laws. Fundamental religious beliefs were confronted by Darwin's theory of evolution, and the argument was played out in the public sphere. As Americans across the country listened to the trial, many were forced to grapple with their religious convictions and reevaluate them in light of the new theories in science.

Azusa Street Revival

In the aftermath of the Scopes trial the Fundamentalist movement began to dwindle. In response to this change, new Christian movements began and moved beyond the boundaries of mainline Protestantism. As Protestant churches began to soften their doctrinal standards by allowing more moderate views regarding biblical authority, several new Christian movements developed to fill the gap. These groups, associated with the holiness movement, were fashioned by the extraordinary meetings held on Azusa Street in Los Angeles, California.

The Pentecostal movement began at 312 Azusa Street, Los Angeles in an abandoned Methodist church building. William Seymour, a black holiness preacher, founded the Apostolic Faith Gospel Mission emphasizing the work of the Holy Spirit in believer's lives. His preaching led to a local revival that captured the attention of the nation, and eventually the world. Seymour's teachings emphasized that the outpouring of the Holy Spirit on all believers led to spiritual gifts, including healing and speaking in tongues (ecstatic spiritual speech). The revival was marked by fervent prayer, healings, new forms of worship, and speaking in tongues. It also emphasized the full participation of women as well as black and Hispanic believers.

Pentecostalism expanded to include the formation of the Assemblies of God churches as well as numerous African-American denominations, including the Church of God in Christ and the African Methodist Episcopal Church. These black denominations offered new types of worship that were similar to what had been practiced in their churches in earlier American history. They also provided educational opportunities for black individuals as well as missionary connections with the world.

The Lost Generation

Challenges to American culture came from other venues in society throughout the 1920s, as well. A group of young writers and artists sought to escape from the materialism and mass culture of American society by creating their own sub-movement. Known as the "Lost Generation," these critics of American society rebelled against what they deemed as a shallow, anti-intellectual, and materialistic culture. They were disgusted with the adoration of American movie stars as well as the industrialism of the age. Wrestling with their own sense of personal alienation and seeking self-fulfillment, these individuals used their works to strip the illusions of success and expose the innate sufferings of life.

Disenchanted and embittered by World War I, the Lost Generation resisted the Victorian cultural mores still alive in the nation and moved overseas to live a life of sexual liberation and hedonism. Writers, such as F. Scott Fitzgerald, E.E. Cummings, and Ernest Hemingway produced one of the most creative periods of American literature. Their works emphasized the belief in progress and exposed the shallowness of materialism as well as the absurdity of war. In all, the works of the Lost Generation became another form of resistance to the developing American culture of the 1920s.

Race Riots

During World War I, the Great Migration continued with the relocation of more African-Americans to the North seeking safety from racial violence in the south and the economic gain of burgeoning cities. Industrialized urban areas in the North needed factory workers and recruited black employees from the South. As a consequence, an estimated one million African-Americans relocated and acquired work in places such as slaughterhouses and factories. These workers were challenged when four million American soldiers returned home after the war seeking employment. The result led to an increase in racial division. Racial prejudices also expanded with the influence of the Harlem Renaissance, the shocking expansion of the Ku Klux Klan, and the unchecked segregation in the south. As a result, the country witnessed a new wave of race riots.

Racial tensions erupted in East St. Louis, Illinois in 1917, as newly arrived black workers assumed available factory positions and developed new neighborhoods. When friction arose due to disputes concerning labor issues, a mob marched on a black neighborhood, leaving over 100 dead. Tensions continued to grow in July 1919, when Eugene Williams, a 17-year-old African-American young man, drowned in Lake Michigan. Williams was swimming with his friends in the lake when he crossed the unofficial segregation barrier in the lake. White adults began to throw stones at him for violating the invisible blockade and Williams drowned. When the Chicago police arrived, they refused to arrest anyone. Black eyewitnesses protested and rioting resulted. The Chicago riots lasted 13 days and left 38 people dead, hundreds wounded, and a 1000 black families without homes. These types of race riots triggered hostility and fear among Americans and fed the spirit of disunity within the nation.

The Instability of the Late 1920s

Economic Instability

As the consumer revolution expanded throughout the 1920s, the use of credit grew proportionally. More people used credit than ever before in an effort to maintain personal success. However, the rise of credit also strained the economic stability of the country and placed numerous Americans in debt. As banks sought to keep up with credit demands they, along with other industries and individuals, invested in the stock market as a means to make money.

Throughout the 1920s, the stock market consistently grew and, by the end of the decade, had long established a bull market. The prolonged gains in the market led many Americans and businesses to invest heavily in stocks. Many investors began to participate in speculation and margin-buying as a way to make quick money. Both of these tactics tend to rely on insider market knowledge as well as the need to turn a profit to maintain success. However, these approaches were also establishing a market with overinflated stocks and risky investments.

Election of 1928

The year 1928 was one of tremendous optimism in the nation as America appeared to be becoming rich. In the presidential election, Republican Herbert Hoover campaigned emphasizing the economic success of the country as well as the need to maintain a pro-business environment. His Democratic opponent, former New York governor, Al Smith, focused on social issues relating to the poor and immigrant populations. As a child of immigrants, he opposed immigration quotas, wanted to end Prohibition, and challenged the status quo as the first Catholic individual to run for president. Hoover won in a landslide, pledging to continue the economic boom of the decade.

The Great Crash of 1929

As Hoover took office in 1929, the American economy was balancing on a thin line. The newly elected president told the American people that he was going to maintain the policies of the previous eight years in an effort to banish poverty from the nation. The strong economy that he touted, however, was distorted and on the verge of collapsing.

The stock market began to collapse in the fall of 1929. Investors started to nervously sell their stocks in an effort to prevent personal loss as the market fell. However, what began as a dip in the market quickly became a rush when on October 24, the day known as Black Thursday, brokers began to sell their stocks in mass panic. Giant financial leaders, such as J.P. Morgan, Jr., worked with other business moguls to find ways to restore confidence in the market. They injected $100 million to boost the market and demonstrate a measure of faith. However, the panic did not subside. The following week, on Black Tuesday, October 29, more selling took place resulting in an almost total stoppage of trade. As American investors scurried to sell their stocks, the value of the market was cut in half in a single day. In short, 16 million shares of stock were traded and more than $30 billion in paper money vanished. In November, the market crashed, and began what came to be known as the Great Depression.

Conclusion

The 1920s was a decade of optimism, change, and challenge. Although America maintained a limited role in world affairs, it played a key position in helping rebuild the international community by means of economic aid, military reductions, and overseeing efforts to end war in the world. The American economy grew substantially and became a global force, so that by the end of the decade, the United States generated a third of total world production. It appeared that America was on the road to even more prosperity.

As American industries set production records, wages increased and working hours declined. More people had disposable income as well as free time than they ever had before. The American culture was created as advertisers lured consumers to new products and the ease of credit. The automobile became the number one demand of most people, and created a new center for the nation's economy. Other forceful changes occurred with the rebirth of African-American culture and entrance of the new woman.

However, the changes also generated friction. Americans balked at the new Prohibition laws and found ways to undermine them. The surge of immigration created an anti-foreign sentiment that filtered throughout the federal government and justice system. And traditional norms of society were confronted by new scientific theories, racial injustices, and alienated intellectuals. Although the 1920s can rightly be described as the Roaring Age, the decade was also complicated and difficult. The issues being debated ushered America into the modern age and set the tone for the conversations that would dominate the twentieth century.

CHAPTER SIXTEEN

Great Depression

Chapter 16: Key Concepts

- Discuss the causes of the Great Depression. How did President Hoover respond? Was it effective?

- Why did the American people choose Franklin D. Roosevelt as their President? What was his approach toward ending the Depression?

- Overall, how effective was the New Deal in ending the Depression? What types of changes did FDR and the New Deal bring to America?

Introduction

The Great Depression brought dramatic changes to the culture and political world of America. Throughout U.S. history men and women seldom looked to the federal government for help or direction. Most Americans agreed that the business of the country needed to remain separate from government intervention and involvement. However, the Great Depression challenged this philosophy. The desperate livelihoods experienced by families and the jobless wanderers vainly searching for work compelled the nation to elect a president who would use the federal government to solve their problems. President Roosevelt and his program, called the New Deal, promised to relieve the suffering and reform the nation. However, he was met with criticisms from various groups of Americans, including those within his own Democratic Party. Roosevelt's actions changed the course of America and charted a new path in its landscape. The scope of the crisis propelled the nation into a new direction on the American Road.

1920s Economy

Most historians agree that the causes of the Great Depression stem from economic problems inherent in the 1920s. The decade witnessed American businesses set production records as wages increased and working hours declined. The stock market grew at an unprecedented rate and unemployment reached a low of 1% in 1926. America became the world's economic leader during the post-World War I years, generating 34% of total world production by 1929. Yet, this decade, captured in the descriptive phrase "the Roaring Twenties," also held several weaknesses that cascaded into the crisis that brought America to its knees.

Causes of the Great Depression

The roots of the Great Depression actually developed in the years surrounding World War I when America was becoming the world's richest country. As its Gross National Product expanded during the Industrial Age as well as its role in global trade, the American market became more influential. This influence created a scenario such that when a ripple hit the U.S. market, the impact was experienced world-wide. Throughout the war, American production lines grew to furnish other nations with war materials and, after it, rebuilding materials. Many European nations went off the gold standard to pay for the costs of the war and reconstruction thus leading to inflation. Still, America continued to maintain levels of economic stability. This rise of American economic influence set the stage for a global depression when its economy fell.

Direct causes of the Great Depression include many things, beginning with the post-war years. After World War I, American industry and farming continued to produce goods based on pre-war needs. Congress also kept tariffs high to protect American industries and its economy. However, the demand for American goods drastically declined after the war, because the devastated European countries could no longer afford them. With the stock market booming, many Americans were tempted to continue to invest in these companies, although sales were decreasing. From 1925 on, with companies producing more goods than they could sell, more and more investors were willing to overlook the inequality so they could invest in the market. This led to an overinflated value on the businesses as well as false sense of wealth.

The stock market played another key role in creating the atmosphere for the Depression. As the stock market continued to go up during the 1920s, more and more investors began to play the bull market. Known as speculators, they pooled their capital to buy and sell stock together as a means to manipulate the market. When the speculators bought large amounts of stock together, the price invariably went up, thus encouraging others to buy. Once the stock reached a new high, the speculators cashed in quickly to make a fast profit and sent the price back to its original amount. This resulted in overinflated values of stock creating a façade of value, while those investors choosing their stocks based on the sound investment of a company, struggled to keep up.

As the late 1920s wore on, speculative activity began to overshadow sound investment causing some Americans to worry over the future of the stock market. Other Americans, however, flocked to the market in an attempt to buy into the inner circle of speculators and make money quickly. As a matter of fact, many stock brokers began to encourage investors to buy stock on margin as a means to get a piece of the profits. Investors who bought on margin paid a small amount for the stock they wanted to purchase (usually 10% of the stock's value) and borrowed the rest of the cost of the stock from a broker or trading house. When the value of the stock inevitably went up, the investor sold his share quickly, reimbursed the stockbroker for the loan and pocketed the rest of the money. Buying on margin became so popular that, by late 1929, broker loans totaled close to seven billion dollars. Many of these investors included banks that were speculating with other people's money, that is, funds from ordinary American's savings accounts. This help explains why, although only 10% of Americans actually owned stock, the careless actions of these speculators resulted in millions of dollars disappearing.

The American economy had several weaknesses that paved the road for the Depression as well. The rise of easy credit led to an artificial belief in individual wealth. Thus, people began to borrow too much money. One of the items in highest demand was the automobile. Throughout the 1920s, American automobile factories more than doubled their production, and by the end of the decade, almost every household had a car. More cars led to more rubber, steel, glass, oil, and petroleum industries. Newly created roads, suburbs, shopping centers, and hotels created jobs out of the overflow of the auto industry and established an economy that revolved, in large part, around automobiles. The result created an unbalanced financial market in the country; when automobile sales began to decline, their mutually dependent sectors were influenced in a similar manner.

The prosperity of the 1920s was not enjoyed by everyone. While the number of millionaires jumped substantially from the previous decade, those living in poverty also grew. The gap between the wealthy and the poor became wider as corporate profits rose significantly but hourly wages only went up minimally. As the decade wound down, consumer buying began to slow. Industries, however, refused to slow down production or lower prices.

Farmers, who experienced high demand, generous prices, and easy credit during the war years also refused to scale back their crop production. The demand for food fell, crop prices subsequently dropped, leaving farmers with heavy debt. The makings of an economic crisis were at hand when, in October 1929, the overinflated stock market bottomed out.

Crash of the Stock Market, 1929

The stock market crash of 1929 took place over a ten-day period in late October as the values of stocks fell drastically. Several events happened throughout the year and climaxed in the autumn months. Throughout 1929 credit slowly began to stretch thin for consumers and foreign countries because lenders began holding onto their money. Creditors' fears concerning the stock market as well as a jump in unemployment sparked concerns that the economy was slowing down. The Federal Reserve also started to encourage banks not to use credit any longer that supported speculative

Crowd of people gather outside the New York Stock Exchange following the Crash of 1929

activities in the stock market. In response, consumers began to grow wary of the American economy as it was slowing down.

In an effort to bolster confidence in the economic system, in the late summer and early fall big investors continued to play the market and make money and encouraged others to also invest. However on Monday, October 20, the stock market began to spiral downward. With the falling stock prices, panic settled in among individual investors and businesses alike. Three days later, on Black Thursday, a record 12.9 million shares of stock changed hands as brokers began to make margin calls and investors quickly sold. On October 29, the day known as Black Tuesday, the stock market convulsed as 16 million shares of stock were either traded or sold and more than 30 billion dollars disappeared. The value of the stock market was cut in half as the true worth of stocks began to be realized. Investors all over the world sold their stocks, causing foreign markets to crumble, and the 10-year ordeal known as the Great Depression began.

President Herbert Hoover

Republican Herbert Hoover won the election of 1928 in a landslide emphasizing the economic success of the 1920s as well as promising to continue the stimulation of business and industry in America. His résumé as a public official was broad, including head of the

Food Administration during World War I and Secretary of Commerce under the Harding and Coolidge administrations. Hoover ran against four-time Democratic governor of New York, Al Smith. Hoover's opponent was a child of immigrants and stood against Prohibition and immigration quotas while focusing on social issues. However, Smith suffered from an anti-Catholic prejudice within the country as well as an association with the corruption of Tammany Hall. The American people responded to Hoover's call to continue the economic growth of the Republican decade.

President Hoover was recognized by many as a logistical genius. His actions as the head of the Food Administration provided food and relief to dispossessed individuals and families affected by World War I in a timely and efficient manner. He also led the relief efforts in Illinois after the Mississippi River flooded and destroyed hundreds of thousands of acres in the state. Thus, when the stock market crashed, Hoover immediately sought to provide a semblance of relief and support for the American economic system.

Hoover's Response

The stock market crashed when Hoover had been in office less than eight months. In the immediate weeks after the crash, he brought together key business and industry leaders to the White House to discuss a viable response and asked them to do their part in preventing an economic depression. He encouraged employers to maintain wages for their workers so families could continue to buy goods. Industry leaders agreed not to lay off workers or cut wages while labor leaders agreed to shorter work days to create more jobs. Hoover also pushed state and local leaders to develop jobs in public works to provide employment for the jobless. These actions did not provide much, if any, relief. Most economists in the 1920s agreed that little involvement by the federal government was needed when the economy was in crisis. They concurred that an economy in crisis should be allowed to fix itself as the weaker businesses and banks went under, allowing the stronger institutions to survive.

Hoover's response was built upon the belief of the importance of voluntarism coupled with the economic philosophy that money must be spent in order to prevent an economic depression. In the first years of the crisis, he cut income taxes by 1% while increasing federal spending by 42%. He greatly increased spending on public works programs as well as subsidizing ship-building programs and encouraged the construction of the Hoover Dam. Hoover also tried to help struggling farmers as the agricultural sector declined. Farmers, straining from the postwar years with overproduction, asked the president for assistance to help maintain farm prices. In response, Hoover established the Federal Farm Board that made loans to farmers to create and strengthen farm cooperatives, hoping they would exert more control over crop production and market distribution. In an effort to stave off a true economic depression, the President also attempted to protect American manufacturing. In June, 1930, he signed the Hawley–Smoot tariff, which raised taxes (tariffs) on foreign imports to the United States.

However, the President did not provide much relief and the Depression continued to deepen. In 1932, at the height of the Depression, Hoover oversaw passages of the Revenue Act and Reconstruction Finance Corporation (RFC). The Revenue Act drastically increased tax rates on the highest incomes in the country, creating up to that point in history, the largest tax increase during peacetime in the United States and providing new revenue for the federal government. The RFC loaned 1.5 billion dollars to large businesses, including banks, insurance companies, and railroads in an attempt to help them prevent bankruptcy. Many of Hoover's attempts fell short. The Hawley–Smoot tariff backfired as other countries retaliated by increasing their own tariffs, thus harming the American economy. Little of the relief efforts associated with the RFC trickled down to workers and many businesses were too burdened with large amounts of debt to endure. Overall, the federal government went from a surplus of 700 million dollars at the beginning of Hoover's term to a 2.6 billion dollar deficit by 1932 with an unemployment rate of 20% and rising.

The Growth of the Depression

Although President Hoover assured the American people that the economy would correct itself soon, the economy continued to worsen. Businesses were not able to absorb the heavy losses following the stock market crash and had to take drastic measures by reducing work hours and wages or laying off their employees. Approximately, one-half of the American industries moved their employees from full-time to part-time in an effort to survive. With the rising unemployment, average income for American families declined by 40% leading to millions of families losing their homes. Consumer spending and investments declined accordingly and the economy continued to shrink.

The collapse of the banking system had the most profound effects on the nation and ensured the economic Depression. By 1930, approximately 800 banks had failed and nine million savings accounts disappeared. Americans throughout the country began to worry that all of the banks would close and swallow their savings accounts. In response to these shocking losses, bank runs began in the autumn of 1930 and continued until 1933. Panicked Americans raced to their banks in an effort to withdraw their saving accounts before the institutions ran out of money and closed their doors. Bank runs often began as rumors spread within a community that the bank was running out of cash and may soon shut down. As cash reserves began to dwindle, many banks were forced to liquidate loans in order to meet the needs of their depositors. However, the cash soon dried up because the banks owed too much money to lenders and customers withdrew their cash too quickly. Eventually, over 9000 banks closed their doors with customers losing more than 2.5 billion dollars

The Great Depression reached its worst year in 1932. The unemployment rate had risen to 25% nationally and jobs became scarce as businesses shut their doors. Historians estimate that between 11 and 15 million workers were unemployed at the height of the Depression. However, since most women and children were dependent on these workers' income, this meant that approximately 30 million people were without income. Around the country, the unemployment rate varied by location. The industrial Northeast was hit hard. In similar manner, the South struggled as sharecroppers and tenant farmers were forced off their land by landlords who went into foreclosure. Without social security or unemployment benefits, families struggled for daily-living necessities as they looked for help from relief agencies and local, state, and federal governments. As Americans struggled, they blamed President Hoover for his policies. Hoover's name soon became associated with some of the most desperate aspects of the Depression.

Hoovervilles

Hooverville in Lower Manhattan

Home foreclosure rates jumped dramatically during the early 1930s as the Depression settled into the nation. Some estimates state that almost 10% of the country's mortgages (or a 1000 homes per day) were forfeited between 1932 and 1933, as homeowners could no longer afford to meet their house payments. Many of these families were forced to leave their homes and search for shelter with family or friends, if those were available. However, those displaced families that had nowhere else to turn carved out a "home" in makeshift shanties.

Displaced families and wandering hobos often found shelter in shantytowns that were erected on the edge of several big cities. These camps were nicknamed "Hoovervilles," in an effort to shame and place blame on President Hoover's perceived lack of concern. The Hooverville located in Central Park in New York City was one of the largest of the kind around the nation. The camps varied in size, from hundreds to thousands of people in population. The shanties were made of everything from cardboard boxes to discarded lumber and tin and located along rivers for water usage. Because of the dense population of some of the Hoovervilles, people living in them often suffered from disease as well as high-crime rates. Hoover's name was also scorned through other descriptive quips during the Depression. "Hoover blankets" were newspapers used to keep the homeless warm, and "Hoover flags" were empty pockets turned inside out.

Effects on the Family

The middle-class American family suffered the most during the Depression. The middle-class substantially retreated from their earlier consumer patterns and stopped buying goods. They began sewing their own clothes and started home businesses, such as laundry or baking, as a means to make money. Marriage and birth rates correspondingly dropped as most could not afford to marry or to have more children. Likewise, divorce rates fell because most did not have enough money to pay for them.

Women found ways to work during the Depression in an effort to help their families. Between 1932 and 1937 it was illegal for more than one member of a family to have a federal job. Thus, most employers were unwilling to hire married women because they believed jobs should be given to men first. Married women found imaginative ways to make money, though. They canned, made crafts, and sewed for income as well as took in boarders for rent money (usually unemployed men looking for work). Unmarried women acquired employment more readily than their counterparts, but their unemployment rate remained high during the Depression. Those unmarried women unable to find enough work usually moved back home with their families or settled into communities with other unmarried women, where they lived together in safety and shared resources.

Hobo waking up from his bed in Imperial Valley, California

African-American families suffered more severely than white families during the Depression. Black men were the first to be fired and last to be hired by employers. Some African-American employees were deliberately laid off to hire white workers in their stead, leading to an unemployment rate more than double that of white Americans. Unemployment in the South rose to over 50% for black workers during the 1930s, as sharecroppers and tenant farmers were forced off the land and Southern factory managers fired black employees first. This prompted a surge of African-American men and women to move North in search of work. This migration was met with resistance, however, by Northern unemployed men competing for jobs.

Crime also increased during the Depression as Americans romanticized the idea of bank robbers seeking vindication for their losses. Folk heroes, such as Bonnie & Clyde and John Dillinger, became household names as ordinary Americans followed their exploits in the newspapers and through radio broadcasts. Bonnie & Clyde became famous for robbing over 12 banks, as well as small gas stations and stores, while Dillinger stole money from two dozen banks and escaped from jail twice.

Escapism

As the Depression continued to wear on, men and women found numerous ways to deal with the realities of life through various forms of escape. The radio produced one of the more intense scenes during the Depression. In October, 1938, Orson Welles captured the American attention with his made-for-radio adaptation of H.G. Wells' *War of the Worlds*. The program, which included realistic-sounding alerts that interrupted the broadcast, reported that Martian aliens had landed near Princeton, New Jersey, and were using death rays to kill people. The episode aired on Sunday night and millions of people were tuned in for the show. As the show unfolded, Wells described a giant meteor that crashed into New Jersey and Martians emerging from a cylinder killing thousands. Wells went on to claim that the cylinders also landed in Chicago and St. Louis. Mass panic broke out around the country as millions of Americans tried to escape and leave town.

The American imagination was captured by other events and people during the 1930s. Newspapers followed the carving of Mount Rushmore in South Dakota as well as the erection of the Golden Gate Bridge in California. These feats challenged the status quo of engineering of the time and provided Americans with a new conversation. African-American Jesse Owens became a national hero in 1936 when he returned home from the Olympics in Berlin, Germany with four gold medals in track and field. His success was highlighted as the world became aware of German leader Adolf Hitler's extreme racism. Owens' victories challenged Hitler's views and exposed him on a national platform while spawning patriotism in the country.

Another American who captured the adulation of the American public during the 1930s was Amelia Earhart. She became famous in 1928 as the first woman to fly across the Atlantic Ocean in an aircraft. She was only a passenger then, but in 1932, she completed the feat on her own by flying from Newfoundland to Ireland, marking the fifth anniversary of Charles Lindbergh's first solo flight. Men and women admired Earhart's courage as a female aviator and followed her story throughout the decade. In 1937, Earhart made national news when she announced her daring "Round the World" flight, set to begin in June. On July 2, as she and her navigator were flying over the Pacific Ocean, they disappeared. Earhart was never heard from again.

Dust Bowl

The USDA-ARS Agricultural Systems Research Unit (ASRU).

Dust Storm approach Stratford Texas, 1935

Farmers were deeply affected by the economic plunge which ushered in the Depression. This disaster was exacerbated by the Dust Bowl. Farmers in the South and Midwest suffered from a terrible drought that lasted 10 years and covered 25,000 miles of farm land, from Texas to the Dakotas. Nicknamed the Dust Bowl, the drought was aggravated by poor farming techniques which resulted in soil unable to contain moisture. Periodic wind storms occurred throughout the 1930s and stirred up millions of tons of soil, which it carried across the United States, destroying farms and killing multitudes of cattle and wildlife.

As residents watched the arrival of the dust storms they barricaded themselves in their homes and held damp cloths over their noses and mouths to prevent suffocation. The Red Cross provided gas masks to some communities in an effort to stave off death. Those animals and individuals who did not seek shelter usually suffered agonizing sicknesses and death.

Almost half a million farmers left their farms in the Midwest during the Dust Bowl and headed to California looking for seasonal agricultural work. These "Okies" (nicknamed because many of them came from Oklahoma) piled all of their personal belongings onto their trucks, gathered up the family, and drove out West. California tried to discourage the emigration of the Okies through billboards declaring, "NO JOBS in California," and through other discriminatory tactics. However, the homeless families continued to pour into the state. The destitute poverty and hopelessness of these families became symbols of the Depression. Photographer, Dorothea Lange, documented their plight through pictures she took throughout the mid-1930s. Lange's photographs captured the suffering of the migrant workers and helped arouse public sympathy. Those farmers who chose to remain on their farms located in the Dust Bowl region eventually received government aid with passage of the Soil Conservation Service in 1935. The Soil Conservation Service helped farmers develop techniques to keep topsoil from blowing away by using crop rotation and retaining rainfall.

Militant Responses

The working class and farmers bore the brunt of the Depression. As the economic crisis worsened during the early 1930s, both of these groups experienced resentment and anger toward the federal government and the President. This anger occasionally generated militant responses as the men and women decided to create ways to combat the perceived insufficient policies of the government. Two of the most prominent militant reactions were those of the Bonus Army and the Farmer's Holiday.

In 1924, a grateful nation promised World War I veterans a bonus for their time of service to the United States. Payment promised was $1.00 for each day served in the States and $1.25 for each day served overseas, which would be paid in 1945. As the Depression grew worse during the 1930s, however, many of these veterans began to demand their bonus money. President Hoover did not respond. Therefore, in June 1932, 20,000 veterans, including their families, marched to Washington, D.C. and set up a squatter's camp near the capital and proclaimed to be the "Bonus Expeditionary Force." Congress voted on a bill allocating the bonus money to the veterans but it did not pass the Senate. The veterans refused to leave, however, and remained in the camp for another month. Hoover demanded that the camp disband in late July. After the Bonus Army refused to leave, the U.S. Army arrived with infantry, cavalry, and tanks, and pushed the veterans out of the city. In the process, two babies were killed and the squatter's camp was burned down. The blame of the events fell to President Hoover, and the American people grew even more disdainful toward him.

In a similar manner, in 1932, farmers in Iowa responded to the growing Depression by taking initiative to protect their livelihoods. Farm income declined by 60% in the first years of the Depression due to dropping prices and approximately one-third of the farmers lost their farms. In response, farmers in Iowa began a grass roots movement that became known as the National Farmer's Holiday. Their efforts led farmers to take a "holiday" from shipping crops to market with the desire to raise prices soon spread to farming communities throughout the Midwest. When some farmers violated the Holiday their shipments of goods were stopped by militants and kept from the market. Overall, the Holiday was not much of a success, as most Americans did not have the money to purchase farm goods at the higher prices desired by the farmers.

Election of 1932

As the presidential election in 1932 drew near, Americans suffered the worst year of the Depression. Unemployment reached a new high of 25%, most major banks had closed, and many factories sat idle. Scores of men were scraping together a living through part-time work or riding the rails looking for jobs, while farmers tried to find ways to survive the climate and economic challenges. Hoovervilles littered the outskirts of several major cities and angst and frustration toward the federal government reached new levels. Many Americans blamed President Hoover and the Republican Party for the Depression and looked for a new face, and a different Party, to help ease the economic troubles in the nation.

The Democratic National Convention took place in Chicago in June of 1932. Democrats knew Americans were ready for a change as nine candidates vied for the nomination. New York governor, Franklin Delano Roosevelt, captured the heart of the Convention with his charisma and optimism for a change. He was widely known for his implementation of new measures as governor of New York which brought some relief to the state in the early years of the Depression. Roosevelt won the nomination as the Democratic contender in the upcoming election.

President Herbert Hoover chose to run again in the election of 1932 believing, that with a little more time, his policies would end the Depression. However his Democratic opponent challenged Hoover's weak attempts at ending the crisis and repeatedly blamed him for the economy. In turn, Roosevelt promised the American people a New Deal. He was convinced that the government could and should help individuals in distress as well as fix the problems in the economy and government. Roosevelt's New Deal promised experimental fixes such as increased public works, regulation of securities, development of new mortgage markets, and the repeal of Prohibition. Roosevelt shrewdly adopted the song, "Happy Days are Here Again," as his campaign song. His vision for the country appealed to the American people, and he won the election in a landslide. Along with Roosevelt's victory the election also ushered in a Democratic majority in both the House and the Senate. The Republicans were soundly defeated, and as the New Deal presidency began with a Democratic majority in Congress, Roosevelt believed the American people handed him a mandate for change.

President Roosevelt and the New Deal

President Roosevelt promised the American people what he called the 3 "R's:" relief, recovery, and reform. He pledged *relief* to the destitute and unemployed, *recovery* of the economy in the farming and business sectors as well as the creation of new jobs, and *reform* in the government to prevent another economic collapse in the country. One of his key beliefs was that consumer under-consumption and the unequal distribution of wealth were main causes of the Depression. Thus he created several of his New Deal policies to remedy these problems. In his inaugural address Roosevelt reassured the American people that "this great Nation will endure as it has endured, will revive and will prosper. So. . . let me assert my firm belief that the only thing we have to fear is fear itself—nameless, unreasoning, unjustified terror which paralyzes needed efforts to convert retreat into advance." Using biblical imagery, Roosevelt blamed the "unscrupulous money changers" who were driven by the desire for higher profits and accused them accordingly. Roosevelt called for government initiative in job creation, changes in agriculture, and strict supervision over financial matters in the United States. He closed his speech with the declaration that the American people want "direct, vigorous action."

Life of Franklin D. Roosevelt

The fifth cousin of former President Theodore Roosevelt, Franklin Delano Roosevelt was born into a wealthy and privileged family in New York in 1882. Franklin grew up sheltered from the threat of poverty and the realities of hard living. After his education at prestigious private schools and elite Ivy League universities, he rose to become a lawyer in a prominent New York City law firm. As an adult, Roosevelt carried an optimistic and confident persona that appealed many people. In 1905, FDR married a distant cousin, Eleanor Roosevelt, the niece of former President Theodore Roosevelt. Throughout FDR's administrations, Elea-

President Franklin D. Roosevelt sitting in his car

Library of Congress, Prints & Photographs Division, photograph by Harris & Ewing, LC-DIG-hec-47235.

nor played a vital role as an ambassador of the New Deal. Although Roosevelt was not faithful in his marriage to Eleanor (he had several long-term affairs), his reliance on his wife to meet with the American people bolstered his popularity in the nation.

In the summer of 1921, at the age of 39 years, Roosevelt contracted polio. The disease paralyzed his legs and, although he tried numerous therapies throughout his life, he never regained the use of them. He was only able to stand with his legs encased in heavy steel braces and walk a few steps leaning on someone else. After he became president, Roosevelt persuaded the nation's press to never photograph him while in his wheelchair. He believed this would portray weakness. The press complied and very few photographs exist of FDR in his wheelchair. He found creative ways to conceal his handicap, including giving speeches while seated in his car and walking to podiums escorted by, and heavily leaning on, his son. In his efforts to find a cure, Roosevelt established a foundation at a therapy facility in Warm Springs, Georgia, to offer rehabilitation aids for polio victims. Ultimately, his dedication to find a cure inspired the March of Dimes program, which eventually developed a polio vaccine.

The New Deal Coalition

Roosevelt did not have a concrete plan for ending the Depression when he became President. However, he had several underlying convictions that guided him in his response and led to many experimental programs through the New Deal. Primarily, Roosevelt believed there were inherent flaws in the capitalist system. In his opinion, the unequal distribution of wealth between the rich and the impoverished were caused by the excesses within capitalism. According to Roosevelt, the government needed to moderate wealth in the nation with programs and assistance to protect the poor. Roosevelt also believed the government needed to remedy the imbalance in consumption and production in the nation. He proposed limiting production to raise prices and establish a balance in supply and demand.

Roosevelt's ideas also created a new base of political partnership which redefined voting behaviors and party alliance for the next several decades. This new political partnership was known as the New Deal Coalition. It was made up of many disparate groups of people, including liberal Democrats, big city machines and bosses, labor unions, minorities (especially Catholic, Jewish, and Black Americans), and farmers. These men and women abandoned the Republican Party as the Democratic leadership provided them considerable government aid and economic oversight. Their voting shifts built an alliance of support for the president and encouraged him to pursue his legislative agenda.

The President also surrounded himself with advisers dedicated to reviving the old Progressive Era practices of government regulation from the early 1900s. These academics, nicknamed "the Brain Trust," supported a bigger federal government that intervened in the nation's economy and in society to improve the quality of American life. The Brain Trust became the sounding board behind FDR's agenda and helped spur the creation of many New Deal policies.

First Hundred Days

President Roosevelt entered office promising the American people reform of the nation's weaknesses as well as relief to the jobless and recovery of the economy. He vowed that, within his first 100 days in office, he and the Democratic Congress would push through major legislative changes to help alleviate the problems and despair. Roosevelt's First Hundred Days witnessed many dynamic changes, including the Cullen-Harrison Act, which reversed Prohibition and culminated with the passage of the 21st Amendment, repealing the 18th Amendment. The First Hundred Days also brought passage of 15 major pieces of legislation at a breath-taking speed, including the creation of the "alphabet agencies." These laws created a sizeable number of agencies and government bureaus which established new forms of government regulation and control in the nation.

Reform

One of President Roosevelt's primary goal was to reform the nation's economy so that another Depression would not occur. He began his First Hundred Days overseeing the passage of several laws in an attempt to shore up the weaknesses within the economy and develop regulations to reform it. These measures included the Emergency Banking Act and the creation of the Securities and Exchange Commission (SEC).

Bank Holiday and Emergency Banking Act

The banking system in America was failing at a rapid pace in 1933. Thousands of banks had closed and those remaining afloat were suffering and on the brink of collapse. After his inauguration, FDR declared an immediate four-day "bank holiday." All of the nation's banks were shut down during the "holiday" as the president worked with New Dealers to draft the Emergency Banking Act. This Act gave the Secretary of the Treasury the authority to decide which banks could safely reopen and rushed two billion dollars in new currency to them. Congress also passed the Glass-Steagall Banking Act, which created the Federal Deposition Insurance Corporation (FDIC). The FDIC guaranteed bank deposits up to $5000, and promised that the federal government would reimburse depositors if their banks failed. When the banks reopened deposits exceeded withdrawals and confidence in the banks began to grow once again.

Securities and Exchange Commission

In his inaugural address Roosevelt blamed the lack of regulation in the stock market for the 1929 crash and promised to fix it. He pressed Congress to establish a commission to regulate the stock market which led to the passage of the Federal Securities Act and the creation of the SEC. The SEC was commissioned to prevent fraud, corruption, and insider trading in Wall Street as well as regulate the stock market through the licensing of investment dealers, monitoring of all stock transactions, and requirement that corporate offices make full disclosures of their companies. Roosevelt chose stock speculator Joseph Kennedy to head the Commission. Kennedy had made millions playing the market in the 1920s, and many criticized the president for his choice. Roosevelt, however, responded with confidence that if the government wanted to catch a thief, they needed to use one. With Kennedy's oversight, Wall Street brokers faced tougher regulations in the market and harsher measures for speculation.

Relief

Throughout American history the federal government was hesitant to assume responsibility and care for the poor and hungry in the nation. However, the high unemployment rate and the large number of destitute farmers during the Depression prompted men and women to clamor for government aid. By 1933, almost 13 million people were unemployed. After receiving reports that jobless Americans were referring to themselves as the "Forgotten Man," (forgotten by government agencies and the president) Roosevelt urged Congress to pass several pieces of legislation that offered relief to the American people. Several of the measures passed during the First Hundred Days catered to Roosevelt's conservation interests as well as his desire to employ young men, who were especially hit hard with the Depression. Roosevelt feared that if no one helped the younger unemployed generation, their discontentment would eventually pose a threat to social order. The key agencies

CCC (Civilian Conservation Corps) boys at work, Beltsville, Maryland

created to facilitate work for the young men as well as others were the Federal Emergency Relief Act (FERA), Civilian Conservation Corps (CCC), Public Works Administration (PWA), and Tennessee Valley Authority (TVA).

Federal Emergency Relief Act (FERA) and Civil Works Administration (CWA)

During the Hundred Days Congress passed the FERA which provided individual states monetary grants and loans to establish and operate relief programs. FERA was commissioned for two years and provided $500 million to the states to feed the hungry and create government-funded, unskilled jobs for the unemployed. States, however, were reluctant to begin local public works programs, so FERA established the federally-funded Civil Works Administration (CWA) in an effort to provide temporary jobs for public works projects. The CWA provided 400,000 shovel-ready jobs between the winter of 1933 and 1934. Four million CWA workers renovated schools, rebuilt roads and bridges, and dug sewers. Roosevelt, however, was skittish to establish long-term government-funded jobs out of fear that the American people would become too reliant on the federal government. Therefore, the CWA ended in March, 1934. Roosevelt and other New Dealers created other public works programs during his First Hundred Days to offset unemployment.

Civilian Conservation Corps (CCC)

In March 1933, the CCC was created to provide jobs to young men for the purpose of helping to preserve the nation's natural resources. Headed by the War Department, the CCC provided work for single, healthy, young men consisting of flood and fire prevention, planting trees, reducing soil erosion, and building parks and taming rivers, among other environmental jobs. The men were collected together and sent to work camps in the countryside for 6–12 month stints. To maintain their jobs, they were required to remain in the camps as well as send a bulk of their income back to their family. The CCC became one of the most popular forms of work relief efforts and eventually employed between two and three million men.

Public Works Administration (PWA)

In June, 1933, Congress appropriated $3.3 billion for the creation of the PWA. This was an attempt to increase employment and business activity by funding and administrating the construction of airports, naval warships, large electricity-generating dams, schools, and hospitals. The PWA remained active throughout the 1930s. Although it employed hundreds of thousands of Americans, the PWA was accused of corruption as it was difficult to account for the distribution of money. Some accused the PWA of diverting money from the private sector and hindering the stimulation of the economy. These critics argued that the creation of private sector jobs were inhibited or destroyed due to the government-initiated work created by the PWA.

Tennessee Valley Authority (TVA)

The Tennessee River Valley suffered severely through the Depression and became one of the most poverty-stricken areas in the country. Congress, under the direction of the president, decided to address the problems in 1933 with the creation of the TVA. The TVA became an ambitious, and yet controversial, program designed to create jobs for the unemployed in the region as well as provide electricity to poor residents living in the Tennessee Valley. Through the erection of dams along the Tennessee River, the TVA extended electricity at a low cost to much of the seven-state Tennessee Valley. Private power companies in the South rallied opposition against the federal power company, proclaiming it hindered free enterprise opportunities as well as leveraged federal funds and power against them. However, the companies continually lost as local residents supported the TVA.

Recovery

During his first Hundred Days, President Roosevelt also promised the American people economic recovery. He desired to create measures that returned the economy to normalcy and find ways to fix the weaknesses in the American system. In his eagerness, Roosevelt persuaded Congress to pass measures that stretched the power of the federal government and, ultimately, challenged the limits of the U.S. Constitution. Two of his most important measures were the Agricultural Adjustment Act (AAA) and National Industrial Recovery Act (NIRA). These were only in place for a few years, as they were soon declared unconstitutional by the Supreme Court.

Agricultural Adjustment Act (AAA)

Congress created the AAA in 1933, the largest of several farm bills. In broad terms, the AAA's purpose was to reduce farm production in an effort to raise prices. The hope was that the decrease in supply would strengthen the demand and raise the overall price. However, the measure was met by the American people with skepticism and, in some cases, anger. The AAA regulated farm production of wheat, corn, cotton, tobacco, and rice as well as the milk industry. In an effort to balance supply and demand the government paid farmers subsidies to limit the growth of these crops or to not grow them at all. Farmers were also paid to destroy crops already planted and slaughter millions of cattle, pigs, sheep, and other livestock to keep supply low. Farmers were also encouraged to "sell" their crops to the government as a means to withhold it from market to wait for higher prices. The government "bought" or loaned farmers money to store the crop and, when prices were high enough, farmers sold the crops and repaid the loan. If the price did not raise high enough, the farmer kept the loan while the government stored the crop. Due to the practices of the AAA, thousands of tenant farmers and sharecroppers were forced off the land as landlords allowed large amounts of acreage to lay fallow. These displaced Americans left their homes and staggered across the nation looking for work.

The AAA ran into criticism across America as many in the public noticed the discrepancy between the storage and destruction of food and crops while men, women, and children went going to bed hungry. Critics also argued that the AAA violated the Constitution because the government was controlling an entire agricultural sector in the American economy, thus obstructing the nation's free enterprise system. In 1936, the Supreme Court ruled that the AAA was unconstitutional. The Court argued that the federal regulation of agriculture violated the rights of the states. Regulation of agriculture was considered a state power, and the federal government superseded their authority.

National Industrial Recovery Act (NIRA) and National Recovery Administration (NRA)

President Roosevelt also tried to reshape the industrial sector of the American system in an effort to alleviate the affects of the Depression. The key to the President's goal was the NIRA. The NIRA was passed in 1933 as a measure to keep wages high for workers while regulating prices and industry within the nation. Because the mass unemployment during the Depression reduced consumer demands and brought many industries to a halt, businesses that tried to survive and continue production had to cut wages and working hours. New Dealers viewed these actions as "unrestricted competition" and believed they were harmful to economic recovery and needed to be curtailed. The NIRA included several measures, such as the creation of a national public works program known as the PWA (see earlier), the right of working people to organize and engage in collective bargaining, and the development of an industrial oversight board.

In an effort to reorganize the industrial sector, the NIRA established the National Recovery Administration (NRA). The NRA created and persuaded many industries to voluntarily develop regulations, known as "codes," that set prices and established fair working conditions, thus minimizing competition and stabilizing existing industries. Industries throughout the United States wrote elaborate codes that set prices, fixed minimum wages, and set maximum weekly work hours. The federal government called for many of these industries to accept a "blanket code:" a minimum wage between 20 and 40 cents an hour, a maximum work week of 35–40 hours, and the abolition of child labor. The President hoped industries would respond to his calls for standard wages for employees and government oversight and found ways to encourage participation. Those businesses that accepted the regulations displayed the NRA Blue Eagle in their front windows, and Americans were encouraged to patronize these and shun those that opted out of the NRA codes.

One motivation behind the NRA codes was to strengthen existing industries and provide their workers with better conditions. The New Dealers were hoping the industries would respond with a social conscience to the benefit of their employees as well as help the economy. However, in contrast to helping industries establish fair codes for the good of the working class, many businesses wrote codes that served their own interests and profit motives. Other business leaders criticized the NRA as government control over private enterprise through the manipulation of fair competition. In 1935, the NIRA was declared unconstitutional by the U.S. Supreme Court. The justices ruled that the NIRA exceeded the powers that Congress could constitutionally regulate. Roosevelt was devastated with the ruling and began to look for a way to rearrange the Supreme Court to meet his needs.

FDR and the American People

President Roosevelt had a robust and charismatic personality that brought reassurance and optimism to many Americans. His promises to help the Forgotten Man as well as bring recovery to the economy helped many people to place their trust in him. Roosevelt also bolstered his connection with the American people in some concrete ways through the use of Fireside Chats and the work of his wife, Eleanor.

Fireside Chats

One of the biggest criticisms of President Hoover was that he was detached from the hardships of the American people during the first years of the Depression. Men and women throughout the nation accused Hoover of ignoring their needs and voices. When Roosevelt ran for president in 1932, he promised Americans that he would walk "hand in hand" with them as they faced the difficult roads ahead and found ways to heal the economy. Therefore, it was only natural that four days after his inauguration, on March 12, 1933, President Roosevelt met with the American people via radio for his first Fireside Chat.

President Franklin D. Roosevelt and his Fireside Chat

Library of Congress, Prints & Photographs Division, photograph by Harris & Ewing, LC-DIG-hec-47251.

Roosevelt called the men and women of the nation to gather around their radios, while he was sitting near the fireside, and listen to him as he explained his plans for the nation. These Fireside Chats became a means to speak candidly and personally to the American people in an informal manner. Roosevelt used simple language and concrete analogies as he spoke and opened his conversations with "my friends." Over the course of his presidency FDR held 30 Chats, from March 1933 to June 1944, with the first one addressing the banking emergency. In this first Fireside Chat, Roosevelt reassured Americans that the new banking measures being adopted in Congress would allow them to put their money safely back into the reopened banks rather than keep it under their mattresses.

Eleanor Roosevelt

Eleanor Roosevelt

Another way President Roosevelt stayed connected with the American people was through the travels and meetings undertaken by his wife. Eleanor Roosevelt met personally with men and women throughout the nation, hearing their stories and seeing where they lived. She broke new ground as First Lady as she traveled over 30,000 miles and met with individuals and groups in meeting halls, church basements, and parlors.

Eleanor's interests moved beyond politics as she became an activist for women's rights, an advocate for African-Americans, and a voice for the working class. She encouraged the advancement of women in the arts and in education. Her determination to include women in the political world led to the first female appointee to a New Deal agency, Ellen Woodward, as the head of the Federal Emergency Relief Administration. She also held her own press conferences, for female reporters only, and wrote a daily syndicated column for newspapers titled, *My Day*.

Eleanor also spent time visiting poverty stricken areas and tried to find ways to alleviate their suffering by encouraging Americans to write to her and share their stories. Scores of individuals and families responded who were left homeless, jobless, and hungry, and she sought to provide a written answer to each letter. Eleanor also focused energy on the youth in the country. She believed their future was directly linked to the response of the current nation's leadership. Eleanor oversaw the creation of the National Youth Administration in 1935, which provided grants to college students who agreed to work part-time and job training for those not currently enrolled in school.

Challenges to the New Deal

Although many programs and agencies were created in the first years of Roosevelt's presidency the Depression continued. Unemployment remained high and a radical mood began to spread in the nation in 1934. Many feared the Depression would never end and began to accuse the president of building huge expectations and not delivering. Various political groups began to challenge the president's policies and present alternative ideas. The nation's spotlight also revealed several radical individuals who confronted the slow economic growth and offered new plans for the nation. Some labor unions began resorting to violence in their demands for more rights and better protection for their workers. In all, the challenges to the New Deal came in various formats and through several distinct individuals. In some instances, Roosevelt responded to and adapted his plans and on other occasions, the President dismissed the challenge.

Political Challenges

The New Deal isolated groups of politicians in both parties. On the right, Republicans argued that the New Deal was too radical and undermined the democratic principles of the nation, including private property and free enterprise. They claimed that the cost of the President's plans as well as the manipulation of the economy choked the natural recovery of the markets and would inevitably create a welfare state. Democrats on the left believed the President was too soft on the corporate greed and powerful monopolies within industrial America, thus continuing the policies that led to the Depression.

In 1934, the American Liberty League was founded on the basis that the New Deal was betraying basic constitutional rights. The League argued that the individualism and freedom were decreasing and the country was moving toward a fascist form of government. Fascism was growing in Europe during this time (in Italy and Germany) and some Americans viewed it as an acceptable alternative to the economic depression in the nation. As proof of the League's claims, they argued that the AAA was a move toward a state-run economy. The League hosted a well-publicized campaign against the New Deal and helped create a gulf between Roosevelt and business leaders in the country.

Challenges to the New Deal also came from groups that promoted alternative forms of governments. The Communist and Socialist Parties were reignited during the 1930s as critics argued that capitalism had failed. These groups declared that the New Deal government worked too closely with the large business moguls which cemented the cycle of poverty in the nation. The American Communist Party (Communist Party, USA) was founded in 1919, on the heels of the Russian Revolution, and grew to its largest size in the 1930s. The Party included tens of thousands of Americans who advocated for the creation and growth of labor unions, the plight of the unemployed, and the need for African-American civil rights. The Communist Party, USA also called for the overthrow of bourgeois democracy and the destruction of capitalism in favor of the Soviet-style form of government. Although politically it did not become a national challenge to the American democratic system, the Party offered a voice for the disenchanted and a place for those alienated by their ideologies.

The Socialist Party in America began in 1901 and grew throughout the industrial age, as members railed against the power of the big monopolies and the oppression of the working class. Although during the Great Depression, the Socialist Party experienced modest growth, there was one state election that captured the attention of the nation. Famed Socialist writer, Upton Sinclair, ran for the governorship of California in 1934. The well-known author of the muckraking book, *The Jungle,* Sinclair campaigned to end poverty in California. Although Sinclair lost the election, historians argue his calls for reform influenced several of the New Deal policies.

One of the most formidable challenges to the New Deal came from within the Democratic Party. Huey Long served as governor of Louisiana from 1928 to 1932 and was elected to the U.S. Senate in 1932. Son of a Louisiana backcountry farmer, Long claimed to

Library of Congress, Prints & Photographs Division, photograph by Harris & Ewing, LC-DIG-hec-38171.

Huey P. Long

represent the voice of Midwestern farmers, poor factory workers, and struggling Southerners. As governor of Louisiana, he built roads, hospitals, and schools while using bully tactics and backroom deals to manipulate the state. Nicknamed "the Kingfish," Long controlled Louisiana by consolidating all of the power of the state government within himself.

As a politician, Long capitalized on people's anger toward the rich and called for limits on the amount of wealth an individual could attain. As a Senator, he proposed a series of bills to "soak the rich" and redistribute the wealth. The bills included bans on annual incomes over $1 million and caps on individual inheritances at $5 million. Anything over these amounts would be seized by the federal government and redistributed to the poor. In 1934, he took his famous "Share Our Wealth" campaign to the national level and began his bid for the presidency. He promoted his campaign with the slogan, "Every man a King, but no one wears a crown." His radical ideas mobilized more than 5 million people in support of his campaign. However, Long's bid for the presidency was cut short. In 1935, at the age of 42, Long was assassinated by the son-in-law of one of his opponents, Judge Benjamin Parvy. Long's ideas are often credited as influencing several of Roosevelt's New-Deal policies during his next term.

Other Challenges to the New Deal

By 1935, many big businesses had become resentful of government intervention and feared the heightened regulations and taxes that were placed upon them. Two of the largest business groups, the National Association of Manufactures and the Chamber of Commerce, openly challenged the New Deal. Businesses also feared the growing power of the labor unions. As Democrats on the Left called for more unions and the destruction of monopolies in the business sector, industrial leaders chose to move away from the President and their New-Deal affiliations.

One of the most prominent challengers to the New Deal was a popular radio priest from Detroit, named Father Charles Coughlin. His radio program, called *The Hour of Power*, drew up to 30 million listeners each week. Coughlin enthusiastically supported Roosevelt during the 1932 election and believed that the New Deal was the only viable solution to the economic depression in the country. He urged his listeners to vote for Roosevelt and hoped, because of his radio influence, that he would have the president's attention. However, after FDR won the election, the President created distance from Coughlin's radical populist ideas. In turn, Coughlin turned against the President and started to use his program to attack New-Deal policies while espousing his own radical ideology.

Coughlin's radio programs were filled with relentless attacks on the elite. He proclaimed himself the spokesman for the "common man" and blamed the financiers and international bankers, especially Jewish ones, for the Depression. Coughlin called for the nationalization of major industries, railroads, and banks in an effort to punish the private sector and free-up money for public consumption. As his radio program continued into the late 1930s, Coughlin's anti-Semitic views began to overshadow his messages. He expressed support of Adolf Hitler's National Socialism and Benito Mussolini's Fascism. Coughlin's influence began to wane near the end of the decade, and he was finally pulled from the radio waves after the start of World War II.

Second Hundred Days

After Congressional victories in 1934, President Roosevelt initiated what has been called the Second Hundred Days. This was another series of legislative reforms that tried to stimulate consumer spending. Roosevelt believed that the federal government bore the responsibility for the welfare of the individual American, and once men and women felt secure, consumer spending would jump and the Depression would end. His goal was to create a safety net so that when forces bore upon citizens that were beyond their control, such as economic depressions or social oppression, the federal government was able to provide them with support and relief. The creation of the welfare state by the President cemented the shifting political alliances of the 1930s. The working class pledged their allegiance to the Democratic Party because of the aid and support they received from the federal government.

Works Progress Administration (WPA)

In 1935, unemployment was still high and Roosevelt acknowledged the need for more jobs. Congress approved $5 billion, and Roosevelt created by executive order the Works Progress Administration (WPA). WPA jobs included public-work programs such as the construction of roads, bridges, parks, and schools as well as the employment of artists, authors, actors, and playwrights to showcase their talents. Historians were paid to write books, artists painted murals in post offices, and actors put on plays

WPA New Deal art the Clarkson S. Fisher Federal Building and U.S. Courthouse, Trenton, NJ.

for the public with WPA funds. Almost every community in the nation had some form of WPA involvement. At its height, the WPA employed 3 million people and pumped billions of dollars into the nation's economy.

However, the WPA was met with criticism from various groups around the country. Some argued that it was rife with corruption and the unequal distribution of jobs. For example, the South with the poorest Americans received the least amount of assistance from the WPA. Accusations also abounded that WPA workers were pressured to support President Roosevelt's candidates and his reelection campaign to stay employed.

Social Security

As New Dealers continued to move toward a bigger federal government with more involvement in the American economy, they shifted their attention to the elderly. Influenced by the radical musings of Huey Long and Father Coughlin, these politicians, humanitarians, and Progressives argued for universal coverage for the elderly through modest, government-funded pensions. Roosevelt, however, was hesitant to provide government money without any form of work and helped remold the plan into a self-financing model. The new model, known as the Social Security Act, was created in 1935 and struck a balance between tax contributions from workers and their employers which were paid into a pension available upon retirement.

Social Security became the keystone of Roosevelt's development of a welfare state. The Act required pensions be funded by tax contributions from workers and their employers and not government. It also issued multimillion dollar grants to states to provide assistance to the elderly, unemployment benefits for the jobless, and financial support to dependent mothers and children. The political battle over Social Security pitted advocates for the elderly and poor, leftists and Progressives against conservatives who feared it would create a population of people dependent on the government.

The Social Security Act, however, did not cover all Americans. It was nearly impossible to collect contributions from individuals employed on an irregular basis, those working in domestic areas, and agricultural laborers. Therefore, farm workers and domestic servants were excluded from these old-age pensions during the first years of the Social Security Act's enforcement. However, the limits on Social Security did not last, and the program soon expanded to include more workers as well as provide benefits to the dependents of deceased recipients. The Social Security Act was challenged for its constitutionality and upheld by the Supreme Court in 1937. It became the prominent safety net for the American people and the most important feature of Roosevelt's creation of a welfare state.

The Wagner Act and Labor Unions

The Wagner Act, officially named the National Labor Relations Act, was passed in 1935 with the purpose of providing the legal right of workers (excluding farmers and domestic workers) to organize or join labor unions with the force of the federal government behind their appeals. The Act authorized the federal government to supervise the formation of unions as well as intervene on behalf of the workers when needed. The Act also created the National Labor Relations Board (NLRB) which was responsible for sponsoring and overseeing elections for union representation. The NLRB was composed of three members, appointed by the President, to enforce employee rights. According to the Act, once the majority of workers within a company voted for a union, that union became the sole bargaining tool for the entire workforce, and the employer was forced to negotiate with its elected leaders.

The Wagner Act oversaw the expansion of union membership by at least 20%. Labor unions expanded as they included the unskilled workers employed at the assembly line factories. The creation of the Committee for Industrial Organization (CIO) was formed in 1935 under the leadership of John Lewis and became the voice for these unskilled workers. The CIO was instrumental in helping several unions expand, including the volatile development of the United Auto Workers. Union expansion usually did not happen without struggles and, sometimes violent encounters between workers and their employers.

Election of 1936

Although there were some visible signs of recovery in the nation by 1936, the Depression continued to linger. Short-term results included temporary relief for suffering Americans with government-funded jobs and federal aid to the poor. However, the jobless rate had only dropped to 17%, with more than 8 million people still unemployed, and many more Americans clamored for help to get out of the cycle of poverty in which they were enveloped. President Roosevelt entered the election of 1936 hopeful and focused on continuing his bold New-Deal programs. He showcased for the American people the successes of the New Deal through economic recovery and government reform.

Republicans chose Kansas Governor, Alfred (Alf) Landon as their presidential nominee for the election. Landon was a moderate Republican who stood against the newly enacted Social Security Act and called for a balanced budget in the federal government. The Social Security Act was very unpopular with the majority of American people and many thought Landon would win, especially after a popular opinion poll, conducted by *Literary Digest*, claimed a Landon victory. However, the election was not even close. Roosevelt won by a landslide, claiming 46 of the 48 states and 60.8% of the popular vote. The President accepted this lop-sided victory as a directive from the American people to not only continue his New-Deal policies but expand them with bold and determined change.

Court Packing

Roosevelt was infuriated when the Court ruled that the NIRA (1935) and AAA (1936) were unconstitutional, and he was fearful that other key pieces of the New Deal would also be overturned. On the docket for the Court were challenges to the constitutionality of the Social Security Act, the Wagner Act, and the SEC. Roosevelt, therefore, proposed in 1937 a reorganization of the judiciary as a means to guarantee the protection of his policies.

Roosevelt argued that the Court opposed his policies because it was filled with older, conservative judges that had been appointed by earlier Republican presidents. These judges had a "horse and buggy" mentality and hindered the progress of the nation. To offset these conservative judges, the President developed a plan that became known as "court packing." Roosevelt proposed adding one new justice for each existing judge who was over 70 years old and had served on the Court for over 10 years. Since six of the nine justices were over the age of 70, the proposal would have allowed Roosevelt to add six more justices, thus packing the Court with his appointees. The President argued that the additional judges would bring a more flexible view of the Constitution, which would help preserve his New-Deal programs.

Roosevelt underestimated the response of the American people to his court-packing scheme. Opposition to the plan was intense, from both Republicans and Democrats, and included some of his New-Deal supporters. His argument that old age hindered progress insulted many elderly Americans and the manipulation of the Court by the executive powerfueled anger and outrage. In response to the storm of protest from the public, Congress quickly defeated the bill. However, the Supreme Court justices received Roosevelt's blatant message. The Court supported the New-Deal acts before them, including the Wagner Act and Social Security Act, and began moving in a more liberal direction. Over the next four years, FDR filled the vacancies of seven justices, who resigned, retired, or died, and inevitably created a more liberal Court that supported his actions.

New-Deal Recession

President Roosevelt's public defeat of his court-packing scheme set him back in his efforts to implement more of his New-Deal policies. The administration was also hit hard by an economic shift in the nation in 1937. Due to a temporary rise in the Gross National Product in early 1937 as well as a decline in unemployment, the President believed that the Depression was finally lifting. As a result, he slowed down some of his New-Deal policies and cut funds to public works projects as well as urged the Federal Reserve to raise interest rates. However, his actions did not bring more stability to the economy. The crisis was not over, and the American nation plunged into an economic recession that last 13 months.

Because the economy had never fully recovered since the crash in 1929, the recession that hit in 1937 was not an ordinary one. During the New-Deal recession, personal incomes dropped and national production declined almost 30%. Farm prices also dropped by 20% and unemployment rate jumped from 14.3% to 19%. The economic gains produced since 1933 dramatically declined in just a few months. Critics blamed the President and his New-Deal policies, claiming that businessmen were holding onto their capital out of fear of the unsound economy. They also argued that the higher taxes many businesses were paying, due to the newly implemented Social Security Act, was hurting the economy and removing money from the market. Critics also argued that the recession proved that New Deal policies did not work because they created primarily government-funded jobs that did not help resurrect the private sector. They argued that the earlier progress created by the New Deal was an illusion.

On the other hand, New Dealers blamed the wealthy businessmen for deliberately refusing to invest their capital, creating what they called a "capital strike." By withholding their money from the economy, they hindered investments which deterred growth in the economy. New Dealers also criticized the President for implementing a more conservative fiscal policy when he tried to balance the budget by cutting public works projects. They pressed that more government involvement was needed to pull the country out of the Depression. They encouraged the President to resurrect federal spending to stimulate the economy.

As arguments swirled regarding the economic course of action for the nation, the theories of British economist, John Maynard Keynes, joined the conversation. Keynes's recently published book, *The General Theory of Employment, Interest, and Money* (1936), argued that government deficit spending would bring soundness to the economy by getting consumers to buy more. Accordingly, as the government intervened and pumped more money into the market consumer buying would revive. He believed that the private sector could not heal the nation on its own; it needed government help, even if the government incurred more debt. Keynes also believed that the President needed to tap into the wealthy businessmen of the nation and use them to help spur economic activity. In a letter he wrote in 1938, Keynes noted that if the President harnessed the "wolves and tigers" of private enterprise, that is, the wealthy businessmen in the country, and treated them better, as "domestic animals by nature, even though they have been badly brought up and not trained as you wish" he could once again encourage their involvement in the economic market. Keynes' work influenced a significant number of the nation's politicians and economists in the years to come. Keynesian economics also became a cornerstone for the Democratic Party.

Neglected Americans under the New Deal

As the implementation of the New Deal continued throughout the 1930s, many working people remained untouched by its initiatives. The New Deal provided its best protection for those workers in major industries and participants of labor unions while millions of other Americans continued to suffer. Analysts argued that the New Deal created a two-tier system of welfare. The top tier included organized workers while the bottom tier included African-Americans, women, children, and the unskilled and uneducated.

African-Americans suffered the most during the Depression with an unemployment rate that doubled the national rate and racial injustices rampant in the nation. The New Deal offered little to help them. Black workers who belonged to unions or lived in the North benefited the most from the government policies. However, those men and women living in the rural South, the majority of the African-American population, endured extreme hardship. Black workers employed by public works programs, such as the WPA, were paid less than white workers and assumed only a handful of the vast supervisory positions available.

The TVA refused to hire black employees and most of the sharecroppers and tenant farmers in the South, who were overlooked in the New-Deal farm programs, were often pushed off their land as farmers were paid by the government to leave large lots of land fallow. Coupled with these neglects was the virile racism in the South.

Domestic workers and women in the textile mills were also neglected under the New Deal. These women worked in unsafe conditions for long hours and little pay and received none of the benefits of government aid or access to unions. Their work was overlooked by the government, as most of the public works jobs were geared toward men and included large construction projects. These "invisible women" were continually slighted throughout the next several decades.

Hispanic Americans and Native Americans were also excluded from New-Deal policies. Hispanics had access to some unions, and those who joined benefited from the laws protecting them. But most Mexicans worked in agricultural areas as low-paying field workers. Their income declined substantially as farmers struggled and lost their land. Local and state governments cracked down on Mexican aliens during the Depression also, and eventually sent 500,000 men and women back to Mexico. Native Americans also suffered as the poorest of the American population and received no help from the President's policies. However, there was a dramatic shift in Indian policy under the New Deal. The Indian Reorganization Act (IRA) was established in 1934 and allowed Indian tribes once again the right to own their land and have greater control over their own affairs. The IRA reversed the Dawes Act of 1887, which removed Native Americans from reservations in an effort to help them assimilate into American culture. The IRA also helped prevent further depletion of reservation resources and create new reservations for those tribes who voted for its application.

Conclusion

The Great Depression challenged the national, political, and economic systems of America. After the crash of the stock market in 1929, most Americans looked to family members and friends for help, believing that the crisis would soon end. However, the Depression worsened. By 1932, men and women began to clamor for relief as many blamed President Hoover for government inaction and the suffering they were enduring. Roosevelt's election, however, brought promises of the relief, recovery, and reform to the nation. His optimism and charisma buoyed the American spirit and his plan called the New Deal promised hope.

President Roosevelt's policies of the New Deal have been debated by historians since their inception. The New Deal drastically increased the power of the federal government with massive spending bills and limited control over various economic sectors. It also shored up sound banks, started large public works programs, and brought a semblance of stability to agriculture. Although the unemployed rate dropped by only 10% (from 25% to 15%) during the 1930s the President argued that his policies would work in time. As the decade wore on, however, he was faced with challenges from the U.S. Supreme Court,

Democrats in his own Party, conservative Republicans, and business leaders. However, Roosevelt continued to forge ahead with his policies and paved the American road for a stronger and more involved federal government.

America's attention began to shift away from the problems at home during the late 1930s as it witnessed the rise of new, and potentially dangerous, powers in Europe. The formation of fascism, under Benito Mussolini in Italy and Adolf Hitler in Germany, began to threaten European and American security. The policies of the National Socialist Party (Nazi) under Hitler catapulted Germany into the international spotlight as it became the first nation out of the Depression and cemented the popularity of the leader. America did not realize it yet, but the year 1939 was about to change its focus from battling against the Depression at home to warring against belligerent nations around the world.

CHAPTER SEVENTEEN

World War II

Chapter 17: Key Concepts

○ What characteristics stand out most as proving vital to defining the European sector of the war and its ultimate outcomes? What is your reasoning for choosing these factors?

○ What characteristics stand out most as proving vital to defining the Asian sector of the war and its ultimate outcomes? What is your reasoning for choosing these factors?

○ Who is the most intriguing historical figure from this time period in your view and what is your reasoning behind the choice?

Introduction

World War II was one of the most volatile periods in world history. There were many actors in this greatest of dramas. It unleashed a myriad of changes after the war's conclusion that are still felt in the present. Throughout the 1930s and 1940s, people around the globe lived and died during the greatest war in history. World War II came at a cost of tens of millions of dead and wounded. The conflict also came at a price of hundreds of billions of dollars. However, sheer numbers can only begin to tell the story. Even for those who never served in harm's way, the reality of the war was always ever present. Some people lost their entire families, fortunes, and even sanity. It was even a more horrible and calamitous event than World War I.

World War II was an era that impacted every common citizen of the world, and a few leaders became icons due to their military service. In the United States, the media coverage of the conflict came to people by way of newspapers, radio broadcasts, and film footage. In these diverse portrayals, battle scenes were explained, and in the case of victories, celebrated. Within the media coverage, the war-tested soldier represented the height of courage and patriotic sacrifice. However, the leading American figures of the period became the most powerful icons representing the western war effort. Among these were Generals Omar Bradley, Dwight Eisenhower, George Marshall, Douglas MacArthur, and George Patton. However, without the many millions of average military and civilian workers, these men would have never reached such tremendous acclaim. Moreover, the war could have turned out in a far different manner.

The Road to War in the European Theater

Isolationism and appeasement were the twin ideologies that most often characterized the pre-war period. Isolationism was an approach to diplomacy where nations took a minimalist approach to global interaction beyond those activities which fit their own specific interests. Such a plan de-emphasized more internationalist strategies such as collective security and global diplomacy. Throughout the 1920s and much of the 1930s, the United States took on a largely isolationist agenda regarding foreign affairs. The concept of appeasement involved approaching global policy with a "lesser of multiple evils" strategy. Appeasement meant compromising with potential enemy combatants instead of confronting them in order to avoid conflict. Ravaged by World War I, the Great Depression, and the costs of maintaining international colonies, England and France took on appeasement as a plan to smooth over growing diplomatic difficulties in the 1930s.

In the 1920s, Germany was governed under a democratic constitutional system. The harsh penalties from the aftermath of World War I had left Germany with a severely weakened military and economy. The Great Depression further brought economic and societal difficulties to Germany's long list of hardships. Surging unemployment, inflation, and food shortages left the German people looking for a new approach to their governing structure. Amid these difficult times, the Nazi Party rose to political power. Adolph Hitler was

Adolph Hitler

the public face and leader of this upstart group. He had served as a corporal in World War I for his native Austria, and then joined the Nazis in the early 1920s. Subsequently, he was arrested as part of a failed government political insurrection in the German region of Bavaria. This incident, popularly known as the Beer Hall Putsch, led to the arrest of Hitler. During his time in jail, he authored a manifesto entitled Mein Kampf (My Struggle). In this work, Hitler explained a comprehensive strategy for building a racially pure Nazi empire.

The Nazis seized on existing racial prejudice and theories about history to build support and define their program. Anti-Semitism was an unfortunate tradition throughout Europe and particularly in Austria where Hitler was raised. For the Nazis, Jews were a foreign people not included in the Volk (the Folk, or the masses) of Germany. Nazis preached that Germans were the true heirs of a pure race called the Aryans, and it was influence by outsiders that kept their nation from dominating the world. To reach global superiority, Hitler encouraged Germans have lots of offspring, and in addition, he endorsed the nation adding more territorial living space to accommodate them. Therefore, Hitler envisioned increasing Germany's borders. Also, Nazism was a form of fascism whereby one pledged total allegiance to the state. Germans would be tutored from birth that service to the mother country was important beyond all other considerations. Hitler's government would become heavily involved in private enterprise to ensure that all efforts were aimed at strengthening Germany. Combined, the Nazi program meant that Germany must be heavily armed, productive in industry, territorially expansive, and free of any group or individuals who were not thought of as naturally belonging to the German "race." This was a disastrous vision for the world.

It is one thing to have a set of goals, as did Hitler, and it is another to successfully put them into practice. Indeed, the Nazis obtained legitimacy in Germany over a short period in the early 1930s. They did so via the German people voting them in as part of a political coalition in the nation's legislative assembly, the Reichstag. Once in power, the Nazis used force and extra-legal persuasion to eliminate other political groups and takeover the German government. Adolph Hitler held the position of chancellor and he was the central figure in what fast developed into a brutal, dictatorial regime.

The democracies of the western world allowed Germany to rebuild their military and economy. The strong sanctions of World War I got cast aside. Instead, nations such as England and France chose to try and appease a potential threat with immediate gratification in the hope it would mean a less likely chance for another total war. In addition, the United States, in its continuing isolated state, focused on domestic economic rebuilding during most of the 1930s. However, the country did have, in President Franklin Roosevelt, a more internationally inclined Commander-in-Chief. Later in the 1930s, this development led to a more active American involvement in the prewar diplomatic process.

Germany found a willing ally in Italy. After World War I, Benito Mussolini's fascist regime came into power. He brought together a nation in want of a return to prosperous times. As had been the case for other European countries after World War I, Italy suffered great economic hardship and political turmoil. Mussolini promised to correct these issues. In reality, he used a fascist dictatorship to preach nationalism and cement his totalitarian rule. Fascism was a doctrine that emphasized loyalty and obedience to state. These types of regimes were by nature militaristic with an extreme nationalist outlook. Nazism and Italian fascism had many similarities but were not the same. The promises Mussolini boldly proclaimed never actually occurred. He aspired to turn Italy into the central piece of a new Mediterranean-based empire. Instead, his advisors implemented a brutal plan of action and provided a compatible secondary wartime partner to Germany. While they played a pertinent role in the conflict, Italy's inferior military armaments, leadership, and number of forces kept them from fulfilling Mussolini's vision.

In Europe, 1937–1938 proved to be a very tenuous and foreboding year. During this time, Germany declared a union with Austria, and in turn, Nazis took over the national government. Then, under the mantra of Germanic unity, the Nazis sought to take over of the Sudetenland region of Czechoslovakia. The area had many Germanic people and a useful industrial base, and therefore, Germany saw it as a good fit for its ongoing prewar building process. The Nazi's aspirations to annex the Sudetenland led to the ultimate example of appeasement diplomacy. With the Munich Pact, four nations: Germany, England, France, and Italy developed an agreement to resolve the growing storm of war in Europe. In total, the Munich Pact allowed Germany to take over the Sudetenland and subsequently the entirety of Czechoslovakia.

Despite France having previously agreed to a mutual security treaty with the Czechs, this new plan dismantled that arrangement. For their part, Germany agreed to stop its growing war plans and maintain a calm diplomatic stance with its fellow European nations. Many international press and diplomatic outlets commended the agreement. Notably, British Prime Minister Neville Chamberlain, who played a very key role in negotiating the plan, stated that the conference had yielded "peace for our time." In reality, the Munich Pact would not serve as a lasting arrangement. Instead, Germany continued readying for achieving greater imperialistic objectives.

Along with the Munich Pact, Germany negotiated another diplomatic agreement with the Soviet Union. The 1939 German Soviet Non-Aggression Pact publically assured a truce between the two countries. Privately, they agreed to divide up Poland along an east/west geographical line. In turn, Germany secured the right to initiate war on their portion of Poland, and the Soviet Union received territorial concessions. This plan worked for the communist government of the Soviet Union. Under the leadership of Josef Stalin, they had enacted an extremely brutal system of mass internal political imprisonment and murders. To many western countries, Soviet communism was every bit as worrisome as Nazi Germany. To Hitler, the Soviet Union was a central piece to establishing a dominant empire in Europe. The nation had the natural resources, land, and population to form an industrial juggernaut. Unbeknownst to Soviet leaders, Germany planned to take these things by force.

Josef Stalin

In September 1939, World War II began in Europe, and Germany's invasion of Poland officially set it into motion. The move forced England and France to declare war on Germany and vice versa. The doctrine of appeasement had allowed Germany to prepare for the conflict in a much better manner than its opponents. Throughout 1940, Germany rolled over European nations. Even a traditionally formidable military power in France was no real match for the onslaught. Germany used a lethal combination of modern armed forces weaponry and frenetic pacing in a strategy dubbed blitzkrieg or "lightening war." It also was implementing a brutal series of air assaults on England. As a result of the ongoing crisis in Europe, England reached out to the United States for assistance. Ultimately, inquiries and communication between the two nations led to the establishment of the 1941 Lend Lease Act. Under the legislation, the United States could send a wide variety of war supplies and funding to England. Later that year, the law was expanded to include another European nation in need of assistance: the Soviet Union.

Germany had long planned to launch a massive invasion of the Soviet Union. Its vast natural resources and population base represented a vital cog in Hitler's designs to rule Europe. In June 1941, this strategy became a reality. Over the next several months, Germany pillaged the Soviet Union with massive levels of destruction and casualties. By late 1941, this caused the United States to increase the Lend Lease program to include the Soviets. Over the war's entirety, the Lend Lease program eventually expanded to several dozen nations and a nearly 50 billion dollar cost.

This expansive assistance effort proved to be a controversial policy. In reaction to the growing emphasis by the Roosevelt administration and other internationalists, those that favored a more isolationist stance went on the offensive. In September 1940, the America' First Committee formed, and its primary agenda was to advocate against the U.S. involvement in World War II. Through public rallies, radio programs, and newspaper articles, the group endorsed their plan for staying out of the growing conflict. The America First Committee endorsed several policies to allow the nation to stand strong and neutral from the quagmire brewing in Europe. These actions included improving American defenses at home to repel against potential foreign invaders and avoiding any assistance or involvement in the ongoing European war. At its peak, the America First Committee claimed more than 800,000 members. While they were vocal and influential, the group did not last past the watershed events of the Japanese bombing of Pearl Harbor. The organization disbanded several days after it took place.

The Road to War in the Pacific Theater

Along with Germany, the United States and other global powers faced a growing 1930s diplomatic crisis in Asia. At the heart of the issue was Japan and its growing intention to become a self-sustaining empire. Over the previous eight decades, Japan and western countries, including the United States, had developed a productive diplomatic and trade relationship. However, in the 1920s and 1930s, a new generation of militaristic, nationalistic, and imperialistic policy makers took over the government. As such, the alliance between Japan and western nations

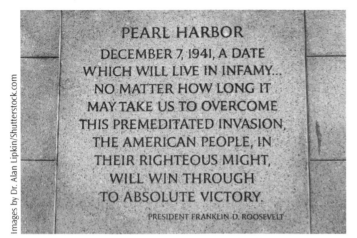

Speech that President Franklin Roosevelt made after Japanese attack on Pearl Harbor is an inscription on the wall of the World War II Memorial on the National Mall in Washington, D.C.

gradually tore apart. Japan's new regime led the government toward a very aggressive path in global affairs. They wanted to be on an even footing with the western powers in all regards. As a result, Japan endeavored for a greater internal base of industrial capabilities, natural resources, agriculturally arable land, and laborers. Thus, Japan began propagandizing and planning for a takeover of the Asian mainland.

Under the guise of cultural and regional betterment, Japan wanted China and other smaller nations to be the heart of a modern empire of epic proportions. The diplomatic and economic consequences of such an agenda gave the United States and other western nations a great deal of collective stress. In 1937 and 1938, Japan ramped up toward war. The July 1937 invasion of China, December 1937 sinking of the U.S. Gunboat Panay, and December 1938 siege of the Chinese city of Nanking all demonstrated Japan was dedicated to an ambitious and violent takeover of Asia. The "Rape of Nanking" resulted in over 200,000 civilian casualties and caused great international outrage. Nonetheless, Japan continued on in its imperial expansion strategy.

During the period 1939–1941, the United States continued to experience heightened tensions with Japan. While diplomatic negotiations proceeded, the two countries continued to hit a figurative wall over Japanese expansion and military aggression in Asia. The United States decided to enact numerous economic sanctions against Japan. Among these very serious measures, America discontinued the trade of steel and petroleum with them. These were both vital elements for the Japanese war machine, and therefore, this new reality led Japan into a mode of taking military action against the United States.

On December 7, 1941 Japan initiated an aerial military attack on American naval and air armed forces personnel in Hawaii. This use of force at Pearl Harbor led to more than 2,400 American casualties. In addition, the incident caused the destruction of 18 American warships and over 300 U.S. airplanes. The Japanese military action also largely solidified American unity toward going to war. Over the next several days, the United States formally declared intentions to enter the global war effort on the side of the Allied Forces. As 1942 dawned, the European theater contained the continent of Europe, North Africa, and the Middle East as primary battle grounds. In the Pacific theater, the continent of Asia and seemingly countless Pacific and Indian Ocean-based nations and territories provided the main areas of conflict. However, one must also include naval and aerial phases as areas of fighting too. Indeed, this was a war that would be fought in all places and ways possible.

The Active War Period: American Involvement in the European Theater

In 1942, the first full year of American involvement in the European theater, major Allied nations consisted of the United States, Great Britain, and the Soviet Union. The United States and Britain spent a great deal of effort battling Germany and Italy in Western Europe, the Mediterranean, Africa, and the Middle East. In Eastern Europe, the Soviet Union served as the primary warfront. In the shared American and British areas of responsibility of the European theater, Allied forces steadily made positive progress in early and mid-1943. By the summer of that year, the Allies readied and began a major military offensive in Italy. Involving more than 500,000 man force, the campaign traveled from south to north into the heart of Italy. Eventually, an over nine-month effort resulted in the Allies taking back the strategic city of Rome. However, the victory came at a high price as the ongoing battles resulted in several hundred thousand Allied casualties. As their plans further evolved, the Allies took back numerous key targets throughout the Mediterranean, North Africa, and the Middle East. Throughout 1943 and 1944, these victorious battles were positioning the landscape for a major western push geared at finalizing Allied victory in Europe.

As the Americans and British made positive inroads, the Soviet Union pushed back against Germany. From 1942 through 1944, the Russian people survived a series of massive military assaults, suffered millions of casualties, and lost many billions of dollars in infrastructure. However, the fire of battle steeled the Russian citizenry, and over time, they managed to take the fight to their German opponents. Over the course of the war, the Soviet Union had created an incredibly strong and modernized industrial economy, and they developed an equally impressive military arsenal. Given these factors, the Soviet Union transitioned from a defensive to offensive philosophy and forced Germany into a steady, violent, and clear retreat. As a result, by the spring of 1944, the campaign that became known as D-Day was being readied in Western Europe and the push from Eastern Europe was firmly in motion, as well.

Omaha Beach after D-Day. Protected by barrage balloons, ships, delivered trucks loaded with supplies. June 7–10, 1944, World War II. Normandy, France

When it came to securing the Western European landscape, the Allies needed to force the German military back eastward to Berlin and out of France. The D-Day operation included an extraordinarily complex level of tactical strategy, covert intelligence gathering, and a plentiful and diverse array of military forces and weaponry. In addition, the level of support logistics and supply gathering was also an unprecedented undertaking. Indeed, this would either be the high point or nadir of the Allied forces' overall war effort. Throughout 1943 and the first part of 1944, the Allies developed a sound strategy and militarily cleared the path for the western push. A big part of this plan included regular aerial bombardment of Germany's industrial sector. In turn, this began draining the German military of the steel, petroleum, and other key resources needed to survive a total war.

After months of meetings and groundwork, June 1944 became the time for launching the D-Day invasion. Throughout the early waves of the attack, the Allies utilized over 150,000 soldiers, 12,000 airplanes, 7,000 naval vessels, and thousands more tanks and other assorted ground-based vehicles. Over the forthcoming months, the Allies deployed several million troops into France. These soldiers risked their lives, and many came home wounded or lost their lives in an incredibly brutal and ultimately successful military campaign.

The D-Day invasion, part of Operation Overlord, was the largest military naval landing in the history of the world. Beaches known as Normandy, Omaha, and others had to be taken one-by-one. The sands were drenched in blood as heavy German guns, snipers, and foot-soldiers barraged Allied forces with storms of deadly fire. Men who made their way onto the beaches knew that many would not make it through the conflict alive. D-Day is one of, if not the, most iconic American military engagements of all time. It was what had to be done to liberate France and conquer Nazi Germany. It also was a major gamble. In wartime, sea landings or crossings always make one vulnerable to a potential disaster. The seas have the power to change at any time, strand, or isolate soldiers. It was the ultimate gamble, but it proved fruitful toward the goal of winning the war.

In the late summer of 1944, Allied forces launched further successful forays in the Mediterranean, and pushed forward to free Belgium and France from German occupation. These efforts yielded great gains, but several more months of arduous warfare lay ahead. In the last weeks of 1944, Germany attacked the Allies near their western border. The Battle of the Bulge represented a final German opportunity to create an offensive strategy against their opponents. The ongoing fight inflicted over 80,000 plus casualties on the Allies. However, they maintained a stable foothold against Germany, and in the end, their side proved victorious in the Battle of the Bulge. In the final months of the war in Europe, the Allies pushed further and squeezed Germany into an eventual surrender. Ultimately, the Nazi regime fell in the spring of 1945.

The Active War Period: American Involvement in the Pacific Theater

While the war in Europe raged forward, the fighting in the Pacific proved just as violent and nightmarish. Both sides consistently demonstrated a strong will to win and at times to just survive. In the aftermath of the attack on Pearl Harbor, the United States joined the Allies against the Japanese in an all-out military campaign. Within the United States, people felt a great deal of rage toward Japan. American newspapers, magazines, cartoons, books, and radio programming railed against Japan in the harshest of terms. The media used patriotic, religious, musical, humorous, and a plethora of other approaches to create written and audio messages lambasting Japan. These collective efforts were a powerful affront to the Japanese while endorsing calls for unity, vengeance, and victory. In the case of Japan's approach to propaganda, their efforts demonstrated a similar multifaceted approach to decrying the United States and endorsing national support of the total war effort.

From the start of active engagement, the Allies sought to retake islands in the Pacific, and over time they wanted to wear down the Japanese military toward an eventual invasion of their home islands. For their part, throughout 1942 the Japanese continued launching further offensives in the Pacific and Asian mainland. Their military invaded and took over areas such as the Philippines, Hong Kong, and Burma. Also, as the year progressed, the Allies and Japan exchanged firepower in a series of key aerial and naval battles. Fought in May 1942, the Battle of the Coral Sea ended with each side sustaining one lost aircraft carrier. In addition, Japan endured significant destruction to several more of their war ships. The Battle of Midway took place in June 1942. During this conflict, Allied forces totally devastated four Japanese aircraft carriers, and in turn, this Allied victory proved to be one of the important turning points in the war.

From these engagements forward, the Allies utilized efficient aerial and naval strategy to develop and keep the upper hand against the Japanese. These ongoing setbacks made it very difficult for Japan to keep a secure territorial foothold. Owing to a lack of natural resources and manufacturing capabilities, the Japanese did not have the quantity of assets needed to continually rebuild their air and naval stockpile. Contrastingly, the Allies, particularly the United States, maintained a significant depth of strength in these vital areas. Thus, this clear advantage went a long way toward securing the Allies eventual victory in the war. However, Japan did not completely abandon its aerial efforts. In lieu of conventional attacks, they deployed suicide air missions to inflict damage on Allied ships. These missions were called Kamikazes, and although only a fraction of them achieved direct impact, the worst ones resulted in destruction, lost vessels, and casualties. However, Allied personnel took many of them down before the intended goal was fulfilled.

USS Bunker Hill aircraft carrier was hit by two Kamikazes in 30 seconds, May 11, 1945

Everett Historical/Shutterstock.com

Throughout 1943, the Allies developed and launched complex attacks on Japanese held strongholds in the Pacific. These offensives utilized air personnel, warships, and land soldiers to steadily take islands in the Pacific. Once secured, the Allies used them as key supply stations and airplane landing strips. By late 1944, Allied troops had regained numerous key islands, and in turn, they were progressing forward in the direction of the Japanese. With their voyage toward Japan, the Allies implemented a strategy deemed island hopping.

This resulted in positive territorial results but also numerous casualties in what was horrific fighting.

In the spring of 1945, the Allies battled Japanese troops at Iwo Jima and Okinawa. These conflicts represented the height of the vicious fighting that characterized the island-hopping campaign. The total casualty count for both sides was more than 46,000 soldiers at Iwo Jima and 165,000 troops at Okinawa. Along with the high casualty rate, island hopping required engaging opposition forces in a maze of jungles, trenches, marsh, garrisons, and several more natural and man-made challenges. This often meant engaging in direct combat amidst unknown and difficult surroundings. The collective rage and fortitude of both sides spilled onto the battle fields as the Japanese grew increasingly desperate. Both sides were committed to sustaining war until the last man standing was eliminated.

The Allies combined retaking of Pacific islands with an aggressive and around the clock series of bombing operations on Japanese urban and industrial sectors. Their mission was to cause total devastation to key military installations, manufacturing areas, and heavily populated confines. As a result, these raids created extremely high civilian casualty totals. This was not a coincidence. Indeed, there was a psychological element to the strategy. Specifically, the Allies wanted to force Japan into a state of despair and then unconditional surrender. Simply put, they sought to bomb them into complete submission. The best example of the nature of this objective occurred on the evenings of March 9 and 10, 1945. Over those two nights, Allied bombing leveled over 16 square miles in and around Tokyo. In addition, the death toll exceeded more than 100,000 people. Throughout the forthcoming months, the Japanese people suffered an extremely high rate of civilian deaths and loss of infrastructure. However, the nation's military and government leaders remained committed to the ongoing war effort.

Harry Truman bronze bust in the Missouri State Capitol, Jefferson City, Missouri

Nagel Photography/Shutterstock.com

Ultimately, the summer of 1945 proved to be the final act of the war in the Pacific. In April 1945, President Roosevelt had passed away. In his place, Vice President Harry Truman came into power. Like the vast majority of Americans, Truman had been in the dark regarding key classified military measures of the ongoing war effort. Among those programs was a program to build an atomic weapon. Upon taking office, Truman found out about the Manhattan Project and its specific parameters. Over several months, he consulted other Allied leaders and his own advisors over the potential of utilizing atomic bombs to force the Japanese into an unconditional surrender.

The alternative plan was to continue implementing a conventional invasion strategy. The continuing bombing efforts of Japan's main land had inflicted a great deal of human and economic damage. However, the concept of an Allied amphibious to ground landing was still several months away. The two part plan was scheduled to be rolled out in the late fall of 1945 (Operation Olympic) and early spring of 1946 (Operation Coronet). In terms of manpower, supplies, and weaponry, it would have been a larger scale version of the D-Day Operation. The war would have likely been extended into 1947, and in turn, could have led to a high casualty rate. The great human loss totals of the island hopping campaign concerned Truman and other key decision makers. The extension of the brutal fighting by one to two more years meant a finish to the conflict would still be well down the road. More than anything else, the risk of losing hundreds of thousands of Allied troops tilted the decision toward the nuclear option.

The Manhattan Project was a classified project aimed at developing nuclear weapons. The main area of production was in Los Alamos, NM. Oak Ridge, TN and Hanford, WA housed other key facilities. These otherwise quiet outposts became the secretive center of revolutionary scientific progress. Between late 1942 and mid-1945, the process of creating an ultimate weapon of destruction took place. The process involved more than 120,000 people and came at a cost of two billion dollars. Owing to the high security measures of the program, only a small group of people involved in its production were aware of the end goal of the process.

Photo of Hiroshima bomb explosion taken in Kure, Japan, August 6, 1945

The Allies decided to use two atomic bombs on the Japanese mainland. The first of these weapons, nicknamed "Little Boy," was dropped on August 6, 1945. The target area was Hiroshima, Japan. Almost instantaneously, a vast majority of the city was leveled. In addition, the bomb led to the immediate deaths of almost 80,000 people, and wounded another 30,000. The powerful blast did not force a submission from the Japanese. A second atomic bomb, nicknamed "Fat Man," was dropped on August 9, 1945. The target area was Nagasaki, Japan. Upon impact, it killed over 60,000 people and caused an untold amount of damage to the surrounding area. Finally, the Japanese government surrendered on August 15, 1945, and this became known as Victory in Japan Day. Several weeks later, Japan signed an official document of surrender agreement on September 2, 1945.

The American Home Front: Economic Developments

Perhaps the biggest advantage America brought to the Allies were enormous capabilities regarding agricultural and industrial production. In turn, igniting these production sectors allowed the U.S. economy to finally escape economic depression. Statistics help to paint the picture of the gap between America and its Axis opponents. For example, by the last year of the war in 1945 the United States manufactured over 88,000 tanks compared to

Germany's output of just over 44,000. In regards to airplane manufacturing, America rolled out just under 300,000 whereas Japan only produced about 70,000.

The federal government exerted a great deal of control and organization regarding overall production of goods for the war. However, officials also realized they needed to be on the same page as major businesses to avoid unwanted conflicts and holdups. As a result, federal planning leaders implemented policies such as: a suspension of competitive bidding, low-interest loans for equipment, and tax incentives for new or expansionary construction projects. For their part, manufacturers adjusted production focus to fit the war effort's needs. For example, Ford Motor Company became a primary producer of military aircraft instead of family automobiles.

The agricultural sector also experienced increased economic growth. The federal government increased the cap on crop prices. This caused agricultural income to experience a growth rate of several hundred percent. One weakness to this financial prosperity is that it tended to favor large farms and agricultural corporations. Therefore, during the war, many smaller farming families chose to trade their agricultural careers for manufacturing jobs. On the whole, Americans' war time income levels rose several hundred percent. This represented a distinct change from the financial doldrums of several years earlier. In total, American job creation exploded, and millions of previously unemployed individuals found work.

However, there was a downside to the period's economic changes. Specifically, there were noticeable inflation increases and product shortages. After 1941, prices rose by nearly 20%. In addition, the military's high level of need for key materials such as glass and steel forced the federal government to suspend manufacturing of regular consumer items. Those items that became temporarily unavailable included vacuums, radios, and automobiles. Rationing efforts included even the smallest of items too, and people had to measure purchases of relatively inexpensive things like tooth paste, coffee, and soap.

Created in 1942, the Office of Price Administration controlled a great deal of policy pertaining to costs and rationing. This authority covered all varieties of products including food, shoes, and gas. Every person in the nation received food ration ledgers. Amounts of food rations were very specific and listed on per person basis. For example, meat rations totaled 28 ounces a week per person. Americans had to adjust to these sacrifices. However, the economic hardships of the previous decade's Great Depression conditioned many people to be capable of surviving with less. In addition, the nation's attitude toward attaining victory in the war built a spirit of unity that made such rationing an acceptable practice.

The American Home Front: Social Developments

One of the most unfortunate domestic issues of the World War II period involved the internment, or forced removal into camps, of Japanese people in America. There was a great deal of paranoia, prejudice, and outright disdain toward anyone of Japanese descent.

Tension ran high enough to make internment camps a reality. In February 1942, President Roosevelt signed an executive order to make this an official policy, and it remained in place through the end of the conflict. Over 127,000 Japanese people became forced occupants of these camps. Over time, there were 10 internment sites spread over 7 states. As camps were being constructed, Japanese people had to stay in various temporary places like horse barns. However, even the permanent encampments did not have acceptable modern living conditions. Things such as living quarters, schools, and cafeterias severely lacked in quality. Those interned had the ability to work for about five dollars a day, and they formed

Interned Japanese American, Sumiko Shigematsu, standing at left, supervises fellow internees working at sewing machines at Manzanar Relocation Center, California

advocacy groups to share complaints and recommendations about the camps. However, these matters often received very little government attention. Ultimately, a federal legal challenge regarding the internment camps went to the U. S. Supreme Court. However, the court ruled in favor of the federal government. Ultimately, Japanese internment occupants did not receive reparation payments until the late 1980s.

Throughout the conflict, women dealt with various changes. The armed forces arranged female-specific jobs and groups of servicewomen. By the end of the war, more than a quarter of a million women had become members of these units. Some of the more prominent ones included the Women's Army Corps (WAC), Women Accepted for Voluntary Emergency Service (WAVES), and the Army and Navy Nursing Corps. The positions designated for women were non-combat in nature. Clerical and nursing jobs became primary professional roles for them in the military. On the American home front, there was a great deal of transition for females, too. Specifically, women entered the workforce in greater numbers than ever before. With the surge of men required for war-time military service, over six million females flooded into various professions.

Millions of African-Americans served in the military and became employed on the home front. They also faced discrimination and segregation in both sectors. The Roosevelt administration responded to political outcry with an executive order that created a group called the Fair Employment Practices Commission. In addition, this spearheaded a policy to prohibit discrimination in defense industry civilian jobs. Moreover, a postwar result became a greater public support for further civil rights reforms. In the immediate years after World War II, integration of the armed forces and a litany of civilian sectors became a reality.

The Tragic Legacy of War Time Atrocities

In the 1930s, the Jewish population of Germany was being stripped of property and generally of their human rights. The United States did not offer a cohesive plan to help them. There were American political leaders that favored lifting a federal cap on foreign refugees, and as such, this could have provided German Jews exile in the United States. However, the ongoing economic depression kept this policy from becoming a reality. Specifically, political leaders believed increasing the total allowed number of refugees would displace American-born workers already struggling to secure work. Moreover, there was a history of prejudice against Jewish people, and this reality also hurt their chances for assistance.

Roll call at Buchenwald concentration camp, ca. 1938–1941. Two prisoners in the foreground are supporting a comrade, as fainting was frequently an excuse for guards to "liquidate" useless inmates

Everett Historical/Shutterstock.com

As the decade progressed, Nazi leaders forced a variety of personal and professional restrictions upon German Jews. These included educational segregation, property confiscation, and baseless imprisonment. As the 1930s came to end, things became worse, and Germany began implementing forced relocation of Jewish people. The Nazis quarantined Jews into sections of German cities that were called ghettos. Then, Nazis began to construct concentration camps to house Jews and others deemed inferior. Soon afterward, this policy extended to Jews from all over Europe. Some of the encampments were work stations where victims endured forced labor on various projects. Within these groups, many people died from exhaustion. Other camps were extermination centers where millions of murders took place, and these mass executions were the most vivid embodiment of the Holocaust. Those killed included people from various ethnic groups as well as homosexuals, the disabled, and others. The highest casualty totals were those of Jewish and Slavic ethnicity. Countless others never made it to camps and were murdered, throughout Europe, by roving Nazi-hit squads.

The discoveries made in the latter part of the war revealed the Nazi prison encampments and all their associated horrors. In Europe, the Nuremberg Trials laid out the historical chronicles of the Holocaust in an in-depth manner. Many of the chief purveyors of the Holocaust were imprisoned and executed. In Asia, there were also many atrocities committed against the civilian populations. Japanese soldiers murdered and pillaged all across the Pacific sector. During the International Military Tribunal for the Far East, war crimes trials led to many Japanese political and military leaders being sentenced to prison time and execution.

Conclusion: A Complex Historical Legacy

The historical legacy of World War II is complex and led to many changes in the world.

A vital part of this heritage was the birth of the Cold War. The aftermath of the conflict saw two nations, the United States and Soviet Union, left standing as the superior global players. As a new super power, The United States wanted to utilize the financial advantages of capitalism and political assets of democracy to attain greater global influence. In contrast, the Soviet Union endeavored to spread the foundational values of communism. Both countries sought to build international trust through the promotion of financial, military, and diplomatic assistance efforts. Both nations built worldwide and regional collective security organizations. This allowed the two new superpowers to share defense armaments, technology, and training with allied nations. In addition, each country provided monetary support through foreign aid to smaller nations, and this gave them banking, business, and infrastructural stability boosts.

The war gave women unprecedented opportunities to join the workforce. A few million women began working industrial jobs due to so many men joining the military. It was not that women did not work before, but many of these jobs had traditionally been reserved for men. American propaganda encouraged women to seek employment in the badly needed fields of producing wartime materials. The classic "Rosie the Riveter" image is one that outlived the end of the war. Ever since, the muscular woman in work clothes has represented the aspirations of females to pursue any career, no matter the type. Rosie became a symbol of feminism, as well. However, after World War II that propaganda turned to urging women to return home so men could fill these jobs. However, there had been irreversible gains in the area of women's rights.

Globally speaking, nations were scrambling to define their positions in the new international community. In the immediate aftermath of the war, the Soviet Union temporarily occupied Eastern Europe. They had agreed with the other Allies to allow people in these areas to hold legitimate elections and establish self-determined political identities. Instead, the Soviet Union forced the occupied territories to build communist governments. On the other hand, the United States used financial support to help countries in Western Europe rebuild their war-torn economies. In addition, they utilized collective security to create a unified military front in the same areas. Like the Soviet Union, the Americans used these tools to attain diplomatic loyalty from their allies. Unlike their Cold War counterparts, the United States did not mandate that these countries directly answer to them.

As with Europe, the fallout from World War II's end and the advent of the Cold War shifted power in Asia, too. Parts of the continent found American capitalism and military assistance to be positive attributes toward building an alliance. Some of the main nations that followed this approach were Japan, Taiwan, and South Korea. On the other hand, nations such as China and North Korea developed diplomatic bonds with the Soviet

Union. Outside of the growing Cold War developments, the most remarkable postwar outcome was Japan's transformation. For several years, the Japanese had an impassioned hatred for the United States and vice versa. However, the nations worked together to mend their diplomatic relationship. They partnered to turn Japan into an international model of peace, prosperity, and stability. In China, the wartime destruction led to tens of millions of casualties. Moreover, their economy and infrastructure were in ruins. It did not help that a civil war reignited between the established national government and rebel communists. Ultimately, in 1949, the communists prevailed in the conflict. This gave the Soviet Union a formidable communist partner in Asia.

One more legacy of World War II was the development of atomic weapons. After generations of industrialization improving modern military armaments, an ultimate weapon of obliteration had finally been invented and used in combat. Just a couple of years after the war, the Soviet Union built an atomic cache. In the ensuing two decades, a number of other nations developed nuclear arsenals. This new reality divided the globe between the haves and have-nots of atomic capabilities. The proliferation of nuclear weapons provided a new level of stress to global affairs. However, this occurrence also forced the concept of war to evolve into a more limited reality. During the Cold War, nuclear weapons made it a necessity to avoid a third installment of complete world war.

In many ways, World War II was the ultimate manifestation of what it meant to wage modern warfare. Technology is often considered a great benefit to humanity, and this is generally true. Although, when one combines mass industrialization, improvements in military capability, science, and the most destructive weapons in the history of mankind, then the world gets something like World War II. Less than 100 years earlier, people were still shooting at each other with muskets. Much had changed in a very short time. The factories of the American mainland had much to do with the Allies winning the war. It suddenly became patriotic to build plane, tank, or jeep parts. This was a different kind of "total war" on a level that dwarfed other American military conflicts like the Civil War and World War I. World War II was the "good war" after all, one in which good and evil were sharply in focus, and one where the United States seemed to save the day. American patriotism would turn to making most of the things that the world consumed. Producing, buying and selling, creating world markets; all of these became part of what it meant to be an American. The Age of America had begun.

CHAPTER EIGHTEEN

The Cold War

Chapter 18: Key Concepts

- What is the biggest American accomplishment during the first several decades of the Cold War and what is your reasoning for this choice?

- What is the most costly American mistake during the first several decades of the Cold War and what is your reasoning for this choice?

- What lessons can students of history take from the Korean and Vietnam conflicts?

The Cold War was a new era in international security, economics, politics, and diplomacy. In the aftermath of World War II, the United States represented a global power that built its system on democracy, free enterprise, and competitive markets. In contrast, the Soviet Union relied on communism to develop itself into a dominant nation. These two had been allies during World War II, and out of necessity formed a successful alliance. However, their perspectives focused on different goals in the conflict's aftermath. In total, these two new superpowers were the next in line to serve as the leading movers of world affairs.

The Early Cold War Years: A New National Security State

Once the war ended, the Soviet Union reneged on previous agreements regarding the post-war transitions of Germany and Europe as a whole. They did not agree with the independent governing and free market solutions favored by their western partners. Instead, they chose to build an organization of communist-run satellite nations in Eastern Europe. Many millions of people that had been under the tyranny of fascism were now facing the harsh rule of communism. Under the Truman administration, the United States began preparing for the new Cold War reality. It involved a major agenda in all aspects of foreign affairs. One aspect of this new era was the American commitment to the United Nations. The organization was modeled to a degree after the League of Nations but with a much more solid foundation of influence. Because the United Nations was a true international body, the United States and Soviet Union both had a role within it. Therefore, each of the two tried to shape its impact on the rest of the world. But the United Nations' larger diplomatic, security, and philanthropic impact often stood apart from the ongoing Cold War.

Both nations' respective world views contrasted sharply in the early Cold War years of policy making. The United States implemented the European Recovery Program, popularly called the Marshall Plan after its creator United States Secretary of State George Marshall, to rebuild war-torn Europe. Once the Soviet Union implemented its plan for taking over the Eastern European block, the Marshall Plan became a clear alternative for the Western European allies of the United States to refocus on postwar reality in a very different manner. From 1947 to 1951, the Marshall Plan sent more than 13 billion dollars to assist 16 European nations in rebuilding their agricultural, industrial, and financial infrastructures. The Marshall Plan secured, from its European participants,

General George Marshall captured in stamp form. He later served as both Secretary of Defense and State. He also pioneered the post-World War II Marshal Plan to rebuild war-torn Europe

diplomatic trust. It demonstrated the power of American wealth used in a productive and helpful fashion to foster democratic growth and financial stability.

Berlin became the earliest center of controversy in the Cold War. In July 1945, the Allies developed four occupation sectors around Berlin and in Germany. The nation and city were both divided along eastern and western lines. During the several years of transition, Germany became two nations that comprised East and West. The Soviet Union heavily influenced East Germany and implemented a communist government. In contrast, the United States and other allies shaped West Germany to align itself within a plan of democracy and a free market financial system. The Berlin Airlift demonstrated the United States' commitment to assuring West Germany's long-term stability. Between July 1948 and May 1949, a humanitarian crisis threatened West Berlin. The Soviet Union implemented a military blockade of all roads to Berlin. The goal was to keep several million Berlin residents from getting basic supplies such as food, water, and other necessities. They also wanted to force total annexation of the city of Berlin. It proved to be a failed power play. The United States and Great Britain flew several hundred thousand air supply missions and carried over 750,000 tons of goods to those in need. In doing so, the "Berlin Airlift" gave the people of the city the supplies they needed to withstand the Soviet policy and demonstrated the West's humanitarian diplomatic initiative. The end result was the Soviet Union stood down and the airlift proved a success.

President Truman endorsed sweeping changes to America's national security state. In August 1946, he worked with Congress to pass the Atomic Energy Act. Under this legislation, the federal government had complete control over all nuclear resources. In addition, there were five appointed members of a new Atomic Energy Commission, and this group helped determine nonmilitary-based nuclear projects. In response to communist attempts to take over Greece and Turkey, President Truman issued the Truman Doctrine. The 1947 edict stated that the United States would contain and fight the spread of communism, by any means, around the globe. Through the 1947 National Security Act, the United States greatly expanded the peace time manpower, weapons, and funding of all branches of the military. The plan implemented a revised civilian leadership structure over the armed forces, and this meant the more powerful Defense Department took the place of the former War Department.

The Truman administration revised and modernized the military to fit the unique needs of a global super power. A new military collaborative leadership group, the Joint Chiefs of Staff, allowed all service branches to have an equal and cohesive strategic voice. In addition, the National Security Council was formed and became a modern body of advisors selected to inform the Commander-in-Chief on global security matters. To assure covert intelligence strategy remained at an elite level, the United States placed a great amount of funding and manpower into the Central Intelligence Agency (CIA). This organization, and the Soviet Union's KGB, became vital parts of the Cold War, which usually included secretive missions of espionage and various covert operations. Both nations gathered intelligence on each other, enemies, and even their strongest allies. A diverse group of diplomatic, armed forces, and civilian specialists worked in dangerous and high-stakes environments in these new roles to assure the United States maintained national security stability.

The official flag of NATO

In April 1949, western countries formed a collective security plan named NATO (North Atlantic Treaty Organization). This new entity provided quick strike conventional and nuclear military capabilities, covert intelligence sharing, and military training in a group effort to solidify Europe versus Soviet machinations. Moreover, NATO provided an outlet for member nations to continually prepare for a potential third world war scenario and a range of regional military conflicts, too. As the need for NATO demonstrated, one of the ongoing realities of the early Cold War was the development and proliferation of nuclear weapons. The United States had built its arsenal for several years after World War II. In September 1949, the Soviet Union tested its first nuclear bomb. President Truman responded by calling for international atomic limits, but he also authorized the development of the more destructive hydrogen bomb. The decades ahead saw thousands of nuclear weapons produced by both superpowers and their respective allied nations.

Throughout the early Cold War, Europe was often the focus of global attention and concern. However, other sectors of the world played a vital role in the period's evolution. None proved a greater center of controversy and intrigue than Asia. In 1949, a major setback for the United States occurred in this theater. Asia's most populous nation, China, had been wartorn for several decades. Along with World War II, the established national government and communist rebel forces fought intermittently for two decades over control of the nation. Despite American diplomatic efforts geared at ending civil war, in 1949 the Communist Party of China seized control of the national government. They pushed the Nationalist Party completely off mainland China, and this group had to flee to Taiwan. These two nations then chose distinctly different sides in the Cold War. Taiwan allied with the United States, and this continued a partnership the nationalists already had with them. In turn, China formed a strong alliance with the Soviet Union. China's large population base and depth of natural resources made, for the Soviet Union, a formidable partner in Asia.

The Korean War: A Major Asian Conflict

In the aftermath of World War II, the nation of Korea was divided along the 38th parallel. With this development, one country became two separate ones: North and South Korea. The Soviet Union supported North Korea, and its leadership structure implemented

Korean War: U.S. Bombers attack Korean side of Sinuiji Bridge, Korea, November 29, 1950

communism. In contrast, South Korea created a more open political structure and, in turn, gained a good deal of assistance from the United States. In June 1950, North Korea invaded South Korea, and this action started a very violent conflict that threatened to turn the Cold War hot. The Soviet Union aided North Korea and gave them a great deal of monetary, armament, and supply assistance. On the other hand, the United Nations stood with South Korea and developed a full multinational military alliance to help win the conflict.

United States General Douglas McArthur led the UN forces, and in the fall of 1950, UN soldiers engaged in a series of campaigns against the North Koreans. MacArthur's forces made extraordinary progress in a short period of time. There appeared a good chance that UN troops would force the communists off the Korean peninsula. To avoid such a cataclysmic scenario, the Soviet Union and North Korea called upon the nearby communist regime in China for assistance. In response, the Chinese sent several hundred thousand soldiers to salvage the war effort. The troop windfall caused the war to become a deadly and entrenched standoff between the two sides.

Within American political and military circles, there was turmoil developing due to the Korean crisis. General McArthur made a number of comments to the media and U.S. politicians that questioned President Truman's military and diplomatic strategy pertaining to Korea and the Cold War. In April 1951, Truman relieved McArthur of command. The whole affair was a black mark for the United States and only offered more controversy while a war was being waged. In July 1953, the Korean War came to a close. The statistical toll of the conflict gives insight into its great monetary and, more importantly, human cost. The United States provided approximately 90% of soldiers used on the UN side of the conflict. In addition, America spent over 67 billion dollars and suffered over 100,000 wounded and 30,000 deaths in the war. In addition, several million from other countries were wounded or killed in the conflict, too.

The Korean War provided the United States with several valuable lessons. The violence of the engagement reaffirmed that nuclear weapons were an option that would only be used as an absolute last resort. The Cold War provided many regional military conflicts. These conflicts ranged from short to long and varied in scope from small engagements to some that caused massive loss of life. Usually, victories of any kind were partial or incremental. Unlike the standard idea of winning complete battles, such as in World War II, the United States considered a limited achievement of goals as a true victory in Korea. The United Nations mandate called for the use of military force to secure South Korea from being overrun by the invading North's military and its associated allies. After three years of combat, this very hard earned victory became a reality.

From General to President: Dwight Eisenhower and Cold War Consensus

Dwight Eisenhower transitioned from acclaimed military achievements to a political career in 1952. Although courted by both primary political parties, Eisenhower chose to run for the presidency as a Republican. He had no previous political experience. However, Eisenhower's leadership style and personal popularity made him an extremely strong candidate. As a result, he swept into office in 1952, and one of the first issues he faced was an ongoing domestic Cold War crisis. For several decades, the political philosophy of communism had been very controversial in the United States. In the 1940s, federal authorities opened several investigations regarding government employees and their ties to communism. In addition, the Truman administration supported these efforts to gain positive momentum for early Cold War policies. Indeed, there was a general national consensus toward rooting out any potential communist threat in American public and private sectors. As the early Cold War years progressed, communists poised legitimate security threats to America and its allies. However, many of the inquiries during these years also surrounded ruining personal and professional reputations of many people that did not have legitimate communist ties. This series of controversial events became known as the Second Red Scare.

As the 1950s began, this movement captured the nation's attention. Political leaders fed this new and growing obsession. In February 1950, Senator Joe McCarthy of Wisconsin claimed to know of two hundred communists working in the United States Department of State. His accusations lacked proof, but the growing public support of anti-communist measures meant people were receptive to his claims. In turn, this meant more media attention and congressional inquiries. The congressional investigations of domestic communism turned controversial, and committee hearings aired to high ratings on national television news broadcasts. There were professional and personal consequences for those investigated, and for a number of these individuals, false communist charges

Dwight David Eisenhower

Zvonimir Atletic /Shutterstock.com

meant the loss of their reputation and being "blacklisted" from one's line of work. Early in his tenure, President Eisenhower spoke out against paranoid anticommunism, also known as McCarthyism. After controversial comments by McCarthy regarding the military being influenced by communists, the U.S. Senate, with Eisenhower's urging, censured him. Eventually, the Second Red Scare became marginalized and discredited.

Eisenhower emphasized a military strategy of massive retaliation, and he based it around conventional and nuclear weapon modernization. As the 1950s progressed, the nuclear arms race between the superpowers frightened the entire world. Throughout the decade, the United States and Soviet Union mass produced thousands of nuclear capable weapons. On both sides, the goal of this prolific growth was to have a huge stockpile of atomic weapons that were capable of hitting targets from several thousand miles away. Moreover, they each placed these armaments strategically around the globe to make this scenario all the more manageable and flexible. As the two nations increased their respective nuclear arsenals, there did not seem to be an end to expansion efforts in sight. The nuclear missile race created an important potentiality called Mutually Assured Destruction (MAD).This scenario predicted that a nuclear war would probably ensure that both the United States and the Soviets would destroy the other. In essence, both nations would launch great numbers of their respective nuclear reserves and end modern civilization. Throughout the Cold War, this nightmare scenario placed a great amount of pressure on the two countries to avoid this through diplomatic and security concerns.

While his nuclear weapon expansion strategy proved controversial, Eisenhower also emphasized the need for responsible use of the energy source for peaceful industrial purposes. During his first term, Eisenhower spoke to the UN General Assembly, and he urged the creation of an international plan and group to oversee the peaceful use of atomic energy. This led to the 1957 creation of the International Atomic Energy Agency. Along with advocating for nuclear power, Eisenhower also emphasized internal improvements and scientific progress as parts of his Cold War plan. This meant improving the national highway system along with developing the National Aeronautics and Space Administration (NASA). The launch of NASA played a great role in the long-term history of the Cold War and beyond. In October 1957, the Soviet Union launched the Sputnik satellite. In January 1958, the United States launched the Explorer One satellite and started NASA the next July. Both powers continued technological progress on satellite and manned space vehicles. Within the context of the Cold War, winning the newly ignited space race became an important focus of financial and scientific planning efforts for each superpower.

While he avoided a large scale military conflict, Eisenhower did use strategic force initiatives to achieve global Cold War objectives. In 1953, the CIA gave aid to British covert security and Iranian military personnel in a coup effort to topple the regime of Iranian Premier Mohammed Mosaddeq. The operation proved successful for the parties involved. In place of the deposed leader, Great Britain and the United States helped the Shah of Iran, Mohammad Reza Pahlavi, take power as the new head of the Iranian government. In exchange for their assistance, the Shah provided United States businesses access to 40% of Iranian oil fields. Within the greater Cold War spectrum, the United States both added new energy capabilities and, in its solidified alliance with Iran, also prevented the Soviet Union from doing likewise. However, in the later Cold War period, this victory proved to have negative long-term consequences for the United States.

In 1954, the CIA supported a coup in Guatemala. The operation targeted President Jacobo Arbenz Guzman. With his election in 1950, Guzman became just the second person to lead the nation as a democratically selected head of state. Despite this fact, the United States believed his regime had too many ties with the Soviet Union. While the coup successfully removed Guzman from power, Guatemala became more politically and militarily unstable. Throughout the Cold War, both the United States and the Soviets continued to use Central and South America as regular areas of proxy warfare and covert measures. Unfortunately, these operations often left many millions of common people in those regions as victims of political and military turmoil.

Another conflict in Asia, specifically Vietnam, developed before and during Eisenhower's presidential tenure. This added further complexities to the Cold War puzzle. In the immediate post-World War II world, France attempted to regain lost territory in Indochina. Between 1946 and 1954, they engaged in the French-Indochina war against opposition insurgents in the region. These nationalist fighters wanted freedom from outside colonizers. Ho Chi Minh directed rebel operations against France. During the Second World War, America assisted him in establishing military opposition against Japanese military troops occupying Indochina. After the war, Minh formed an alliance with the Soviet Union and embraced communism. Subsequently, the United States provided France with more than two and a half billion dollars of aid during the French-Indochina conflict. Ultimately, France could not defeat the revolutionary forces, and in 1954, a multi-nation diplomatic conference took place in Geneva, Switzerland to resolve the conflict.

At this summit, the Indochina territorial regions of Cambodia, Laos, and Vietnam received independence from France. The United States believed elections in Vietnam would result in Minh and his regime taking power. As part of an anticommunism strategy in the region, the United States supported the creation of an independent government in South Vietnam. This regime was both anticommunist and friendly to American foreign policy interests in Asia. North Vietnam still wanted a unified nation, and throughout the rest of the 1950s and into the 1960s, they continued fighting for this to take place. In response, the United States steadily increased their monetary, supply, and military strategic support of South Vietnam. This proved an ongoing quagmire for the Eisenhower administration and grew into a much bigger problem for his next several predecessors.

Other Cold War foreign policy situations brought varying degrees of criticism and praise for the Eisenhower administration. In October 1956, Israel sent military troops into Egypt, and they did this as a response to the Egyptian government's decision to nationalize the Suez Canal. The canal provided a vital trade connection between the Mediterranean and the Red Sea. Since Egyptian nationalization threatened its accessibility to outside nations, Israel received military support from Great Britain and France. In opposition to these developments, the Soviet Union, as an ally of Egypt, threatened military intervention on their behalf. Eisenhower warned both sides of causing the situation to regress into a major military conflict. The United States also threatened its usually solid trio of allies (France, Great Britain, and Israel) with economic sanctions if a diplomatic solution was not sought and reached. Ultimately, a United Nations ceasefire over the Suez Canal conflict halted a potential war. While Eisenhower achieved a diplomatic solution to the Suez situation, he also temporarily damaged close alliances.

In 1957, the popular president issued the Eisenhower doctrine. It called on the United States to, under the request of an allied government, utilize armed assistance versus a communist group. The 1958 Taiwan Strait Crisis was the most relevant example of this doctrine being put into action. Specifically, China began bombing islands near Taiwan and threatened to invade the nation itself. Under the doctrine's mandate, Eisenhower's administration sent U.S. Naval forces in to provide support for Taiwan. This act proved enough to cause China to think twice, and in addition, the exercise proved the doctrine effective.

Eisenhower's last year in office proved controversial and historically important. In May 1960, the Soviet Union shot down a United States U-2 reconnaissance plane. Ultimately, it was revealed the plane was part of a four-year spying program. The incident ruined a planned Paris diplomatic summit scheduled for the two nations. Eisenhower eventually issued an apology for the international embarrassment. He left office warning of the dangers of the military-industrial complex. These were the various relationships between the private sector and the military that could serve to make more weapons and thus drive the continuation of the Cold War.

The Early 1960s: Cuba, Berlin, and Vietnam

The next president, at least in style, was far different from "Ike" Eisenhower. In November 1960, John Kennedy became the youngest ever person elected President of the United States. He had the difficult task of following one of the more popular figures to ever hold the office. Despite his age, Kennedy had some significant professional experience. He had served with distinction in the Second World War. Then, he returned to his native Massachusetts and made a successful transition into politics. Kennedy served six years in the United States House of Representatives and seven years in the United States Senate. Early in his presidential tenure, Kennedy faced a foreign affairs crisis. The origins of the matter developed out of United States intentions to oust Fidel Castro's communist regime in Cuba. Castro rose to power in 1959, and he received a great deal of financial and military assistance from the Soviet Union. Due to this strong alliance, Castro's removal became a top priority of the United States national security organizations.

In April 1961, a force of CIA backed Cuban exiles failed to topple the Fidel Castro regime in Cuba. In the debacle's aftermath, the Cuban government imprisoned over a thousand of them. The affair became known as the Bay of Pigs incident. This failed coup attempt stained Kennedy's still young Cold War record. However, he had some other earlier success. In 1961, Kennedy launched the United States Peace Corps to promote American participation in international service projects dedicated to improving impoverished global communities. In addition, his administration began the Alliance for Progress which was aimed at developing South American nations. These initiatives promoted American values positively in the third world. In addition, both programs provided financial support toward influencing the socio-economic classes of the underdeveloped world lest they fall under the sway of Soviet communism.

In June 1961, Kennedy met with Soviet Premier Nikita Khrushchev in Vienna, Austria but without any real results. The failed meeting did not add any positive momentum to the ongoing Cold War standoff. Furthermore, the completion of a Soviet approved structure to divide East Germany and West Germany further damaged Cold War diplomacy between the two superpowers. This dividing line became known as the Berlin Wall. From 1949 to 1961, many thousands of people moved from East to West Berlin. Across the board, these people found West German policy based around capitalism and democracy to be preferable to East German communism. By 1961, 30,000 German citizens per month made the migration, and the Soviet Union found this to be an unacceptable trend. As a result, the Berlin Wall's development broke ground in June 1961. By its completion in August of that year, the Berlin Wall became the most visible physical line between the two main world views of the Cold War. It also kept countless German families and friends apart for the next several decades.

In October 1962, President Kennedy faced the greatest challenge of his tenure. The Cuban Missile Crisis became the best example of nuclear brinksmanship during the Cold War. The United States discovered that the Soviet Union was gathering and storing nuclear materials in Cuba. A development of armaments of that nature less than one hundred miles off the American coast proved an unacceptable security risk. For a week, the two sides negotiated in secret and without a great deal of progress. Then, the United States broke the news to the world of this serious issue. Kennedy stood firm on the Soviet Union removing their entire nuclear stockpile from Cuba. He ordered an American naval quarantine of Cuba, and in addition, publicly stated that Soviet action toward the naval maneuver meant an initiation of war. After 13 days of negotiations, the two nations finally reached a diplomatic agreement to end the standoff. The Soviet Union evacuated the nuclear cache from Cuba, and the United States agreed to remove a NATO arsenal encampment in Turkey. Kennedy won praise for his calm and organized approach to resolving the situation. The next year both sides, wary of future close calls, began a steady progression toward lessening the global danger of nuclear weapons. In August 1963, Great Britain, the Soviet Union, and the United States

Berlin Wall

Antlio/Shutterstock.com

signed the Limited Test Ban Treaty. This diplomatic resolution marked an important step forward in the Cold War. Policy wise, the pact banned nuclear weapons' tests in the planet's atmosphere, space, and under water. The next several decades saw follow up accords geared at a more progressive policy of preventing the spread and use of nuclear devices.

Throughout the Kennedy administration, America made a fateful new commitment to Vietnam. The assistance included money, military supplies, and thousands of armed forces advisors. In the summer and fall of 1963, there were several negative forces that diminished possibilities of U.S. success in the region. The power of television showed a growing number of revealing public protests in South Vietnam. The most notable and visually disturbing was that of Vietnamese Buddhists committing suicide via self-inflicted burning. These horrific displays protested ongoing corruption and violence in the South Vietnamese government. Another pertinent development occurred when a military coup overthrew the troubled Ngo Dinh Diem regime in South Vietnam. This also resulted in President Diem's death. Increasingly, unstable and unscrupulous leadership in South Vietnam became commonplace.

In November 1963, President Kennedy was assassinated, and the tragedy sparked a national period of grief. His murderer, Lee Harvey Oswald, was a former member of the U.S. Marines that had previously moved to the Soviet Union and developed communist sympathies. Oswald's death occurred just two days after the Kennedy killing. Dallas businessman Jack Ruby shot him at close range, and the entire act aired live on national television. Ruby's widely-seen act of vengeance and Oswald's background story added intrigue to the entire affair. Cold War conspiracies aside, the 1964 Warren Commission Report determined the facts of the case showed Kennedy's death to be at the hands of Oswald alone.

The Vietnam War: A True Quagmire

Amidst the national mourning, Vice President Lyndon Johnson succeeded President Kennedy. His professional political background and presidential policy objectives primarily revolved around domestic matters. However, Johnson inherited a growing national security crisis in the form of continuing negative developments in Vietnam. By Johnson's time in office, several billion dollars and thousands of military advisors had been sent to Asia. The greater international community did not endorse these actions. As such, the growing support of South Vietnam became a largely singular endeavor. On August 2 and 4, 1964, two American naval destroyers, the Maddox and the Turner Joy, reported separate attacks by North Vietnam forces. The apparent North Vietnamese aggression provided enough justification for Congress to pass the Gulf of Tonkin Resolution. This act gave President Johnson authority to greatly increase the use of military force in Vietnam. America had officially entered the active phase of warfare in Vietnam.

The main focus of Johnson's national security policy was the Vietnam War. In February 1965, Johnson ordered bombing raids of North Vietnam targets. In June 1965, U.S. ground troops were activated against North Vietnam. Throughout Johnson's term, tens of thousands of American military draft eligible males and their loved ones fled to other countries to avoid serving in the conflict. Along with those that migrated to places such as Canada

Lyndon B. Johnson (left) being sworn in as president of the United States by Chief Justice Earl Warren

or Europe, millions more Americans participated in anti-war protests. On the other hand, the Vietnam War gained support from millions of other people in the United States. These backers of the campaign served in the military, participated in patriotic rallies, and became the other side of a long, polarizing, and national period of turmoil.

From 1966 to 1968, there were stop and start peace efforts with no real progress made between the various parties. As the war dragged on, by 1968 the United States reached the half million troop mark in Vietnam. It appeared the nation was entrenched in the ongoing venture for the long haul. However, North Vietnam launched a series of coordinate campaigns that year and drastically altered American plans. In January 1968, North Vietnamese troops launched the Tet Offensive against Saigon and 30 total South Vietnam cities. Caught off guard, President Johnson bore the negative political fallout from a growing American frustration with the seemingly never-ending Vietnam situation. In March 1968, he made two very critical announcements. Johnson declared he would not run for reelection in that year's Democratic Party primaries. In addition, he called for a targeted stoppage in U.S. bombings of North Vietnam, and Johnson's goal was to gain peace talk progress. By October 1968, diplomatic negotiations remained stagnant. At that time, Johnson announced a total bombing halt in North Vietnam, and he did this in hope of it leading to more peace talk progress. However, this did not occur.

In November 1968, Richard Nixon won the presidency, and in his victorious campaign platform there was a promise of a secret plan to achieve a victorious and honorable Vietnam peace agreement. In June 1969, Nixon announced the first gradual withdrawal of 25,000 American troops, and this was set to occur by September 1969. This initial pledge began a strategy called Vietnamization. In the previous years of the war, the Nixon administration felt the United States had taken on too much of the active fighting burden from South Vietnam. This needed to be altered, and in exchange, America would supply South Vietnam with ample weapons, money, and supplies. Over time, America would eventually pull out all active military personnel.

Two bombs tumble from a Vietnamese Air Force A-1E Skyraider over a burning North Vietnam hideout in 1967

While the Vietnamization plan gradually became a reality, Nixon's greater war strategy took several controversial turns. In early 1970, a military coup forced communist leadership in Cambodia out of office. As a result, a civil war broke out in the nation. President Nixon announced an invasion of Cambodia by American and South Vietnamese troops to deter North Vietnamese military interference and stop supply routes. Congress set June 1970 as the deadline for the Cambodian military campaign's end. In addition, they voted to cut off all funds for further combat actions in Cambodia on June 30, 1970. The Cambodian episode proved a controversial expansion of the Vietnam War, and it led to a political, media, and public outcry.

In June 1971, Congress passed an extended military draft, and they also passed a resolution to withdraw all American military personnel from Vietnam by 1972. Throughout 1972, there were peace talks. In May and December 1972, President Nixon used increased bombing efforts of North Vietnam to try and force more favorable diplomatic results. As diplomacy progressed in January 1973, President Nixon stopped bombing missions in North Vietnam. On January 27, 1973 negotiators reached a cease fire agreement. President Nixon had secretly promised North Vietnamese leaders several billion dollars in aid as a diplomatic incentive. However, eventual hostilities between North and South Vietnam and Nixon's own troubles with the Watergate Scandal kept this pledge from becoming a reality.

During the Vietnam War, America was embroiled in a national security crisis that seemed to be without a realistic end game. The period represented the nadir for the United States in the Cold War. The Vietnam War tore apart the American people along opposing lines of support and protest. In addition, the global community viewed the engagement as a very negative and unnecessary endeavor. In total, the war led to several million Vietnamese and over 58,000 American deaths. The power of televised news regularly reinforced that the war was not going well. Ultimately, it took several years for the nation to reconstruct its international reputation, domestic unity, and Cold War agenda.

Other Major Cold War Issues: Chinese Detente, Middle East Turmoil, Outer Space Advancements, and Nuclear Diplomacy

The 1960s and 1970s proved to be busy times for the United States' Cold War leadership. While the Vietnam War became the main national defense and diplomatic concern for many Americans, other areas provided diverse challenges and positive advancements. Over several presidential administrations, great strategic emphasis was placed on geographical hotbeds such as China and the Middle East. In addition, technological innovations pertaining to the space race and international security concerns regarding nuclear arsenal containment were priorities. All of these areas had unique figures, events, and themes that proved critical pieces to the greater Cold War puzzle.

During the 1960s, United States' national security sectors learned about a growing division between China and the Soviet Union. Under the Nixon administration, the United States made a secretive priority of engaging with Chinese leaders. Finally, in 1972 the two nations went public with their ongoing foreign policy negotiations. Under President Nixon, the United States secured a détente with China. Several decades of mutual hostility turned into a more cooperative relationship. From then through the end of the Cold War, China and the United States negotiated a diverse array of cultural, diplomatic, economic, and military partnerships. These developments left a rift between the Chinese and the Soviet Union. It gave the Soviet Union another potential Cold War adversary to have to account for on the global scene, and the development opened America to a range of new beneficial foreign policy avenues. Furthermore, after several decades of poorly managing Asian policy, the United States finally developed a strong strategic formula in a crucial area of the world.

In the 1960s and 1970s, the Middle East was a turbulent and war- torn region. The primary concerns in the area ranged from religious conflict to control of oil resources. The Soviet Union and United States often intervened, at a variety of levels, in these disputes. Two of the predominant nations who shaped policy in the Middle East were Egypt and Israel. In June 1967, Egypt organized other nations from the Middle East for a military campaign versus Israel. The military conflict became known as the Six Days War. With a mixture of great planning and superior armaments, Israel achieved a decisive win over its enemies.

Library of Congress, Prints & Photographs Division, U.S. News & World Report Magazine Collection, LC-DIG-ds-07190.

President Richard Nixon with (left to right) Soviet leader Leonid Brezhnev, Soviet Minister of Foreign Affairs Andrei Gromyko, and Secretary of State William P. Rogers, toasting the signing of agreements between the two countries on oceanography, transportation, and cultural exchange in 1973

Astronaut with flag on the Moon

The United States provided Israel with a plethora of financial support and military supplies. In turn, the Six Days War represented the ultimate result of that ongoing partnership. However, Israel also claimed territorial gains from the war and ultimately, the cauldron of Middle East conflict became hotter.

In October 1973, the Yom Kippur War once again pitted Israel against Egypt and its Middle Eastern allies. Both up to and through the war, the United States backed Israel and the Soviet Union supported the Arabic coalition with weapons and aid. The Yom Kippur War lasted three weeks, and it was a less decisive Israeli victory than the Six Days War. In the long run, the United States urged both Egypt and Israel to come together diplomatically toward establishing a more stable Middle East. By the end of the 1970s, this more peaceful approach led to the two nations reaching an agreement. As with China earlier in the decade, the United States used diplomacy to eventually achieve a positive long-term strategy in a volatile area of the world.

Throughout the 1960s, the Soviet Union and United States brought the Cold War outside the earth's atmosphere via a full blown space race. Both nations funded scientific scholars and programs toward advancing this objective. The competition had both tangible and propagandistic effects on the Cold War. From a policy perspective, both countries made progress in areas such as satellites, weapons systems, and computer technology. From a symbolic standpoint, the goal of the space race was about who could become the first nation to achieve a successful moon landing. In July 1969, America achieved this goal, and as a result, they reached a significant high point. With the moon race win, the United States claimed the global reputation as the world's leader in technology.

In the 1960s and 1970s, both Cold War powers gained beneficial results from negotiating agreements on nuclear arsenal restriction and reduction. These developments originated with the 1963 Limited Test Ban Treaty. With the 1968 Nuclear Non-Proliferation Treaty, multination antinuclear diplomacy reached another successful accord. This agreement limited the global proliferation of military capable nuclear equipment. With the May 1972 Strategic Arms Limitations Treaty, the Soviet Union and United States halted production of long range nuclear weapons for five years. These agreements provided positive policy developments toward a more permanent peace in the Cold War.

Conclusion

The Cold War ultimately affected almost everything in the United States. It was about culture as much as policy, war, and international intrigue. Through instructional videos, children were taught how to "duck and cover" under their school-desks in case of a nuclear scare. Largely this culture was full of paranoia. Average people built fall-out shelters under-ground to live and avoid radiation. Stanley Kubrick's 1964 *Dr. Strangelove or: How I Learned to Stop Worrying and Love the Bomb* embodied what often appeared as a world gone mad. It increasingly seemed that the Cold War could likely bring about an Armageddon of some sort. In addition the whole spy movie genre is a result of the Cold War. Indeed, there would be no James Bond without it.

The culture of the Cold War inspired a kind of super-American patriotism. In the vari-ous propaganda campaigns, it was important for the government to define how America was different and better than Soviet Russia. In the American telling, Soviets were author-itarian, antiquated, communal, brutish, and without religious belief. The "godless com-munists" theme was probably the most important. Americans emphasized that they were good Christians and had rugged individualism. It is no coincidence that John Wayne was an icon during the Cold War and made movies that exemplified the quintessential Ameri-can hero. The Cold War, due to trying to create a consensus against the Soviets, introduced a kind of hyper-patriotism that was unique and still influences the nation to the present.

Paradoxically, the Cold War also helped create many people who questioned patriotism and no longer trusted their leaders. The United States would never be exactly the same after Vietnam. This was the first war on television. News anchors, like Walter Cronkite, reported daily on casualties and other developments. It was not clear to many people why Amer-ican young men had to die in a far-away land. War protests gained momentum. On col-lege campuses, especially, young people called for an end to the Vietnam War. Musicians contributed with all sorts of songs about Vietnam. The war, combined with the Watergate scandal, made many either question America itself or forever distrust politicians in Wash-ington. This was a far cry from the age of Eisenhower, who perpetuated the image of a favorite uncle or grandfather. Everyone liked "Ike," but that era seemed a long way from the post-Vietnam world.

The Cold War resulted in a series of highs and lows for the United States. As a new superpower, America developed a different approach to national security. Before the Cold War, the national mindset had never favored a large peacetime military. Instead, America now focused on completely revamping all areas of the armed forces. Bases were estab-lished on every part of the globe, military funding increased dramatically, technological advancements became a priority, and nuclear weapons became the ever present ultimate concern. Owing to Cold War competition, the United States sought to build global alliances and maintain a consensus of unity domestically. The areas of concern shifted from Europe to Asia and even outer space. American leaders managed regional wars, covert opera-tions, foreign aid, and nuclear diplomacy. In total, the United States withstood failures and successes, but through many moments of crisis, the nation maintained and solidified its superpower status. For the country, the American road to prosperity and world leadership remained intact.

CHAPTER NINETEEN

The 1950s and 1960s

Chapter 19: Key Concepts

- What were the factors that brought about the economic boom in the United States between 1945 and 1960?

- What were the origins of Rock and Roll and why was it so provocative?

- What were the key moments of the civil rights movement between 1954 and 1968?

- In what ways did white southerners resist the civil rights movement?

- What social protest movements piggybacked off the civil rights movement?

In Act 3 of William Shakespeare's *Hamlet*, Hamlet discourses on the nature of life after death. He muses that, upon death, humanity travels into "the undiscovered country." This metaphor could be expanded into describing the paths the United States traveled in the quarter century after World War II. Truly, the country launched into undiscovered territories. The postwar era economy reached heretofore unknown heights. The population exploded from 132 million people in 1940 to 180 million two decades later. Americans embraced new technologies like air conditioning and the television. American teenagers danced to a new form of music, Rock and Roll. African-Americans rejected Jim Crow segregation and sought to make America live up to its ideals of equality, freedom, and economic opportunity for all. Throughout the 1950s and 1960s, the country faced the threat of Soviet Communism. While U.S. troops fought in the rice paddies of Vietnam in the 1960s, and African-Americans and other minorities endured violence and oppression in their fight for equality, America's young people began to question the old verities. This led to protests over the war, over civil rights, and over the establishment itself. By 1968, many older Americans rejected the new paths taken by the younger generation and called for a return to the older, more conservative ways. This led to the election of Richard M. Nixon as President. The undiscovered country that Americans entered during the postwar era led to great improvements but also created social, political, and cultural fissures that last until this day.

The Baby Boom

In the two decades after Japan surrendered, the American population skyrocketed. Over 16 million soldiers came home ready to start families and embark on new careers. Between 1946 and 1964, Americans experienced what came to be known as the "Baby Boom." Over 76 million babies were born. This broke down from 3.4 million to 4 million children born every year during this period. These births made up over 40% of the population.

Economic Boom Time

The economy rose to unprecedented heights during these two decades. With unemployment hovering between 15% and 25% in the 1930s, few had money to buy anything. During World War II, more people had money but saved it because companies produced fighter planes and other war materials. No new consumer products hit the market. Between 1945 and 1960, companies unleashed a vast array of products that in turn were gobbled up by hungry consumers. Spending money became the name of the game.

What drove this economic dynamo? An active war and a cold war primed the pump. World War II and the subsequent Cold War with Soviet Russia required massive outlays of government funds. Both conflicts demanded and gave free reign to innovation. While spending began to decrease as World War II wound down, the ensuing Cold War once again prompted massive government spending. Scientific breakthroughs came in areas like nuclear physics and aerospace engineering, as well as advances in chemistry and electronics. The U.S. government invested millions in research. This translated to massive employment in both the public and private sectors.

The country's Gross National Product (the total value a country produces and the services a country provides in one year) increased by 250% in the 15 years after the war. American workers income increased more during this span than it had in the first half century. Before the war, the average worker earned just over $1,500 per year. By 1960, the average salary reached $2,800. With more money to spend, consumers rushed to get the latest automobile, a new house, washer/dryers, and countless other appliances.

The G.I. Bill

Returning veterans benefitted greatly from this economic upswing. The nickname for the U.S. soldier was G.I., which stood for Government Issue. The nickname came from the concept that as a soldier, the government issued you a rifle, a canteen, traveling orders, and the like. With 16 million men returning home from military service, the U.S. government wanted to ease their transition. The Serviceman's Readjustment Act of 1944, commonly known as the G.I. Bill, sought to provide benefits for these veterans. This included business loans from the Veteran's Administration for up to $2,000. Also, the program provided former soldiers monetary allotments for going back to school. Whether they chose to be a doctor or a car mechanic, the G.I. Bill led to a more professional working class. Former soldiers also got low interest loans from the Veteran's Administration in order to buy homes.

Suburbanization

Housing shortages and the ability to purchase a home plagued a large portion of America before World War II. In 1940, only 40% of American families owned their own homes. As low interest loans and affordable housing became available after the war, home ownership skyrocketed to 60% by 1960. Returning vets with families wanted affordable homes. Entrepreneurs like William J. Levitt capitalized on this need. During World War II, Levitt served in the Pacific Theatre with the Seabees, the construction arm of the U.S. Navy. As the U.S. forces took over islands, Levitt worked with crews that went in and quickly constructed airfields and living quarters. He had worked in the construction industry before the war, and he experimented with different methods during his tour of duty. Upon returning home, Levitt honed methods for the creation of low-cost housing. His crews used preformed materials, and working in efficient teams, they built houses quickly. The first subdivision, dubbed "Levittown," went up in Long Island, New York. Later Levitt constructed neighborhoods in Pennsylvania and New Jersey. Other contractors across the country soon copied the Levittown model. With affordable housing outside the cities, America experienced a massive demographic shift in the generation after the war. Between 1950 and 1960, 13 million homes were built. Eleven million of these were erected in communities outside the city in what came to be known as the suburbs. The trend continued well after 1960. Between 1950 and 1980, 18 of the top 25 cities in the United States lost population and over 60 million people moved into the suburbs.

The Sun Belt

In the decade and a half after the war, millions of Americans moved south and west in what came to be known as the Sun Belt. Stretching from North Carolina to California, under the 36th parallel line of latitude, families and businesses relocated. What helped bring about this shift? Manufacturing industries moved to these states lured by cheaper labor and lower taxes. Aerospace companies, plastics plants, computer and electronic manufacturers, along with other industrial research hubs grew in southern states like North Carolina, Florida, California, and Texas.

An aerial view of the Levittown housing project in Pennsylvania

With low labor costs and no unions, new industries thrived. The warmer climate proved inviting, and the lower cost of living brought many away from the colder, crowded, more expensive cities. Affordable air conditioning also served as a key component. Air conditioning had been invented in the early part of the twentieth century, but automobiles did not have air-conditioning units, and affordable AC units for homes and businesses did not evolve until the early 1950s. Midway through the twentieth century, car manufacturers began to put in AC units as standard components. In 1951, a new hotel franchise, Holiday Inn, put window AC units in their rooms. This soon became the standard for all hotels. Homeowners began to buy the individual window units for their homes. This allowed people to move south and west and live and work comfortably in the humid heat of Georgia or the desert heat of Arizona. With all these factors, cities like Phoenix, Arizona grew from 65,000 to three quarters of a million people. Houston, Texas exploded from a large city of 300,000 to a metropolis of over a million and a half people. The Sun Belt states also became magnets for tourist attractions like Disneyland and retirement communities for senior citizens who wanted to escape the cold brutal winters of the Northeast and upper Midwest.

Television

During the 1950s, not only did Americans enjoy the new technology of air conditioning to keep them cool, they also embraced the new technology of television to keep them entertained. Invented in the 1930s, television served as a toy mostly for the well-to-do throughout the 1940s. Less than one half percent of American homes possessed a television in 1948. As televisions were more affordable, the programming increased, and thus the numbers of television sold skyrocketed. By 1954, over half the households in the United States owned a TV. The number climbed to 83% by 1958. By the mid-1950s, the average American family took in four and a half hours of programming a day. Instead of listening to Franklin Roosevelt's soothing voice on the radio or hear a Joe Louis fight, Americans could now see President Dwight Eisenhower speak on important issues or see Willie Mays hit a home run. Advertisers paid for the programming, and in return, ran commercials for their products. Children enjoyed shows like the Mickey Mouse Club and the puppet show Howdy Doody Time. Adults laughed at comedies such as I Love Lucy and the Milton Berle Show. Young people tuned into American Bandstand, a national dance music program. Television gave Americans insight into the world but also provided an avenue for developing a cohesive culture.

Rock and Roll

Young people watched American Bandstand because they had fallen in love with a new style of music known as Rock and Roll. Rock and Roll originated from the black experience in the Jim Crow South. This musical genre evolved from the black Blues and Gospel traditions. In these songs, musicians poured out their hearts concerning themes like broken romances, poverty, racism, and drinking. In the 1930s and 1940s, thousands of these African American musicians migrated to northern cities including New York and Chicago. In night clubs, black and white patrons heard these musical styles. This new genre came to be known as rhythm and blues. The music wildly diverged from the tame mainstream faire most Americans consumed. Rhythm and Blues was provocative, raw, experimental, and overtly sexual. The terms "Rock and Roll" or "rock me baby" found in many of the lyrics originally referred to sexual intercourse, as in "You and me baby gonna rock and roll all night long." Because of segregation, black rhythm and blues musicians got little if any airplay on white radio stations, but the music heard in nightclubs or on independent radio stations began to influence many white musicians. White imitators of this black cultural contribution soon emerged and found an audience. The soulful voice of Elvis Presley, a young white truck driver who came of age in Memphis, Tennessee, captured America's attention in 1956. With hits like "Hound Dog" and "Jailhouse Rock," Presley brought black rhythm and blues to the American mainstream. He was soon followed by other flamboyant musicians including Jerry Lee Lewis, Carl Perkins, and Buddy Holly. A Cleveland, Ohio disc jockey named Alan Freed coined the term Rock and Roll for this new kind of music. With greater white acceptance, black musicians

Pierre-Jean Durieu/Shutterstock.com

Regarded as one of the most significant cultural icons of the 20th century, Elvis Presley is often referred to as "the King"

like Little Richard, Fats Domino, and Chuck Berry also found radio airplay and subsequent fame. In mid 1960s, a number of groups from England, including the Beatles and the Rolling Stones, came on the scene and brought their music to America. This "British Invasion" took Rock and Roll to new directions.

Many adults found Rock and Roll tasteless and appalling. They rejected what they saw as suggestive lyrics and even more suggestive dancing. To many adults, Rock and Roll produced conditions and conduct that loosened society's moral fiber. Politicians and ministers denounced it as Satan's music or part of a Communist plot. Many white adults rejected it because it originated from the black segment of society. For these adults, Rock and Roll did not represent proper music for a polite society. Young people on the other hand, white and black, loved it and believed Rock and Roll was here to stay. The music did stay, and while it evolved into a number of different styles, it became an accepted form of music.

The Struggle Against Jim Crow— The Civil Rights Movement

In the 25 years after World War II, African-Americans also took the initiative and sought to carve out for themselves a new road that would culminate in social, legal, and political equality as well as economic opportunity. The Civil Rights Movement was the greatest social movement of the twentieth century. In one sense, the civil rights movement started when the first 20 African slaves debarked from a Dutch ship in Jamestown harbor in 1619. From that point, African-Americans have struggled for freedom, equality, and economic opportunity. After coming out of slavery in 1865, blacks embraced the 14th Amendment which gave them citizenship, and the 15th Amendment which gave black men the vote. The window of opportunity soon closed with the institution of Jim Crow segregation in the 1870s and throughout the rest of the nineteenth century.

NAACP and Brown v. Board of Education

Founded in 1909 during the Progressive Era, the National Association for the Advancement of Colored People (NAACP) sought ways to combat legal, economic, and social oppression aimed at black people. The main strategy employed by the NAACP consisted of attacking the legal underpinnings of Jim Crow, namely the 1896 *Plessy v. Ferguson* decision which made it legal for states to create separate but equal facilities in regards to public accommodations. *Plessy* and later Supreme Court decisions guaranteed the legal and economic separation of African-Americans in all aspects of life. Thus from 1909 onward, NAACP lawyers tried to demonstrate in court that state and local institutions may have been separate, but they certainly did not live up to the equal part. For example, in the early twentieth century, state legislatures such as Mississippi's apportioned five times the money for white schools as opposed to black schools. Between 1935 and 1953, NAACP lawyers took on several cases to demonstrate that southern states were not living up to the separate but equal principle. NAACP lawyers won several precedents that began to chip away at *Plessy*. These precedents led to the monumental *Brown v. Board of Education of Topeka, Kansas* case in 1954. Here, the court ruled for black parents in Kansas who charged that the public school system of Topeka discriminated against their children based on race. The court overturned *Plessy* and declared that segregation was unconstitutional. While things did not change overnight, *Brown* did mark the beginning of the end for Jim Crow segregation.

White Citizens' Council, Southern Manifesto, and Massive Resistance

While the Supreme Court struck a blow at Jim Crow segregation through the *Brown* decision, the racist system was far from dead. White southerners had overthrown or watered down Reconstruction gains in the nineteenth century, and they vowed to resist all measures that would lead to legal, social, and political equality for black southerners in the twentieth century. *Brown* galvanized a counter movement among white southerners. Using a slogan coined by Harry F. Byrd, the U.S. Senator from Virginia, many whites in the South enacted various strategies of "massive resistance" to thwart the possibility of civil rights gains.

The state of Mississippi took the lead as they did at the end of the Reconstruction era. Whites in Mississippi used open violence and terrorism in 1875 to overthrow the leadership of white and black Republican officials. Other southern states soon adopted this "Mississippi Plan." In 1954, white civic leaders in Mississippi developed another plan to quash any hint of black legal or social equality. In the town of Indianola, Mississippi, the leading cotton planters, doctors, lawyers, and merchants formed the first chapter of the White Citizens' Council (WCC). While agreeing in racial sentiment with terrorist groups like the Ku Klux Klan, the WCC publicly eschewed open violence. Instead, the WCC claimed that they would use all legal means to stop the threat of integration. In reality, the WCC used economic intimidation, public exposure, voter fraud, and covert violence, if necessary, to prevent blacks from gaining the vote, economic opportunity, or justice in the state's legal system. One Mississippi journalist called the WCC the "Uptown Klan." WCC chapters multiplied across the state. Blacks in Mississippi who petitioned for integrated schools or tried to register to vote lost their jobs or became the targets of attack or victims of assassination. The WCC quickly shut down civil rights activity in Mississippi or at least forced it to go underground in the 1950s. Other Deep South states like Alabama and Louisiana followed Mississippi's example with WCC chapters of their own. Whether or not other southern states created their own WCC chapters, they did throw up a multitude of roadblocks to prevent full black participation in southern life.

This determination to resist came to full fruition on March 12, 1957, when 19 southern Senators and 77 Representatives of the U.S. Congress signed and published *The Southern Manifesto*. The document denounced the *Brown* decision as an "unwarranted decision of the Supreme Court," and a substitution of "naked power for established law." These legislators argued that the Constitution did not make mention of public schools, and that the issue belonged to the states. In their mind, *Plessy v. Ferguson* had established segregation as the law of the land. Thus, the current Supreme Court had no right to overturn it. These Congressmen vowed to employ all lawful means to overthrow *Brown*. In reality, this meant blacks in the South, whether at a local or state level, faced all kinds of obstacles ranging from police brutality, economic intimidation, and unjust laws guaranteed to prevent them from exercising their full rights as citizens.

Despite the seemingly unbending wall of resistance, African-Americans pushed in a variety of ways to gain their civil rights. In the popular mindset, the Civil Rights Movement was a social phenomenon solely led by great leaders like Dr. Martin Luther King, Jr. This viewpoint also relies on the idea that marches and protests served as the main weapon in the arsenal of civil-rights activists. This mistaken notion also promotes the idea that all civil-rights activists were on the same page. In reality, civil-rights activists ranged from urban teenagers to middle-aged farmers. The Civil Rights Movement consisted of millions of individuals who strove for equality in various venues using various methods.

Rosa Parks and the Montgomery Bus Boycott 1955

One of the most well-known attempts by African-Americans to challenge Jim Crow segregation came in December 1955 with the Montgomery, Alabama bus boycott. Rosa Parks, a seamstress by trade and secretary of the local NAACP chapter, was arrested when she refused to give up her seat on the bus to a white patron.

In reality, many black patrons before Rosa Parks had refused to give up their bus seats to whites in Montgomery. They were usually fined. What made the Parks arrest unique was the context in which it occurred. The United States was battling Soviet Russia in a propaganda war. The United States could not boast of being a democratic country while allowing its own citizens to be denied equal treatment under the law. Also, civil-rights activists could get their message and their struggle out to the growing American media which consisted of newspapers, television, and radio stations. The Montgomery NAACP mailed out thousands of fliers in protest over Parks' arrest. This led to a 381-day boycott by blacks against the public transit system and created national headlines.

One of the leaders who arose from the boycott was a young 26-year-old minister named Martin Luther King, Jr. King's father, Dr. Martin Luther

Rosa Parks

Neftali/Shutterstock.com

King, Sr., headed the NAACP in Atlanta and pastored the Ebenezer Baptist Church in Atlanta. The younger King earned a PhD in Theology from Boston University in 1955. He had come to pastor Dexter Street Baptist Church in Montgomery in 1954. Led by King and others, the boycott economically crippled the Montgomery transit system and forced the white establishment to make concessions to African-American patrons. This small victory helped encourage other African-Americans across the South to strike a blow for freedom.

Little Rock 1957

In September 1957, civil rights activists in Little Rock, Arkansas sought to make *Brown* a reality through the integration of the all-white Central High School. With the aid of Daisy Bates, the head of the NAACP in Arkansas, nine black teenagers sought to integrate the school. They were rebuffed by Arkansas Governor, Orval Faubus, who said he would call in the Arkansas National Guard to prevent the matriculation of the black students. Eight of the students showed up together for the first day of school but were turned away by the National Guard. One student, Elizabeth Eckford, arrived alone by mistake, and was turned away while facing a screaming mob of angry white adults and students. National reporters caught on film and in photographs the young girl's ordeal. With the national spotlight on the case, President Dwight David Eisenhower intervened to enforce the law. He nationalized the National Guard and sent in over 1,000 members of the 101st Airborne Division of the U.S. Army to guarantee the entrance and safety of the young black students. The students faced harassment in school, and their parents faced harassment as well. Ernest Green, the oldest of the nine, graduated from Central High School in 1958. Governor Faubus closed the school in September 1958 to prevent more integration. The citizens of Little Rock voted to keep the school closed, and it remained closed until the next year. The remaining eight students were forced to complete their studies through correspondence courses. These young people and their parents forced the federal government to act on their behalf, but the struggle was far from over.

Hate Crimes—Emmett Till

In the decade after *Brown*, the country not only became aware of civil rights concerns through events like boycotts and school integration attempts, Americans also began to recognize the plight of black Americans because of a number of racially based murders. Several stand out. One was the murder of Emmett Till in Mississippi in 1955. The year 1963 had two horrific episodes. Medgar Evers, Mississippi Field Secretary of the NAACP, was assassinated in his driveway in June by a fanatical white supremacist. A few months later, Klansmen planted and detonated a bomb in the 16th Street Baptist Church in Birmingham, Alabama killing four black teenage girls and severely wounding another.

Emmett Till was a 14-year-old teenager who came from his home in Chicago to Mississippi for a summer visit with relatives in the sleepy little community of Money. While in a county store, Till supposedly whistled and made suggestive remarks to the owner of the store, a white woman named Carolyn Bryant. Bryant later told her husband Roy about the matter. He and his half-brother, J.W. Milam, went to the residence of Till's grandfather and kidnapped the teenager at gunpoint. They took the young man to a secluded barn where they beat him repeatedly, and then shot Till in the head. The murderers tied Till's corpse to an old cotton gin fan and dumped it into the nearby Tallahatchie River. A fisherman later discovered the bloated and disfigured body. Upon receiving the body back in Chicago, Till's mother refused to have the corpse repaired for burial. She wanted the nation to see what had happened to her son. Bryant and Milam were arrested, tried, and found innocent of the murder, despite Till's grandfather identifying them in court. A reporter from *Look* magazine later interviewed Bryant and Milam and got them to confess to the murders. Because of double jeopardy, they could not be tried again, but the case shed light on the vicious and antidemocratic system that was Jim Crow.

Lunch Counters and Sit-Ins—1960

As the country entered the 1960s, civil-rights activists could see no light at the end of the tunnel, but they were determined to continue. Four students at a Greensboro, North Carolina college, Joseph McNeil, Franklin McCain, Ezell Blair, Jr., and David Richmond, decided to take on Jim Crow themselves. Tired of facing discrimination in public places such as restaurants, they decided to buck the racial norms. On February 1, 1960, the four students went to the "whites only" lunch counter in the local F.W. Woolworth store. The store's owner denied the young men service and asked them to leave. The young men remained until closing, and then went and rallied supporters at the college. The next day, the 4 students and 26 others sat in the Woolworth Diner. Within two weeks, students were staging sit-ins in Durham and Winston-Salem, North Carolina. By March 1960, the sit-in movement had spread to over 55 cities in 13 states. Over 70,000 people ultimately took part in the sit-ins and over 3,000 were arrested. By July 1960, Woolworths announced that it would allow all patrons. This movement helped spawn other protests such as kneel-ins in segregated churches, dive-ins in segregated hotel pools, and read-ins in segregated libraries.

Freedom Riders 1961

Legally, Jim Crow segregation was beginning to crumble by 1960. Practically, it stood firm in many ways across the South. In 1961, the Freedom Riders stood as another attempt to tear down the wall of racial segregation. In 1960, the Supreme Court decision, *Boynton v. Virginia*, ruled that segregated interstate bus stations were unconstitutional. Law was one thing, reality was another. Put together by the civil-rights group, the Congress of Racial Equality (CORE), a group of 13 black and white activists traveled by bus from Virginia to Alabama. They arrived in Anniston, Alabama on May 14, 1961. An angry white crowd of over 200 tried to stop the vehicle, but it continued on past the stop. Many of the 200 whites got in their cars and followed the civil-rights activists. Someone from the mob threw an incendiary device into the bus, catching it on fire. When the Freedom Riders debarked, the mob attacked and beat them. A second Freedom Riders group traveled to Birmingham and experienced similar treatment. Ten days later, a third group of Freedom Riders took a bus to Jackson, Mississippi where they were beaten, arrested, and then sent 200 miles north to Parchman Prison, a maximum security facility. A local judge gave the activists a 30-day jail sentences but it was later overturned by the Supreme Court. Time and again, activists were willing to suffer life-threatening situations to bring national spotlight on the plight of blacks in the South.

Affirmative Action—The First Steps

School integration attempts, sit-ins, and freedom rides helped push a sluggish federal government into a modicum of action. By 1961, civil rights agitation had shined a spotlight on the needs of African-Americans and spurred the federal government to take more action. On March 6, 1961, President John F. Kennedy signed Executive Order #10925. This decree banned government contractors from practicing job discrimination based on "race, creed, color, or national origin." This was the first act that used the term "affirmative action." The decree ordered federal contractors to "take affirmative action" in order to insure that none of the aforementioned barriers were used to weed out possible job candidates. In 1965, President Lyndon Johnson issued Executive Order #11246 and took the issue a step further. Not only were federal contractors forbidden to discriminate against job applicants, they were expected to develop a positive action plan and a timetable to rectify inequalities. These Affirmative Action standards expanded into the Vocational Rehabilitation Act of 1973 that ordered federal contractors to take affirmative action concerning the hiring of Americans with disabilities. The Veterans Readjustment Act of 1974 called for federal contractors to take affirmative action concerning the hiring of Vietnam War veterans. Thus, the Civil Rights Movement had a far reaching affect outside of its own concerns.

James Meredith and Ole Miss 1962

These far reaching effects did not occur without the tremendous efforts of individual African-Americans. James Meredith, a 29-year-old African-American and Air Force veteran, tried to integrate the University of Mississippi. Despite the foot dragging by Mississippi officials throughout the Spring and Summer of 1962, the federal courts ruled that Meredith be allowed entry. Stirred up to a frenzy by the rabid segregationist Governor Ross Barnett, a large group of angry whites, many from out of state, descended upon the campus at Oxford, Mississippi. On September 30, 1962, federal marshals accompanied Meredith to the school. While he was safely hidden on campus in a dorm room, a large crowd assaulted the Marshals in front of the Lyceum, the campus administration building. Many of the Marshals suffered bullet wounds or cuts from projectiles. They returned fire with tear gas. The riot forced President John Kennedy to send in over 5,000 federal troops. When the smoke had cleared, two people were found dead; a young white man from Oxford who was shot when he came to investigate the riot, and a French journalist found shot in the back of the head, execution style. Meredith graduated from the university the next year. By 1962, it was becoming clear that African-Americans would not stop pushing for civil rights, and that the federal government was going to have to play a greater role in the black struggle.

MLK and I have a Dream

The next three years (1963–1965) revealed great highs and horrifying lows in the black attempt to gain civil rights. The greatest event of 1963 was the March on Washington. On August 28 of that year, over 200,000 blacks and whites marched in solidarity in the nation's capital for civil rights. The event ended with the landmark "I Have a Dream" speech by Dr. Martin Luther King, Jr. King called for the United States to live up to its creed, "We hold these truths to be self-evident, that all men are created equal." King proclaimed that he had a dream that his four children would "one day live in a nation where they will not be judged by the color of their skin but by the content of their character." King uttered these stirring words in the context of obscene violence. Two months before the speech in June and less than three weeks after

Martin Luther King, Jr.

the speech in September, the nation recoiled in horror at the murder of Medgar Evers and four innocent children all in the name of white supremacy and the maintenance of Jim Crow segregation.

Medgar Evers

Medgar Evers had worked for the NAACP in Mississippi since the early 1950s and kept national media outlets informed of the goings on in the state. As he pulled into his driveway in Jackson, Mississippi on June 11, 1963, a sniper waited in the bushes across the street. Byron De La Beckwith, an avowed white supremacist, shot Evers in the back, killing him almost instantly. Beckwith left his rifle at the scene of the crime with his fingerprints on it. Prosecutors had little problem building a case against Beckwith especially since he later boasted several times of committing the murder. Beckwith escaped justice with two hung juries in the 1960s, but was finally was convicted of Evers' murder in 1994.

Birmingham 1963

Birmingham was a hotbed of civil-rights activity in 1963. As blacks marched and protested, Eugene "Bull" Connor, the Commissioner of Public Safety, unleashed fire hoses and police attack dogs on the protestors. Many of them were teenagers. News photographers and camera men captured images and film of the attacks for the entire country to see. Birmingham possessed a reputation as a center for intense Klan activity. On September 15, 1963, Klansmen set off a bomb just before the 11 a.m. service at the black 16th Street Baptist Church. That service that morning featured the congregation's children. In the recovery effort, rescuers found four young women dead in the basement rubble. Three were 14 years of age. Their names were Addie Mae Collins, Cynthia Wesley, and Carole Robertson. Eleven-year-old Denise McNair also perished. Sarah Collins, the younger sister of Addie Mae Collins, lost her eye, and 20 more suffered wounds from the blast. The dream was far from being realized.

The Civil Rights Act of 1964

The nation saw hope and horror again in 1964. For over a decade, blacks and sympathetic whites had pushed for the United States to fully embrace its ideals of democracy and freedom. Their efforts bore fruit when after a lengthy battle, Congress passed the Civil Rights Act on July 2, 1964. After the violence in Birmingham in 1963, President John F. Kennedy promoted the idea of the legislation, but he was assassinated in November of that same year. President Lyndon B. Johnson carried the effort to fruition. Despite great resistance by southern and border Democrats, the Act became law. It banned segregation from all public places based on race, national origin, or religion. This included areas like courthouses, bus stations, movie theatres, and restaurants. It also banned discrimination in the work force and created an Equal Employment Opportunity Commission that adjudicated lawsuits from workers who believed that they had been discriminated against. It had taken almost a century since the abolition of slavery, but the federal government was finally trying to live up to its obligations to its black citizens as well as other minorities.

Freedom Summer 1964

While the Civil Rights Act brought some hope, more horror came to light in August of 1964 in Mississippi with the discovery of the bodies of three missing civil rights workers: James Chaney, Michael Schwerner, and Andrew Goodman. All three had been murdered and hidden in an earthen levee near the south Mississippi town of Philadelphia where the young men had worked as a part of the Freedom Summer Project. The project had been put together by civil-rights groups like CORE and the Student Non-Violent Coordinating Committee (SNCC), better known by its nickname "Snick." SNCC workers had attempted voter-registration projects as early as late 1962, but faced surveillance and beatings by organized mobs and law officials. The project entailed the training and sending of over 1,000 volunteers to Mississippi for voter-registration projects. White college students made up the majority of these project participants. The Freedom Summer leadership chose Mississippi because it had earned the reputation as the citadel of Jim Crow. Like the SNCC workers before them, the Freedom Summer participants and local activists endured beatings, arrests by the police, and the burning of dozens of black churches which served as the headquarters of local civil-rights activity. In June 1964, Chaney, Schwerner, and Goodman were arrested on trumped-up charges and held in the Neshoba County Jail in Philadelphia. James Chaney, an African-American, was a native of Mississippi. Andrew Goodman and Michael Schwerner came from New York City. Cecil Price, a Neshoba County deputy sheriff, and member of the Klan, released the three young men late at night, but then apprehended them again before they got out of town. Price was soon joined by two cars carrying his fellow Klansmen. The deputy and his gang took the young men to a secluded spot, shot them in the head, and buried the bodies in an earthen levee. The disappearance of the three activists remained a mystery for over two months before the Federal Bureau of Investigation got an informant to reveal the location of the bodies on August 4, 1964. Federal prosecutors charged the 19 men for violating the activists' civil rights. The U.S. officials knew that no white jury in the area would convict the men of murder. By 1967, Price and six other men, including a Grand Dragon of the Ku Klux Klan, were sentenced to prison terms from 3 to 10 years. A small victory, but this was the first time that white men had been convicted for crimes against civil-rights workers.

Selma

Civil rights activists knew that the national media spotlight was their ally in demonstrating the undemocratic and frightening nature of Jim Crow segregation. Protestors for civil rights proved this reality again on Sunday, March 7, 1965. Hundreds of black protestors, along with a number of sympathetic whites, sought to march peacefully for voting rights from the south Alabama town of Selma to the state capital of Montgomery. As the marchers started, they were met with deputies on horseback and Alabama Highway Patrolmen in full riot gear. When the marchers refused to disperse, the law officials waded into the crowd with tear gas and beat activists with billy clubs. Once again, national media outlets caught the violence with video and photographs.

Monument dedicated to Selma, Montgomery

The event horrified President Lyndon B. Johnson. Eight days after what came to known as "Bloody Sunday," he addressed a joint session of Congress and called for sweeping voting rights legislation. On August 6, 1965, Johnson signed the Voting Rights Act. This was one of the most sweeping civil-rights laws in U.S. history. It banned the use of literacy tests which had been a potent tool for denying blacks, literate or not, the franchise. The measure called for the Justice Department to send officials into areas where over 50% of the nonwhite voting age public was not registered to vote. It also allowed the Justice Department to investigate the use of poll taxes: small fees required to vote. These would be outlawed by the Supreme Court in 1966. This legislation and its enforcement meant that Deep South states with large black populations saw significant increases in voter registration. In a little over a decade, civ-il-rights activists had made enormous strides in dismantling and reshaping a society once based on discrimination. These countless millions had turned the United States down a road of new possibilities.

Changes had come, but the road toward full equality was still fraught with detours and landmines. Many people had joined the civil-rights movement with a faith in the basic goodness and decency of the United States. They thought that white American would change, but for many activists, the struggle had been constantly grueling and many times frightful. The movement suffered from internal disputes as well as a growing anger against virulent racists and even white allies who wanted to tone down or control the protests.

Black Nationalism

Some African-American activists parted ways with the nonviolent and cooperation mentality of Martin Luther King, Jr. One of these was Malcolm X. A spokesman for the African-American group, the Nation of Islam, Malcolm X called for black separation and vigorous self-defense. He rejected cooperation with whites and called for black pride and the formation of black businesses. In 1964, he went to Mecca, Saudi Arabia, the spiritual home of the religion of Islam. Seeing Muslims of all colors broadened his understanding concerning prejudice and racism. While just as militant against racism in America, he began to work with people he once separated himself from. He had a falling out with the Nation of Islam and was assassinated by a member of the organization in New York City on February 21, 1965. *The Autobiography of Malcolm X* came out later that year and influenced a lot of young African-Americans toward a more radical answer in the fight against racism.

Many young activists also fell out with the strategies of Martin Luther King, Jr. While voting rights were being gained, many of these young people still saw problems like violence against protestors, police brutality, slums in the inner cities, grinding poverty in rural areas, and terrible healthcare for the majority of black people. Facing all these problems, they saw no solutions in sight. This anger led many African-Americans to denounce white America as corrupt and impervious to change. These young people called for a more militant reaction. Under the slogan of Black Power, these angry African-Americans called for the dismantling of American capitalism in exchange for economic socialism. They called for a renewed pride in African culture, solidarity amongst blacks, and a separation from whites.

America saw black anger erupt into riots hundreds of times between 1965 and 1968. In August 1965, blacks in the Watts neighborhood of Los Angeles, California rioted over police brutality. The effects were shocking. Thirty four people died, the police arrested over 4,000 others, and the riot resulted in over 35 million dollars in property damage. Forty American cities experienced riots in 1966. Newark, New Jersey and Detroit, Michigan exploded with massive riots in 1967. The Civil Rights Movement had created massive change, but it did not seem enough to millions still mired in economic deprivation.

LBJ and the Great Society

President Lyndon B. Johnson recognized this reality and sought to provide solutions to not only elevate minorities in regards to voting rights, but also directing the federal government to provide tools to help end poverty. The stark reality facing the nation was that over 20% of its population lived below the poverty level. Johnson declared in 1964 that the U.S. government was going to wage a war on poverty and challenged the country to create a "Great Society." Congress passed a dizzying array of programs under this umbrella title. One of these was the Economic Opportunity Act of 1964. This act created the Office for Economic Opportunity, and this agency created a job corps which provided vocational training. The Economic Opportunity Act also provided funds for the creation of Volunteers in Service to America (VISTA). Trained VISTA participants went into impoverished areas for one year to work on projects aimed toward fighting poverty. Other Great Society programs included Medicare and Medicaid. Medicare provided health insurance to people over age 65, and Medicaid provided health insurance to people at certain low income levels. The Food Stamp Act provided government assistance for poor people to purchase greater quantities of essential foodstuffs. Head Start programs sought to provide enrichment activities for low income preschoolers in order to prepare them for kindergarten. These and other legislative acts made Johnson's administration the most active concerning social legislation since the presidency of Franklin D. Roosevelt. Like Roosevelt's New Deal, the Great Society came under intense scrutiny and attack. Johnson's programs did decrease poverty, but it also increased the number of Americans receiving welfare payments instead of seeking jobs. Many of the programs spent too much money or were mismanaged. At the same time, many Americans received educational and vocational aid, and the elderly and the poor received help in paying their medical bills. The Great Society further expanded government in ways that many thought were positive, while a growing number of Americans considered Johnson's programs as government run amok.

Earl Warren and the Supreme Court

Whether through the actions of civil rights protestors or legislation pushed by Presidents, the late 1950s and 1960s saw massive social change. The U.S. Supreme Court helped facilitate much of the alteration to the social and political landscape. In 1953, President Dwight D. Eisenhower appointed Earl Warren, a former Governor of California, as Chief Justice of the Supreme Court. In his 16 years on the bench (1953–1969), Warren led the court in making massive changes concerning the equality of minorities, the nature of church state relations in regards to public schools, and the treatment of individuals under legal arrest. Warren's court is most known for the 1954 *Brown* decision which declared segregation unconstitutional. During his tenure, the Supreme Court consistently upheld civil rights legislation passed by Congress. In a 1962 decision, *Engel v. Vitale*, the court ruled that public school officials could not begin the school day with mandatory religious services written and sponsored by the state. This violated the establishment clause of the First Amendment to the Constitution. In 1963, the Court ruled in *Gideon v. Wainright* that impoverished defendants required legal representation. In 1966, the Court issued the *Miranda v. Arizona* judgment. This decision declared that legal authorities had to inform detainees of their right to silence and their right to legal counsel even if they could not afford a lawyer. While hailed by many, the Warren decisions came under attack by religious and legal conservatives. Many saw *Brown* as government overreach in regards to a state's control of its education system. *Engel* shocked many ministers and church goers as taking God out of the public school system. For many in the legal and law enforcement communities, decisions like *Miranda* hog-tied the police in the performance of their duty while also coddling criminals. Despite the criticisms, most saw the Warren Court as having a positive influence on the country.

The Feminist Movement

With so much social change occurring in the late 1950s and early 1960s, it was only natural that this spirit of change affected other minority groups with their own concerns. The 1960s saw the rise of a militant feminist movement. Women had a long history in America of fighting for their rights and the rights of others. This included the gaining of the right to own property, protesting for the abolition of slavery, and exercising the right to vote. Women had made significant gains by the 1960s, but traditional views still consigned most women to the domestic sphere. Many women found this limitation to be stifling. In 1963, Betty Friedan's book, *The Feminine Mystique,* revealed that a number of American women wanted more for their lives than simply being wives and homemakers. The book challenged women to expand their horizons by going to college and finding careers for themselves. Many young women had already taken an active role in the Civil Rights Movement. Others would join the protest against the war in Vietnam. By 1960, the first oral contraceptive, commonly known as the pill, came on the market, and it allowed women (and men) to have sex in or outside of marriage without worrying about pregnancy. Many found this socially liberating. This added to the spirit of the times where women sought more opportunities and found greater freedom for themselves. Women's rights groups like the National Organization for Women (NOW), founded in 1966, challenged social norms and political traditions. By piggybacking on the gains made by civil-rights activists, women in the 1960s began to carve out for themselves a greater slice of the American dream.

First Women's March for Equality. 5th Ave. NYC

© JP Laffont/Sygma/Corbis.

Gay Rights

The 1960s also saw the emergence of other minority groups who also used the strategies of the Civil Rights Movement to further their own concerns. The Gay Rights Movement served as an example. Religious traditionalists deemed homosexuality a sin and in 1953, the American Psychiatric Society declared being gay a sociopathic disorder. Yet, the 1948 Alfred Kinsey study, *Sexual Behavior in the Human Male*, revealed that almost 40% of the men surveyed for the study admitted to having some kind of homosexual experience. Gays were banned from U.S. government positions in 1953 by

Painted white bronze sculptures by artist entitled "Gay Liberation" George Segal are on the campus of Stanford University.

an Executive Order from President Dwight Eisenhower. Although some gay-rights groups emerged in the 1950s and early 1960s, little had changed.

June 28, 1969 is considered the traditional date for the start of the Gay Rights Movement. Forty-nine out of 50 states had outlawed sex between people of the same gender. In cities like New York City, police made over 100 arrests per week in clubs and other areas where gay New Yorkers congregated. Patrons at the Stonewall Inn, a gay bar in the Greenwich Village section of New York City, regularly received harassment by the police. On June 28, 1969, the police began to roust patrons in the bar, but many fought back. The battle grew so intense that more police were sent in full riot gear. The protest lasted a week. On June 28, 1970, Gay New Yorkers hosted the first Gay Pride parade in honor of the Stonewall Inn riot. It would take decades, but this was the first step toward greater acceptance.

El Movimíento—The Chicano Movement

Mexican Americans, also known as Chicanos, used the civil-rights strategies of the 1950s and 1960s to further their aims as well. Known as El Movimíento or "the movement," Chicano activists gained traction as early as the 1940s. All across the Southwest, Chicanos faced barriers such as segregation, legal inequality, and job exploitation. One of the first gains for Chicanos came with the 1947 Supreme Court decision, *Mendez v. Westminister* which declared that Chicano children could not be segregated in public schools. The 1954 *Hernandez v. Texas* decision declared that the 14th Amendment's call for equal protection included all minority groups. Most Chicanos in states like Texas and California earned their living in the agricultural industry and faced various forms of discrimination. In the 1960s, activists like Cesar Chavez, Dolores Huerta, and Philip Vera Cruz helped form the United Farm

Workers Union. Mirroring other civil-rights activists, Chicanos employed nonviolent protests, boycotts, and strikes to engender change. Many school-age Mexican-Americans worked in what they called the Chicano Student Movement. They battled school segregation and protested over issues like quality textbooks, more Chicano teachers, and classes that spotlighted Chicano culture.

Student Protests and the Counter Culture

The Civil Rights protests of the late 1950s and early 1960s energized many baby boomers coming of age. Unlike their parents, these young Americans had not face the twin crises of the Great Depression and World War II. Many of these young people were the first in their family to attend college. Almost 44% of all 18 to 22-year-olds in the United States attended college by the early 1960s, and three fourths of these students came from homes where the parents' earnings stood above the national median.

Students for a Democratic Society members outside the White House picketing against U.S. policy in Vietnam

With less concerns about finances, this allowed scores of young people, especially white kids, greater time for reflection. Many became concerned about America's plunge into mass consumerism. Students began to voice concerns about the growth of corporate and government funding of research projects in dozens of colleges. Thousands of college-age Americans were stirred by the idealism of John F. Kennedy and his famous inaugural exhortation, "Ask not what your country can do for you, but what you can do for your country." Many white college students joined their black compatriots in the civil rights movement.

What these students saw and experienced proved shocking. They saw the grinding poverty blacks faced in the Deep South. As many took part in projects like the Freedom Riders, or Sit-Ins, or Freedom Summer, these young white people viewed firsthand the mistreatment of blacks. They themselves encountered police brutality and mob violence and saw the legal authority either turn a blind eye or personally take part in the oppression. These experiences radicalized many of these students.

The student protestors came to be known as the New Left because they served as antagonists to conservative values and demanded radical changes to what was considered the traditional American way of life. The first organized group to follow this route was known as the Students for a Democratic Society (SDS). Founded at the University of Michigan in 1960, SDS students denounced racism, corporatism, and militarism. In 1962, they issued the Port Huron statement which criticized a litany of social injustices. By 1964, students at the University of California at Berkeley tangled with college officials over the distribution of civil rights leaflets near the campus. This led to the Free Speech Movement concerning student involvement in political demonstrations on campus. SDS chapters popped up on many American college campuses. These activists denounced the slowness of the federal government to get involved in the Civil Rights Movement, they decried the growing American involvement in the Vietnam War, and they argued that President Johnson's Great Society programs did not go far enough toward eliminating poverty. By the late 1960s, student protestors managed to put together anti-war demonstrations with several hundred thousand participants in cities like New York. In 1968, over 200 anti-Vietnam War rallies took place.

Protests against societal evils like racism and a questionable war stood as a part of what became known as the Counter Culture. The questioning of authority led many young people to experiment in new, and sometimes shocking, expressions of life. While certainly not a majority, many young people grew their hair long, experimented with marijuana and hallucinogenic drugs like LSD. They wore nontraditional fashions, listened to psychedelic rock bands like the Doors or the Jimi Hendrix Experience, and indulged in sexual abandon. The availability of the birth-control pill allowed for the latter with little fear of pregnancy. Many Americans from the Depression and/or World War II generation grew appalled at the attitudes and actions of the nation's youth.

King and Kennedy Assassinations 1968

By 1968, it appeared to many older Americans that the country's social fabric was coming apart at the seams. The country had suffered through the assassination of an idealistic president, John F. Kennedy. African-Americans felt an ever-growing frustration at the limits of civil-rights protest. This frustration led to riots across hundreds of American cities. The Vietnam War appeared to be a morass from which there was no exit. The cost of the war and Lyndon Johnson's Great Society programs inflicted a massive financial burden on taxpayers. Young people seemed to be throwing off all traditions. Could things get much worse? They did. In April and June of 1968, the country recoiled in horror at the assassinations of Dr. Martin Luther King, Jr. and Robert F. Kennedy.

In April, King journeyed to Memphis, Tennessee to stand in solidarity with striking black sanitation workers. King himself had become more radical. He had fallen out with younger black activists who rejected nonviolence and promoted Black Power. While still promoting nonviolence, King criticized the Vietnam War and angered President Johnson. He saw the limitations of civil rights legislation and sought to address the economic concerns of impoverished black Americans. As he stepped out on the second floor balcony of the Lorraine Motel on April 4, 1968, a rifle shot rang out. A bullet hit King in the chest and killed him. His assailant, a white man named James Earl Ray, was soon captured and imprisoned. The news of King's death led to over 100 riots across the country.

Robert F. Kennedy, the former Attorney General and brother of the slain President, was running for the office of Chief Executive when he heard the news of King's death. Addressing a crowd in Indianapolis, Indiana, Kennedy called for calm and told the crowd that he understood the pain of having a loved one murdered. Two months later on June 5, 1968, Kennedy also met his end by an assassin's bullet while campaigning in Los Angeles. Sirhan Sirhan, an immigrant from Jordan, claimed he committed the deed because he considered Kennedy a promoter of the nation of Israel and an enemy of all Palestinians under Israeli occupation. For a lot of Americans, the deaths of King and Kennedy came as crushing blows. Both charismatic and idealistic, many thought these two might lead the country into a better place. Instead, they served as examples of the ever growing chaos of the 1960s.

Richard Nixon and the "Silent Majority"

By 1968, many Americans were tired of the unrest and hoped for a change. The Vietnam War had turned into a fiasco and ruined the presidency of Lyndon Johnson. He refused to run for reelection. Many Democrats had pinned their hopes on the campaign of Robert Kennedy. He was opposed by Senator Eugene McCarthy and Vice President Hubert Humphrey. With Kennedy's death in June 1968, Democratic support swung toward Humphrey. Humphrey won the nomination at the Democratic convention in Chicago, Illinois, but a great deal of national attention turned toward the Vietnam protestors who infiltrated the convention hall as well as protesting outside. News cameras caught Chicago police officers beating protestors with nightsticks and herding them into police paddy wagons. The chaos seemed far from over.

Richard Nixon, the Republican nominee, ran as a counterweight candidate promising to restore order amidst the turmoil. Nixon promised to end the Vietnam War and vowed to listen to the "silent majority" who had grown tired of the war and all the social upheaval. A large number middle class white Americans chose Nixon and gave him a narrow victory over Humphries in November 1968. This "silent majority" rejected the changes brought in the 1960s. They thought that the old verities were being overthrown, and they wanted to rectify the situation. In the minds of many Americans, the clamoring of war protestors, sexual libertines, civil rights activists, and feminists served to undermine traditions like patriotism, work ethic, God, and marriage. Those that voted for Nixon hoped for a reviving of America's fortunes at home and abroad. In reality, as the United States entered the 1970s, the turmoil and social chaos would only increase.

CHAPTER TWENTY

The Rise of Conservatism

Chapter 20: Key Concepts

- What was the Watergate scandal about, and how did it diminish the office of the President?

- What were the domestic and foreign problems that soured Americans on the Presidency of Jimmy Carter?

- What were the successes and failures of the presidency of Ronald Reagan?

- What were the key domestic issues and foreign problems during the Bill Clinton administration?

- What were the crises of George Bush's presidency that affect us to the present?

If any one word can describe an era, then the word "divided" aptly describes the 1960s. The country divided over the Vietnam War and over issues such as the direction of the civil rights movement and gender equality. Young people coming out of the Baby Boom generation disagreed with their parents over what constituted acceptable behavior and what made good citizens. Americans divided over the nature of government itself, an age old argument going back to the days of Thomas Jefferson and Alexander Hamilton. By 1968, many Americans wanted a turning back of the clock. They wanted a return to small government which meant less interference in people's lives and less tax dollars from their pockets. Millions of Americans wanted a president who could reunite the country. Richard Nixon promised to do all that. He claimed that the goal of his presidency was "to bring the American people together."

Richard M. Nixon

Library of Congress, Prints & Photographs Division, LC-USZ62-13037

Nixon's election marked a significant turn in American history. From 1968 to 2008, the United States underwent a more conservative turn in politics. Republican Presidents led the country 28 of 40 years. While Bill Clinton (1993–2001) was a Democrat, even he had to govern more as a centrist than previous Democratic Presidents.

Nixon (1969–1974)

In the 36-year period between 1933 and 1969, only one Republican served in the Oval Office, namely Dwight D. Eisenhower (1953–1961). As President, Eisenhower kept many of the New Deal and Fair Deal policies of Franklin Roosevelt and Harry S. Truman. Yet, by 1964, there was a growing conservative backlash against the entrenched Democratic vision for the country. Barry Goldwater, a Republican Senator from Arizona, ran a hard right campaign against President Lyndon Johnson in 1964. Goldwater denounced many of the established New Deal programs like Social Security. He shocked many by saying that atomic weapons served as one of the U.S. options in the growing Vietnam conflict. He also did not support the Civil Rights Act of 1964. Goldwater, however, proved too extreme for most Americans. Johnson crushed Goldwater by 16 million votes. The President tallied every state's electoral vote except Goldwater's home state of Arizona and the Deep South states of Louisiana, Mississippi, Alabama, Georgia, and South Carolina.

While many saw Goldwater as extreme, the next four years (1965 through late 1968) seethed with conflict and caused many to reconsider or further push for a more conservative ideology. By the election of 1968, many Americans had grown disillusioned with the direction of the country. The growing quagmire that was the Vietnam War, the civil rights protests and urban unrest, the counter culture movement, and the cost of Lyndon

Johnson's Great Society programs alarmed many conservative, traditional Americans. They wanted a candidate who would resolve the Vietnam conflict as well as promote traditional values like faith in God, patriotism, and self-reliance. Former Vice President Richard M. Nixon promised to fit that bill. Nixon narrowly defeated Hubert Humphrey who had served as Lyndon Johnson's Vice President. While Nixon did not carry all the Deep South in 1968, more and more Deep South states began voting Republican. Between 1968 and the early 1980s, a trend emerged where former southern Democratic strongholds began to go almost exclusively Republican in Presidential elections.

Nixon had to change his modus operandi in the 1968 election. As a Congressman from California, he had earned a reputation as a ruthless Communist hunter during the Second Red Scare of the late 1940s and early 1950s. He served as a dutiful Vice President under Eisenhower, and he narrowly lost the Presidency to John F. Kennedy in 1960. Nixon also lost the governorship of California in 1962. In 1968, he ran as the "New Nixon," one who was a responsible, sensible candidate, and one who could lead the country out of the turmoil of the 1960s.

Vietnam Protests

As seen in the last chapter, Nixon's actions in Vietnam contradicted his campaign claims to reduce the U.S. effort in the overseas conflict. As with the Johnson administration, war protesters denounced Nixon for ratcheting up the war effort. Two of these protests led to bloodshed. On May 4, 1970, at Kent State University in Ohio, National Guardsmen shot and killed four anti-war protesters. On May 14, two black students died after being shot by state Highway Patrolmen at Jackson State College in Jackson, Mississippi.

Oil Embargo

While Nixon was trying to wind down the war, another foreign crisis came to bear heavily upon the U.S. economy. In October 1973, Egypt and Syria unleashed a surprise attack on the nation of Israel. These two states, along with many other Muslim countries, had been at odds with Israel since its founding in 1948. The United States tried to diffuse the situation but also provided Israel with military aid. Despite heavy losses, the Israelis successfully repelled the invasion. In retaliation, the Organization of Petroleum Exporting Countries (OPEC), which included Muslim countries like Saudi Arabia, Iraq, and Iran, launched an oil embargo against the United States. The lack of oil sent fuel prices skyrocketing which also led to high inflation. This meant that a person's income bought fewer items. Negotiations eventually ended the embargo in the Spring of 1974, but the crisis revealed a U.S. weakness concerning our dependence on foreign oil and led to such measures as the creation of a Strategic Petroleum Preserve, lowered speed limits on American highways, and the creation of more fuel-efficient automobiles.

Despite his campaign rhetoric about cutting back government influence, Nixon actually put forth several measures that increased government impact in certain aspects of

American life. He expanded the number of people covered by Social Security. Through an executive order, he created the Environmental Protection Agency (EPA). This government agency sought to regulate businesses in regards to pollution as well as clean up the environment. In 1972, the EPA successfully put forth its first legislation, the Clean Air Act. Concerning civil rights, Nixon's Labor Department enacted Affirmative Action timetables in 1969 to insure that businesses that held government contracts move toward the hiring of qualified minority candidates.

Equal Rights Amendment

Other social concerns of the 1960s continued to garner attention during Nixon's tenure. Women's Liberation activists pushed for and got Congress to pass the Equal Rights Amendment in 1972. The amendment stated in very simple language, "Equality of rights under the law shall not be denied or abridged by the United States or by any state on account of sex." Thirty-five states eventually approved the amendment, but it needed 38 to have the three-quarters vote needed to get ratification. As the country entered the 1980s, the amendment still lacked the three votes.

Watergate

Nixon's hopes of acquiring a sufficient number of reelection votes in 1972 appeared bright, but he and his advisers planted the seeds for their own destruction. On June 17, 1972, Washington D.C. police caught five inept burglars inside the Democratic National Headquarters in the Watergate Building. The complex held an array of offices and personal apartments. James McCord, Jr., one of the five intruders, served as Chief of Security for Nixon's Committee to Reelect the President, called CREEP by critics. Nixon deflected any connection to the break in and crushed liberal Democrat George McGovern in the 1972 election. Nixon won every state's electoral votes but Massachusetts along with 60% of the popular vote.

Washington Post investigative reporter Bob Woodward proved to be one of the key contributors to unraveling the Watergate scandal

The Watergate scandal did not go away, however, but only grew bigger. Three of the Watergate burglars pleaded guilty, and the other two were convicted. Robert Woodward and Carl Bernstein, reporters for the *Washington Post*, began to investigate the story. Over the rest of 1972 and 1973, they and others uncovered an array of illegal activities that implicated several of Nixon's campaign staff, advisers in his administration, and even the President himself. This led to Congressional hearings and multiple members of the Nixon administration resigning and later being indicted. Nixon taped all of his office meetings, and eventually Congress subpoenaed the tapes. The tapes clearly revealed that in many ways Nixon was involved in the cover-up.

By 1973, multiple scandals inundated the Nixon administration. In the October of that year, Vice President Spiro Agnew had to resign because of his own dishonor. An investigation revealed that he had taken bribes while serving as the Governor of Maryland. He pled no contest to tax evasion. Gerald R. Ford, a Congressman from Michigan, became Vice President. By the time the Watergate scandal came to full fruition, a total of 40 government officials came under indictment. Many of Nixon's closest advisers were convicted and served time in prison.

By the summer of 1974, it became clear that Congress was going to bring articles of impeachment against President Nixon. He had not ordered the Watergate break in, but he clearly took part in the cover up. To escape the disgrace of impeachment, Nixon resigned on August 9, 1974.

Gerald Ford (1974–1976)

Gerald Ford was sworn in as President, and subsequently committed a blunder that marred his presidency. He did not think the country needed to see a disgraced president tried in court, so Ford pardoned Nixon from all wrongdoing. He claimed "our long national nightmare is over." His act outraged a large number of Americans. What Ford actually did was guarantee that he would not be elected President in his own right.

Ford's brief tenure as president (August 1974–January 1977) took place during traumatic foreign and domestic crises. On April 30, 1975, North Vietnamese forces stormed into the South Vietnamese capital city of Saigon, unifying Vietnam under Communist rule. News cameras caught U.S. service personnel fleeing the U.S. embassy by helicopter. The United States had waged war against the North Vietnamese since 1964. The fall of Saigon served as a great embarrassment for the country and the great loss of life, over 58,000 deaths, damaged many Americans' faith in the military. At home, the country was still reeling from the Watergate scandal as well as a terrible economic downturn. Along with the oil embargo, the economy suffered from high inflation and the unemployment rate doubled from less than 5% to over 8%.

Jimmy Carter (1977–1981)

All of these factors led American voters to reach out in a new direction. In the same year that the country celebrated its 200th anniversary in July 1976, James Earl Carter, Jr., better known as Jimmy, won the presidency in November. A former Democratic Governor of Georgia, Carter ran as an outsider and brought a warmth and sincerity that many voters gravitated toward. Yet, the same economic problems that plagued Ford, also weighed down Carter's administration. The economy stagnated with interest rates reaching 20% as well as high inflation. Carter's policies failed to overcome these conditions.

Human Rights and Camp David Accords

Concerning foreign issues, Carter sought to bring a new spirit into the White House. He emphasized human rights and denounced oppression, especially for those behind the Iron Curtain. Needless to say, his call for more humane treatment was met with indifference by Soviet Russia and other nations. Carter's major foreign achievement came in 1979 with the Camp David Accords. Carter tried to bring together the warring countries of Egypt and Israel. By late 1978, Carter got Egyptian President, Anwar El Sadat, and Israeli Prime Minister, Menachem Begin, to meet at Camp David, the presidential retreat in Maryland. On

Egyptian President Anwar Sadat and Israeli Prime Minister Menachem Begin acknowledge applause during a Joint Session of Congress in which President Jimmy Carter announced the results of the Camp David Accords

March 26, 1979, Sadat and Begin signed a peace treaty known as the Camp David Accords. Egypt formally recognized Israel, and Israel pledged to gradually remove its troops from the Sinai Peninsula, the border between the two countries. Both pledged to conduct trade and diplomacy with each other. The Camp David accords angered many in the Arab world, but worldwide, Carter's efforts were seen as a major diplomatic coup. Also during Carter's presidency, the United States formally recognized the People's Republic of China.

Afghanistan and the Iran Hostage Crisis

Despite some foreign success, a bad economy and two major foreign policy setbacks helped set the stage for Carter being a one-term president. In 1979, any hope of better relations with the Soviet Union evaporated when the Soviets invaded Afghanistan and installed a Communist government. Protestations from the United States did little. Symbolically, the height of U.S. resistance concerning the invasion came when Carter ordered the U.S. Olympic team to boycott the 1980 Summer Olympics in Moscow.

The event that came to indelibly stamp the Carter presidency also came in 1979 with the takeover of the U.S. embassy in Iran by Muslim extremists. In 1953, the United States helped covertly overthrow Mohammad Mossadegh, the legitimate leader of Iran, when he threatened to nationalize Iran's oil industry. The United States and Britain had controlled most of the oil production. Once Mossadegh was overthrown, the United States installed a pro-western ruler, the Shah (Mohammad Reza Pahlavi). The Shah allowed the United States and Britain to continue to profit from Iran's oil production. While pro-American, the

Shah brutalized his own people with secret police and economic policies that hurt Iranians while he personally lived in luxury. He was ousted in 1979, and the United States allowed him into the country for cancer treatments. This enraged student revolutionaries in the capital city of Teheran. Under the direction of radical Islamic leader, Ayatollah Ruhollah Khomeini, Iranian students stormed the U.S. Embassy on November 4, 1979. Originally, 66 people were taken hostage. Later 14 people were released (women, African-Americans, and foreign nationals). Fifty-two Americans were held hostage for 444 days until January 21, 1981. Carter ordered U.S. banks to freeze Iranian assets and sought negotiations, but nothing worked. By the Spring of 1980, Carter sent in a covert military rescue team, but a helicopter crashed killing eight U.S. servicemen. While a decent man and a real humanitarian, Carter appeared weak in regards to our sworn Cold War enemy and powerless to rescue Americans from the clutches of extremists. These disappointments, plus a stagnating economy, paved the way for a conservative Republican resurgence in 1980. Ronald Reagan, a former Hollywood actor, and two-term Governor of California, led the way.

The country's national psyche had taken numerous hits in the 17 years leading up to 1980. President John F. Kennedy had been killed in 1963. His brother and presidential hopeful, Robert Kennedy, also died from as assassin's bullet in 1968. Malcolm X and Martin Luther King, Jr., both civil-rights icons, met bloody ends in the 1960s. The country endured a decade long war in Vietnam that left 58,000 dead, over 300,000 wounded, a disheartened military, and a country divided. The Soviet Union still loomed as a large threat to freedom and democracy over large parts of the world. African-Americans and other minorities made great strides in the area of civil rights, but still faced economic and legal oppression. Our highest office, the Presidency, fell under disgrace through the mechanizations of Richard Nixon. The economy deteriorated in the latter part of the 1970s, and many Americans, Republican and Democrat alike, thought government influence was too far reaching, too bloated with bureaucracy, and too free with its spending. It's safe to say that by 1980, many Americans had grown discouraged about the paths the nation had taken in the past and questioned where it was headed in the future.

Ronald Reagan (1981–1988)

Ronald Reagan ran for President in 1980 and promised to return America to its former greatness. His message rang true with millions of Americans across the country. Only 17 days shy of turning 70 at his inauguration in January 20, 1981, he was the oldest man to become President. Reagan talked tough but always had a smile. He declared that "government is not the solution to our problems, government is the problem!" Reagan ran a conservative campaign, calling for spending cuts in federal programs. With interest rates hovering at 20%, Reagan promoted government deregulation and tax cuts. His rationale revolved around the idea that tax cuts would allow businesses to keep more income and thus spur greater productivity. On a personal level, if people paid fewer taxes, then they would have more money in their pockets to spend. According to Reagan's philosophy, tax cuts would stimulate the economy.

Concerning foreign diplomacy, the "Great Communicator," as he was later called, promised to get the release of the American hostages in Iran. Reagan believed in a robust push back to the spread of Soviet Communist influence. He called for the strengthening of U.S. defenses and helping allies around the world fight Communism whether overtly or covertly. Reagan's charisma and rhetoric helped him capture 51% of the popular vote and the electoral votes of forty-five states. The election of Ronald Reagan marked a conservative resurgence in the United States.

The country seemed to be on an upswing the day Reagan was inaugurated. On January 21, 1981, as Reagan took the oath of office as President, Iran released the 52 American hostages.

President Ronald Reagan in his office

Library of Congress, Prints & Photographs Division, photograph by Carol M. Highsmith, LC-DIG-highsm-15747.

Reagan did not have anything directly to do with the release, but the timing could not have been more perfect. A couple of months later, a would-be assassin shot Reagan. His popularity went up when word got out that while the President lay on the operating table, he quipped to the surgical staff, "I hope you are all Republicans."

Tax Cuts, Deregulation, and Disparity of Wealth

Domestically, Reagan got Republicans and many Democrats to support much of his agenda. Congress cut back government regulations for businesses and lowered tax rates. Reaganomics, the moniker given to the President's economic policies, did lead to a major economic upswing. The highest tax rate dropped from 70% to 28%. This led to more business investment which in turn led to more higher paying jobs. Two years into Reagan's term, Americans saw inflation and unemployment drop below 10%. On the other hand, Reagan's policies led to deep cuts in many programs geared toward helping the poor and other areas like student loans. Reagan's policies did benefit a lot of Americans, but they helped the richest Americans the most. The 400 richest families in the United States saw their wealth increase three fold in the 1980s. The gap between the rich and poor regressed to World War II levels. The prosperity that Reagan promised in the 1980s did trickle down to a great number of Americans, but it did not reach down to those on the bottom.

Concerning civil and gender rights, Reagan opposed the extension of the 1965 Voting Rights Act. His administration sought to end many Affirmative Action programs. Many of his judicial appointees wanted to scale back civil rights initiatives. He did appoint the first woman to the U.S. Supreme Court, Sandra Day O'Connor. Yet, the conservative turn of many in the country resulted in the failure of the Equal Rights Amendment to be ratified by the 1982 deadline.

Reagan and Gorbachev—*Glastnost and Perestroika*

While running for President, Ronald Reagan called a building up of the American military presence around the world and a greater push back against Soviet Russia. In both he was successful. During his presidency, the United States invaded the small Caribbean island of Grenada in 1983 to repel Cuban forces. In 1986, U.S. bombers attacked two cities in the African country of Libya. The bombers tried to take out Libya's leader Muammar Gadaffi for his support of terrorist acts against the United States and its allies. In regards to Communism, Reagan demanded that the Soviet Union tear down the Berlin Wall, the symbol of the Iron Curtain and oppression. While talking tough, Reagan actually reached out to the leader of Soviet Russia, Mikhail Gorbachev. The two men became close. The Soviets had spent so much money on defense that their economy teetered on the verge of collapse. Gorbachev saw that it made sense to cut back on defensive measures. Gorbachev put forth a policy known as *Glastnost* which meant "openness." He called for the Russian economy to be "restructured," *Perestroika* in Russian. This new economic outlook meant that the Soviet Union would be more open to western capitalism. Relations between the two countries improved so much that in 1987, Reagan and Gorbachev signed the Intermediate-Range Nuclear Forces (INF) Treaty. This agreement called for the destruction of 2,500 U.S. and Soviet missiles in Europe.

While seeing some success, Reagan's tax cuts and military buildup came with a high price. Cutting taxes helped individuals and corporations, but it did not bring as much revenue into the federal coffers as projected. The decreased revenue plus heavy defense spending significantly increased the national deficit. That is the amount by which the government spends more than it takes in per year. Deficit spending increased almost three fold from 80 billion dollars a year to 221 billion dollars a year between 1980 and 1986. The deficit spending also tripled the national debt, the amount the government owes to its creditors. The debt increased from slightly less than one trillion dollars in 1980 to over 2.7 trillion dollars by 1986. Reagan promised to reign in government, but he actually increased government spending dramatically.

Iran-Contra Affair

One major political scandal marred Ronald Reagan's eight years in office. Nicknamed the Iran/Contra affair, the scandal revolved around a covert Central Intelligence Agency (CIA) operation that connected the Middle Eastern countries of Iran and Lebanon with the Central American country of Nicaragua. In the early 1980s, Iran fought in a bloody struggle with its neighbor Iraq. On the verge of defeat, Iran needed missiles. At the same time, a radical Muslim organization known as Hezbollah held Americans hostages in the country of Lebanon. Members of Hezbollah were loyal to Ayatollah Khomeini in Iran. U.S. intelligence officials offered to sell missiles to Iran exchange for the release of the American hostages in Lebanon. The deal was struck, and then U.S. intelligence officials used the proceeds from the missile deal to fund anti-Communist guerillas, known as Contras, in their attempt to overthrow the pro-Communist government in Nicaragua. This effort violated

U.S. neutrality laws. The deal became public by the fall of 1986. After lengthy Congressional hearings, several high officials in the Reagan administration were either indicted or convicted, but many were later pardoned by President George Bush. No direct evidence ever tied Reagan to the orchestration of the affair.

Despite the scandal, it did not damage the President's popularity. When Reagan stepped down in January 1989, his approval rating hovered at 60%. He came into the White House with an economy in tatters and a Cold War still raging. He argued that the country needed to be rejuvenated. His charisma and personality helped restore America's confidence in itself. He helped bring about a great economic recovery, and he is to be given a lot of credit for helping end the Cold War.

George H. W. Bush (1989–1993)

Reagan's popularity paved the way for Vice President George Herbert Walker Bush to reach the Presidency in 1988. Bush served in the 1960s and 1970s in various government positions. He served two terms in the U.S. House of Representatives as a part of the Texas delegation. President Nixon chose him to be the U.S. Ambassador to the United Nations, and later President Ford appointed him as the Director of the Central Intelligence Agency.

Berlin Wall and the End of the Cold War

Bush's tenure as President (1989–1992) was mostly known for foreign affairs. By 1989, a groundswell of discontent had arisen across Eastern Europe. Gorbachev's policy of Glasnost or openness was actually a response to the already existing unrest in countries such as Poland, Czechoslovakia, and Hungary. By 1989, both Poland and Czechoslovakia held elections for President. In the fall of 1989, East German officials announced that its citizens could travel unhindered into West Germany. This unleashed a flood of East Germans traveling to see friends and family whom many had not seen since 1961 when the Berlin wall was built. This led to the tearing down of the Berlin Wall, the symbol of Soviet oppression. The momentum spread to other countries formally controlled by Soviet Russia. Like President Reagan, George Bush sought to increase relations between the United States and the Soviet Union. In 1991, both countries signed the Strategic Arms Reduction Treaty (START) which called for the dismantling of long-range nuclear weapons. Later in 1991, the Soviet Union disbanded, and the Cold War was over.

Remains of the Berlin Wall

Ewais/Shutterstock.com

Operation Desert Storm

While the Cold War was ending, other foreign crises tested the Bush administration. In 1990, Iraq, led by its ruthless dictator Saddam Hussein, invaded their neighbor Kuwait. The crisis concerned the flow of oil out of the Middle East through the Persian Gulf. The United States, along with a coalition of nearly 30 nations, joined a military alliance to oust the Iraqi Army. The coalition effort was called Operation Desert Shield. The United States and its allies gave Iraq a deadline for its withdrawal from Kuwait. Hussein boasted that the United States and its allies better be ready for "the mother of all wars." In January 1991, Operation Desert Shield became Operation Desert Storm as coalition planes began a heavy air bombardment of Baghdad, the Iraqi capital, and key Iraqi defensive positions. By early February 1991, coalition ground forces invaded Kuwait. In less than 100 hours, the United States and its allies routed the Iraqi Army and drove them out of Kuwait. The United States decided the mission was over and chose not to invade Iraq, thus Saddam Hussein remained in power. Bush's approval rating soared to 92%. The bitter taste left by Vietnam seemed to dissipate for many with a clear cut example of U.S. military might and precision.

Approval ratings are fickle things. The economy took a downturn in 1991 and 1992 as the country entered a recession. Bush's approval rating dropped. He had run for President on the slogan, "Read My Lips, No New Taxes." This mantra came back to haunt him. Deficit spending had increased under Bush. Many Democrats called for the raising of taxes to make up for the shortfall. In 1992, Bush approved a Congressional tax increase of $134 Billion over five years. This angered many in the Republican Party. The country's economic woes would open the door for the eventual 1992 Democratic nominee for President, William Jefferson "Bill" Clinton.

Bill Clinton (1993–2001)

A Rhodes Scholar and multi-term Governor of Arkansas, Bill Clinton challenged Bush over the economy. His slogan during the campaign of 1992 was "It's the economy stupid." Bush not only faced his Democratic rival in the election, he also faced a third party candidate, billionaire Ross Perot from Texas. Perot ran on a platform of reducing the federal deficit by cutting spending instead of raising taxes. Perot tried to draw supporters from both parties. He dropped out of the campaign in July 1992, but then soon reentered it. Clinton won the election with 43% of the popular vote. Thirty-nine million people chose Bush, but he was hindered by Perot tallying 20 million ballots. Clinton won 370 electoral votes. Republican dissatisfaction with Bush over the tax increase and Perot's third party campaign doomed the President's reelection bid. Perot created the Reform Party and ran again in 1996 but got less than half the votes he received in 1992.

Don't Ask Don't Tell and Health Care

Clinton came into the White House in 1993 seeking to establish traditional Democratic policies, but he suffered several defeats at the hands of Congress during his first two years in office. He sought to get the ban lifted on open homosexuals in the military. He received push back from conservative Democrats, Republicans, and military officials. In 1993, he signed a compromise measure that still carried a ban on open homosexuals but allowed gay men and women to remain in the military if they did not profess publicly their orientation. Their superiors could not ask their sexual orientation or harass gay servicemen and women. The directive required that military personnel "don't ask, don't tell, don't pursue, and don't harass." Clinton also sought to reform the health care system in the United States, something Democrats had tried to accomplish since President Harry S. Truman in the late 1940s. Clinton appointed his wife Hillary to head up a task force to develop a nationwide comprehensive health care system. The effort proved to be a disaster. The plan was too complicated, and it never got out of the House of Representatives.

Rodney King and O. J. Simpson

While the country appeared to be moving, however incrementally, toward a greater acceptance of homosexuals, the age old problem of race relations reminded Americans it was still alive in the early and mid-1990s. One incident happened in the latter half of George H. W. Bush's tenure (1991 and 1992), while the other occurred during the first term of the Bill Clinton administration. Both episodes gripped the nation. In 1991, a paroled felon named Rodney King led police on a high speed chase in Los Angeles, California. King, an African-American, refused to obey police

LAPD advance upon protester on the south lawn of City Hall while police car burns during night one of the Rodney King Riots on April 20, 1992 in Los Angles, CA.

commands. Using batons, three white officers beat King and kicked him repeatedly while another officer stood by. A passerby captured the beating on film with a new technology, the video camcorder. The three officers who actually beat King were later indicted for assault with a deadly weapon and excessive use of force. A jury in the predominantly white town of Simi Valley outside of Los Angeles County acquitted the officers in the Spring of 1992. No African-Americans served on the jury. The verdict sparked outrage in the black community in south central Los Angeles. Better known as Watts, this area had already erupted in violence over police brutality back in 1965. It happened again after the King verdict. Rioters attacked and beat passing motorists, many severely. Stores were looted and burned. Rioting continued for three days culminating in 55 deaths, 4,000 buildings damaged, 7,000 arrests, and 2,000 injuries. The riot incurred over $1 Billion in damage. The four policemen were tried in federal court for violating King's civil rights. The court sentenced two of the four police officers to brief stints in prison.

The other racial episode that polarized the nation involved one of America's most beloved sports heroes, and one of the most well-known African-Americans in the country, O. J. Simpson. Simpson was a former Heisman Trophy winner and one of the greatest running backs in National Football League (NFL) history. He spent most of his playing career with the Buffalo Bills. After his professional football career ended in the late 1970s, Simpson continued to earn national notoriety for almost two decades as a commercial spokesman, actor, and sports commentator. In June of 1994, headlines broke concerning the grisly murder of Nicole Brown Simpson, the running back's estranged wife, and a waiter named Ron Goldman. Both victims were white, and both were found slashed to death outside the woman's house in a neighborhood in Los Angeles. Eventually, the police turned their attention to O. J. Simpson and issued an arrest warrant. Simpson did not turn himself into the authorities. Millions of Americans sat enraptured before their television sets watching Simpson and his friend Al Cowlings lead a cavalcade of police cars down several miles of Los Angeles freeway. Cowlings drove Simpson's white Ford Bronco and told police via cell phone that Simpson held a gun to his own head and threatened to kill himself. Eventually the police convinced Simpson to surrender, and he was taken into custody. What unfolded for the next year was one of the most famous murder trials in U.S. history; mainly because Simpson was black and famous, and his wife was white. Also, Americans could watch the entire trial live on television. Simpson hired a crack team of lawyers and forensic specialists. The jury acquitted Simpson of both murders in September 1995. Most blacks who were polled rejoiced over Simpson's acquittal, and polls showed that most whites thought Simpson to be guilty. The case revealed the deep racial divide that still existed in the country and how blacks and whites held divergent views toward institutions like the police and the judicial system.

Domestic Terrorism—World Trade Center and Oklahoma City

The country in the early 1990s not only saw the aftermath of a race riot, the United States came to experience the horror of domestic terrorism in 1993 and 1995. In February 1993, radical Muslim terrorists detonated a rental van packed with explosives in the parking garage of the North Tower of the World Trade Center in New York City. Six people died and over 1,000 received injuries. That same Spring, agents with the federal Bureau of Alcohol, Tobacco, and Firearms (ATF) tried to serve a warrant on the Waco, Texas compound of a religious group known as the Branch Davidians. The Branch Davidian community promoted an apocalyptic end times philosophy and had been suspected of abusing children in their care as well as stockpiling a large cache of weapons. The group resisted when the federal agents arrived, and the conflict led to a 51-day siege of the compound by federal agents. As they stormed the premises on April 19, 1993, fire broke out in the compound killing over 80 men, women, and children. Timothy McVeigh, a Persian Gulf War veteran, and his partner, Terry Nichols, blamed the U.S. government for the Waco showdown. They saw the U.S. government as an oppressive tyrant. Thus, on April 19, 1995, on the two-year anniversary of the Branch Davidian incident, McVeigh drove a rented Ryder truck stuffed with explosives and stopped it in front of the Alfred P. Murrah Federal Building in Oklahoma City, Oklahoma. The massive explosion tore off half of the building and killed 168 people as well as injuring over 600. McVeigh and Nichols were eventually tracked down and arrested. McVeigh was executed in 2001, and Nichols received 161 life sentences. Even greater acts of domestic terrorism would shock the nation in the decade to come.

The Internet and Personal Computers

The 1990s were not only known for these serious social issues but also as a period of great economic prosperity. The boom times of the 1990s were directly tied to technological innovations. The driving force for economic improvement centered on the public release of the internet and the widespread use of personal computers. Once solely used by the military, the internet, or World Wide Web as it came to be called, allowed computers all over the country to communicate with each other. Per-

A personal computer represented the growth of technology

kavalenkau/Shutterstock.com

sonal computers from the companies Microsoft and Apple found their way into a majority of American homes. More and more people began to communicate and do business on wireless cellular phones. These technological innovations served as a boom for corporations and all kinds of businesses, which in turn helped bring a substantial increase in the value of the U.S. stock market.

The Contract with America

In 1994, Clinton and the Democratic Party suffered a setback when Republicans took over Congressional seats previously held by Democrats and gained control of both Houses of Congress. Led by Newt Gingrich, the Speaker of the House, Republicans issued a new political strategy known as the Contract for America. This measure called for the passage of a constitutional amendment that would require a balanced budget Amendment. Republicans did not get Clinton to go that far, but they did get him to agree to over a trillion dollars in cuts between 1995 and 2002. Clinton also signed a Welfare Reform Bill which required able-bodied people, who were receiving welfare, to find employment. Clinton recognized the significance of the midterm losses of 1994 and moved toward the center. This benefitted his administration. He boasted of falling deficits and a prosperous economy and cruised to reelection over Republican nominee Robert Dole in 1996.

Mogadishu, Rwanda, and the Balkans

Bill Clinton's foreign diplomacy proved less successful. He sent in U.S. forces into the east African country of Somalia. Clinton intervened in the country's civil war by sending in U.S. troops as a part of a UN peacekeeping force. On October 3 and 4, 1993, two U.S. Blackhawk helicopters were shot down over the city of Mogadishu by Somali militia forces loyal to the self-proclaimed President, Mohammed Farrah Aidid. The rescue effort by the U.S. Army and other UN forces led to a two-day firefight. Eighteen U.S. soldiers died and 84 were wounded. Clinton quickly pulled the U.S. detachment out of Somalia.

In 1994, a civil war broke out in the African country of Rwanda where the majority Hutu tried to eliminate the minority group known as the Tutsi. Stung by the fiasco in Somalia, Clinton and the United Nations did not send in an armed peacekeeping group. Hutus attacked and murdered up to a million Tutsis before the slaughter subsided. Clinton said later that this was one of the biggest mistakes of his presidency.

In 1995, Clinton sent in U.S. forces as a part of a UN peacekeeping detachment into the Balkan countries in Eastern Europe. These states became independent after the breakup of Communist Yugoslavia. One of the new countries, known as Bosnia, contained a majority of Muslims and a minority of Orthodox Christian Bosnians who claimed allegiance with the neighboring country of Serbia. The Bosnian Serbs joined forces with the Serbian military to attack the Bosnian Muslims (known as Bosniaks). Experts estimate that over 100,000 people died in the civil war. The UN peacekeeping group tried to provide order and protection.

Monica Lewinsky and Impeachment

Clinton was riding a massive wave of popularity when a sexual scandal broke in early 1998. It was alleged that Clinton had a sexual relationship with a young intern named Monica Lewinsky in 1995 and 1996. Some of their meetings supposedly happened in the Oval Office. Clinton had already been under investigation for sexual harassment against a woman named Paula Jones while he served as Governor of Arkansas. Janet Reno, the Attorney General of the United States, appointed Kenneth Starr as Independent Counsel to investigate. This led to Clinton testifying before a grand jury in January 1998. He denied wrongdoing under oath. A few days later, Clinton went before the national media and sternly protested the charges and claimed that he had never engaged "in sexual relations with that woman" meaning Lewinsky. Investigators continued to find more evidence of the sexual affair, and finally on August 15, Clinton admitted before a television audience of his affair with the intern. While admitting moral failure, Clinton adamantly insisted that he had done nothing illegal. Starr presented his findings to Congress and concluded that Clinton had perjured himself before the grand jury. Republicans pounced on this and brought impeachment charges against Clinton. Democrats came to the President's defense and argued that while Clinton committed a moral offense, that of adultery, his actions did not reach the "high crimes and misdemeanors" standard given in the Constitution that is necessary for impeachment. The House brought impeachment charges of perjury and obstruction of justice against Clinton in December 1998. The Republicans held a majority in the House and sustained both charges with a 228-206 vote for perjury and a 221-212 vote for obstruction of justice. Clinton became only the second President in history to be impeached.

Seen as a partisan battle by many Americans, the impeachment process then moved to the Senate. The Senate had to vote on whether or not Clinton should actually be removed from office. The verdict fell well below the 2/3 vote needed for removal. Ten Republicans joined their Democratic colleagues and voted 55-45 against the charge of perjury. The Senate then split 50-50 on the obstruction of justice charge. Two factors helped Clinton get an acquittal. One, the battle in Congress was seen by many as politically motivated, but probably more importantly, Clinton benefitted from a booming economy and was overall a popular President. When Clinton stepped down at the end of his second term in 2001, he held an approval rating of 66%.

George W. Bush (2001–2009)

With Clinton's second term ending, the question arose concerning who would be the next President. Vice President Al Gore captured the Democratic nomination, and Governor George W. Bush from Texas won the Republican nomination. He was the son of former President, George H.W. Bush. Gore and Bush took part in one of the most controversial elections in American history. According to the U.S. Constitution, the candidate who wins the most popular votes in a state receives the state's electoral votes. A state's amount of electoral votes is based on the number of U.S. Representatives and Senators it has. There are a total of 538 electoral votes, and the candidate who wins at least 270, wins the election. In the election of 2000, Gore and Bush ran a neck and neck race. It all came down to who won the Florida election and its 25 electoral votes. Gore was ahead of Bush by several hundred thousand votes in the popular tally, but could still lose the election if Bush won Florida. Ironically, if Gore had won his home state of Tennessee, Florida's tally would have been inconsequential. The final total in Florida fell into dispute over voting irregularities and faulty voting machines that produced mangled ballots that could not be clearly read by machine or human counters. At first, the vote was given to George Bush. Gore's election campaign demanded a recount. The case eventually made it to the Supreme Court. And in what many saw as a partisan vote, Chief Justice William Rehnquist and four other justices voted for the recount to stop which meant Bush was declared President. Many viewed the vote as partisan because all five Justices had been appointed by Republican Presidents; Richard Nixon, Ronald Reagan, and George H.W. Bush. George W. Bush became only the second son in U.S. history to follow his father into the White House. He became the 43rd President, and his father served as the 41st. The other father/son Presidents were John Adams, the second President, and John Quincy Adams, the sixth.

9/11 and the Patriot Act

The Memorial Wall, located at FDNY Engine 10 Ladder 10, directly across from the World Trade Center site. It is dedicated to the 343 members of the NYFD who died on 9/11.

There have been many major turning points in U.S. history. The first shot of the American Revolution on April 19, 1775 pushed the 13 colonies war with England. The Declaration of Independence, on July 4, 1776, signaled our cleavage from Great Britain. The first shot of the Civil War was fired on April 12, 1865, leading to the end of chattel slavery. Americans recoiled in horror as the radio blared that the Japanese had bombed the U.S. Naval base at Pearl Harbor in Hawaii on December 7, 1941. This catapulted the country into World War II.

As the country entered the twenty-first century, it experienced a horrible event that is no doubt going to define generations to come. On September 11, 2001, 19 radical Muslim terrorists hijacked four U.S. airliners. Two hit the World Trade Center Towers in the heart of New York's financial district. Both buildings collapsed killing thousands, including more than 300 fire, police, and transit authority officers on the scene to help the wounded. Another plane hit the Pentagon, the headquarters of the Defense Department in Washington, D.C. The hijackers planned for the fourth plane to hit the White House, the residence and office of the President. The brave passengers on the plane fought to regain control, but the plane crashed in Pennsylvania, killing all aboard. The orchestrated terror attack stunned the country. The death toll reached over 3,000 people and was the worst act of terrorism in U.S. history.

U.S. intelligence officials discovered that the coordinated attacks came at the hands of a radical Muslim group known as Al Qaeda. A Saudi Arabian national named Osama Bin Ladin fronted the organization. It was believed that Bin Ladin kept his base of operations in the country of Afghanistan. Another radical group known as the Taliban ruled Afghanistan and gave support to Bin Ladin. Ironically, the United States had supported the Taliban faction when they were fighting Soviet invaders in the 1980s. The terrorists' rationale behind the attacks focused on the United States' support of Israel and the United States' involvement in the affairs of the Middle East. For these extremists, the United States stood as an evil force, and enemy of Islam, and a dragon to be slain. The Cold War had ended, but now the United States faced an enemy unlike ever before.

President Bush vowed that the United States would hunt down the terrorists and exact vengeance. In less than six weeks after the attacks, the Congress passed the USA PATRIOT ACT which is a 10-letter acronym for "Uniting and Strengthening America by Providing

Appropriate Tools Required to Intercept and Obstruct Terrorism Act." This legislation gave the U.S. government widespread powers to use surveillance in the monitoring and arrest of suspected terrorists. The government created a new cabinet position, that of the Department of Homeland Security. This agency sought to coordinate security efforts and guarantee cooperation between government departments.

Afghanistan and Iraq Wars

In October 2001, the United States, Great Britain, and contingents from other nations, invaded Afghanistan. The United States and its allies quickly overwhelmed the Taliban government and destroyed a great number of Al Qaeda camps. While pockets of Taliban and Al Qaeda resistance remained, a new government took over, and elections were held. Osama Bin Ladin remained at large until U.S. forces killed him in Pakistan 2011. Between 2001 and 2014, over 800,000 U.S. military personnel served in Afghanistan. Almost 2,200 lost their lives and almost 20,000 were wounded.

In 2003, President Bush presented his case to the American people that the United States possessed evidence that Saddam Hussein, the dictator of Iraq, was working to acquire chemical, biological, or nuclear weapons. Bush used the term "weapons of mass destruction" (WMD). In 1991, at the end of the Persian Gulf War, the United Nations had forced Hussein to sign an agreement that limited Iraq's military capabilities, but Hussein had systematically prevented UN inspectors from verifying his fulfillment of the agreement. President Bush declared to the American people that the U.S. war on terrorism demanded, if necessary, preemptive strikes. In other words, we must hit our enemies before they hit us first. Iraq was seen as such a threat. Saddam Hussein refused to adhere to U.S. demands, and thus in 2003, the United States and Great Britain, along with other allies, invaded Iraq. Much like 1991, coalition forces quickly overwhelmed the Iraqi army. Hussein and his key advisers were soon captured. An Iraqi tribunal found Hussein guilty of crimes against the Iraqi people and executed him in 2006. Despite President Bush's claims, no weapons of mass destruction were found. The last U.S. forces left Iraq in 2011. Over 1.5 million men and women served in the conflict. The war left over 4,400 U.S. soldiers dead and over 31,000 wounded. The war's cost has run over a trillion dollars, and the country is still racked with instability and violence.

Housing Bubble and Recession

The first decade of the twenty-first century not only saw the United States involved in two wars, but also plunge into a terrible financial crisis. In 2008, very close to a new presidential election, the United States entered a financial recession. This financial downturn came about because the housing bubble popped. Beginning in 2001, the country underwent a housing boom. Because interest rates lowered, lenders watered down loan qualification parameters. Banks and lending agencies lent billions of dollars to home applicants who really were not qualified. These applicants had a weak or bad credit rating and stood a good chance of defaulting on their loans. Millions of Americans took on more debt than they could afford. Investment bankers bought up these loans and developed packages to be used as collateral for financial investments. People began to see homes as investment properties, and not just residences. By mid-decade, over 40% of all homeowners bought residences for either vacation getaways or investment opportunities. By 2006, the housing market slowed down. Thus, an enormous amount of properties went unsold. Many of the questionable lenders began to default on their loans. The speculation bubble burst. Many real estate investors began to default because they could not keep up with their multiple mortgages. Millions of Americans began to see the value of their homes drop dramatically below what they had paid for them. This financial backlash recoiled upon the banks. Washington Mutual became the largest bank failure in U.S. history. Lehman Brothers, a Wall Street financial firm, went bankrupt. This was the largest bankruptcy in U.S. history. The country teetered on the brink of a major economic depression. Of course, the ripple effect hit the entire country with an economic slowdown which meant high unemployment, less wages, and higher prices. In October 2008, President George Bush signed the Troubled Asset Relief Plan (TARP). TARP was a $700 billion effort to help the economy. The U.S. government bought the stock of many of the faltering financial organizations to keep them afloat until the crisis was over. In early 2009, Congress approved an $800 Billion stimulus package. This was the largest spending bill in U.S. history. This colossal outlay of funds significantly increased the national debt. While the country has navigated out of the recession, many of the effects are still being felt.

Election of Barack Obama 2008

Library of Congress, Prints & Photographs Division, LC-DIG-ppbd-00358

President Barack Obama

In 2008, the country seemed to turn a racial corner. In November of that year, Senator Barack Hussein Obama from Illinois, became the first African-American to be elected President. He defeated Hillary Rodham Clinton in the Democratic primary, and then went on to soundly beat Republican nominee John McCain from Arizona. The country had undergone a conservative resurgence with Ronald Reagan in 1980, but it appeared that many in the country were ready for a new direction. Obama was reelected in 2012.

Since the end of the Civil War in 1865, the United States has traveled down many roads. Some paths like isolationism, laissez faire government, and Jim Crow racism have proved to be dead ends. Thus, the country has taken detours and developed new routes. Instead of isolationism, the country is now a leading player in international affairs and has the largest military presence in the world.

In the half century after the Civil War, the U.S. government directly impacted its citizens in a very limited way. Through events like the Great Depression, World War II, and the Civil Rights Movement, the government became more involved in ever increasing spheres of American life. Yet, this road has contained alternating exits between the call for less government or more government. Technology has taken Americans down new roads of exploration. We have put a man on the Moon and connected the nation through the World Wide Web. As the United States moves deeper into the twenty-first century these questions confront us concerning what path the country will take. How do we deal with the continuing threat of terrorism? What steps need to be taken to improve our economic standing? What is our place in the world at large? Where will technology next take us? Finally, after almost 240 years of existence, what does it mean to be an American? Thomas Jefferson penned in the Declaration of Independence, "We hold these truths to be self-evident, that all men are created equal." The Pledge of Allegiance vows that the United States is a place that promotes "liberty and justice for all." It is the task of Americans in the twenty-first century to clear a path in the future to make these sentiments a continuing reality.

INDEX